# Crisis Investor

*Turning Financial Calamities into Profitable Opportunities Successfully*

By

# James J. Hobart

# Crisis Investor

*Turning Financial Calamities into*
*Profitable Opportunities Successfully*

**James J. Hobart**

**Editor: Thomas Hauck**

Editor: Thomas Hauck

First Printing: 2016

ISBN   978-0-578-17883-7

James J. Hobart Publishing
Contact: james.jh.publishing@gmail.com

Special discounts are available on quantity purchases by corporations, associations, educators, and others. For details, contact the publisher at the above listed address.

First Edition

*I dedicate my book to my Loving Father and Mother, thank you.*

*I also dedicate my life works to free markets, free enterprise, and to the free people of the world. Long live Capitalism!*

# Contents

# Acknowledgements

I would like to recognize my parents for the love and support they have shown me. Thank you so much!

Many inspiring teachers have greatly influenced my life. Thank you Mr. Werpney, Coach Ragsdale, Mrs. Nichols, Mrs. Neuding, Doc Murray, Dr. George, and many others. I appreciate all of the lessons you have taught me.

I want to also recognize many individuals who have influenced my investing and business philosophy: Kyle Bass, Les Brown, Warren Buffett, Andrew Carnegie, Doug Casey, Mark Cuban, Bill Gates, Ben Graham, Steve Jobs, Charles Koch, David Koch, John Mackey, Mike Maloney, Chris Martenson, Elon Musk, Kevin O'leary, General George S. Patton, Dan Pena, James G. Rickards, Brian Rose, Rick Rule, Peter Sage, Peter Schiff, Jack Welch, and many more. Many are in the resource section of this book as well, or are quoted.

Also, I want to thank and acknowledge my mentors who have helped with my progress as an entrepreneur. Thank you Uncle Jim, Mr. Fortunato, and Mr. Lamsens. Thank you to all of my Scoutmasters and advisors. A special thank you to my Eagle Scout advisor Mrs. Tull.

I would also like to thank "Matt the Math Guy," as he would like to be referred to, for reading over the early rough drafts of my book.

I also want to recognize and thank my editor Thomas Hauck for all of the wonderful work he performed to transform my fourth draft of this book, and into a professional formatted investing book. Thank you.

Thanks to everyone for influencing me, helping me, and supporting me on my journey.

– James J. Hobart

# Letter to The Reader

The Financial Crisis of 2008 ignited the motivation for this book. It had a profound impact on me, my family, members of my community, and the world. I saw many friends, family members, and people in the world affected by The Financial Crisis of 2008. Oxford conducted a study and found more than 10,000 suicides were linked to The Financial Crisis of 2008[1]. My purpose for writing this book is to help individuals protect themselves and their families from personal financial calamities as well as the world financial crises that I believe we will see in the future. I never want to see someone going through the pain and suffering that I saw in 2008. I had a family member commit suicide due to personal financial struggles, and my friend's mother committed suicide after losing her job as a result of the financial crisis.

Let me briefly introduce myself. I am an Eagle Scout, an entrepreneur, and a college student pursuing a triple major in accounting, business information systems, and supply chain management. I was elected by a Boy Scout Troop of 108 boys to hold the office of Senior Patrol Leader, and I have found many successes in life. I will one day graduate with my master of business administration, master of accounting, and become a certified public accountant. My life's dream is to operate a successful real estate development company that builds ranch and farm estates. One of my favorite pastimes is to study financial and monetary history, my father's financial lessons sparked my curiosity at an early age.

I was fourteen years old when the Financial Crisis of 2008 unfolded. Our community, which had a median income of $115,000, was dumbfounded by the amount of suicides committed in 2008 and 2009. The effects of losing wonderful people in our community were so horrific and overwhelming that the high school dedicated a day to lecture us and present videos to educate us kids on what was going on, and how we could help prevent this by talking to our parents about the subject. Seeing the parents of friends and classmates

---

[1] "More than 10,000 Suicides across Europe, North America Occurred During Recession, Study." University Herald RSS. N.p., 12 June 2014. Web. 02 Feb. 2016. http://www.universityherald.com/articles/9884/20140612/suicides-europe-america-recession-financial-oxford-men.htm

commit suicide drove me to find out why the Financial Crisis of 2008 occurred, why we always see one or two financial crises every decade, and how these financial calamities form.

I have devoted thousands of hours of time to understanding financial crises and have educated myself on the topic. I read books, watched hours of YouTube videos and presentations, read online articles, and listened to podcasts and any other sources to learn about financial calamities. However, I found that there was not a single book, video, or podcast that was dedicated solely to educating people about financial calamities, financial crisis, or crisis investing. I did not find a single source formatted to present economic principles, followed by historical information as a foundation for a person's knowledge, subsequently backed by professional investors insight, and with a guide for individuals to utilize in their personal finances.

I've written this book to help you protect and profit from the financial crisis that we all know is coming.

Sincerely,
James J. Hobart

# Introduction

In this book I hope to make economics understandable, present historical background information, show you my own as well as others' investing principles and concepts, and then create a formatted step-by-step guide as a tool to help protect yourself and your family. I talk directly and honestly, make a point, move straight to the next point, and bring the economy, business, investing, and personal finances altogether. I wrote this book specifically for anyone who wants to learn how to protect themselves, possibly generate generational wealth, and become a blessing for their families, communities, and the world by accomplishing their personal and entrepreneurial dreams and activities.

I want to be as accurate as possible with the information that I provide. One thing I dislike is perpetuating misinformation. I have read and watched all kinds of information from many different economists, investors, business persons, and entrepreneurs. Economists such as Murray Rothbard, Milton Friedman, Paul Krugman, and Ben Bernanke write books and mathematical formulas that make economics sound so complex and so convoluted. The normal person does not have the time to read, study, and interpret these economic formulae and theories that have little to do with the economic principles of investing during an economic crisis. What these economists are trying to do is write over each other's heads to impress each other and win the Nobel Prize in Economics. They make economics so complex that average people can't understand what they are talking about; an average person doesn't want to hear or try to figure out all of these theories, formulas, and ideologies. People who are trying to get by in their daily lives just want an understanding of how the economy works and how to protect themselves and their family from these horrific financial crises. As an area of study, economics can be very simple if the information is boiled down to its fundamental principles. My mission is to help as many people as possible understand basic economics to better protect themselves from future financial calamities.

A few Christmases ago, I did not want to give any of my friends or family gifts that had microscopic value or benefit in their lives. I also did not want to give them any cash. Instead, I wanted to inform them about constitutional silver, and America's story of money. So, I purchased constitutional silver (referred to as 90% Silver U.S. coinage at Gold & Silver stores) and wrote a Christmas letter with the title *America's Story of Money*. My letter was the foundation for Chapter 4. I elaborated on the subject and went into more detail in the chapter. I hope you enjoy Chapter 4 as much as my friends, relatives, and I do.

I will boil economics down to these five fundamental principles: the law of supply and demand (not some abstract theory); the four economic resources; the tools of how people exchange value in society, money and currency; economic cycles; and human behavior or mindset of fear or euphoria. When you see these events in the news, on the Internet, or hear about them in speaking engagements, you'll be able to break it down to these five fundamental principles, to enable you to understand what these economists, businesspeople, and investors are saying. I know that life is hectic and non-stop, so your time is very important to you. The time that you devote to financial education is precious. So, I know I have to get right to the point!

Here's a quick preview of my book. I expect you to read this book in a few sittings, not one sitting, so if you read a chapter a night, great! If you read a few chapters, great! There are a few places to take a break at in the book. Chapters 1-3 focus on mindset and basic economic principles, which will allow your foundation of knowledge to understand the more advanced subjects in the latter part of this book. Chapters 4-6 are the chapters that go over monetary history, financial history, and how people like you protected themselves and built massive fortunes. Chapters 7-9 concentrate on the subjects of identifying, protecting, and how to turn financial calamities into profitable opportunities. Chapters 10 and 11 discuss the topics of my predictions and how I would formulate my game plan for the financial road ahead. Chapters 12-15 are my thoughts regarding how the advancements in energy, agriculture, and technology will affect your life. Not only the effects these advancements will have, but also the opportunities that lie ahead. Let's start building that solid foundation of economic knowledge.

# Chapter 1: Catastrophe Is Always Around the Corner

Have you ever wondered how investors, business persons, and entrepreneurs became billionaires out of the Financial Crisis of 2008? Have you ever pondered why there were more millionaires created out of the Great Depression than at any other time in U.S. history? How did these successful people do it? What if you could do it also? Maybe not becoming a billionaire, but what if you could protect your family from financial calamities? Possibly increase your net worth significantly from profiting from the coming economic boom? Would you do it? This book is devoted to informing you the reader about the mindset, knowledge, history, and information about how to succeed in a financial calamity.

Financial calamities occur with disturbing regularity. In the late 1980s we had the Savings and Loan Crisis, followed by the Tequila Crisis in 1994, the Long-Term Capital Management (LTCM) Crisis in 1998, which coincided with the Russian Financial Crisis, and then the Dotcom Bust in 2001, followed by the 2003 recession. The most recent crisis we saw began in 2008 and, many believe, is still lingering today.

Just when everything seems to be going fine, we encounter speed bumps in the road ahead. That's just life! However, those are just setbacks, and your future success in life lies ahead. Your life is guided by the choices you make. Knowledge gives you choices, and choices give you power. Empowerment of your self, whether it is mind, body, or soul, creates the foundation for a fulfilled life. My purpose in this book is to allow you to understand how these crises form, how to protect yourself, and, more importantly, how to turn these calamities into profitable opportunities.

To get a clearer perspective, let's take a look at the list of previous financial disasters throughout history.

## A Partial List of Financial Calamities

1637 Tulip Mania
1720 The South Sea Bubble

The Mississippi Bubble
Crisis of 1772
Panic of 1792
Panic of 1796-1797
Danish state bankruptcy of 1813
U.S. Panics of 1819, 1825, 1837, 1847, 1857, 1866
Panic of 1873 (Long Depression)
U.S. Panics of 1884, 1890, 1893, 1896, 1901, 1907, 1910-1911
Australian Banking Crisis of 1893
1910 Shanghai Rubber Stock Market Crisis
U.S. Depression of 1920
U.S. Great Depression of 1929-1933
The Dollar Devaluation in 1933
Recession of 1937
1973 Oil Crisis
Secondary Banking Crisis of 1973-1975 in the United Kingdom
1980s Latin American Debt Crisis
1980 Gold and Silver Bubbles Bursting
Bank Stock Crisis (Israel 1983)
1987 Black Monday
1989-1991 Savings and Loan Crisis
1990 Japanese Asset Bubble
Scandinavian Banking Crisis
Early 1990s Recession
1992 Black Wednesday
1994 Mexican Debt Crisis (Tequila Crisis)
1997 Asian Financial Crisis
1998 Russian Financial Crisis
2001 Turkish Economic Crisis
2001 Dotcom Bubble
2002 Argentine Economic Crisis
2003 U.S. Economic Recession
2008 Financial Crisis
2008-2011 Icelandic Financial Crisis
2010 European Sovereign Debt Crisis
2014 Russian Ruble Crisis
There is a list dedicated to hyperinflation!

# Concept #1

The first lesson to understand that there will always be a financial catastrophe waiting around the corner. The economy operates in cycles, and these cycles are driven by activities in the economy. Rick Rule said, "Bull markets are the authors of bear markets, and bear markets are the authors of bull markets."[i] Every investor, entrepreneur, business person, or wealth creator needs to have knowledge of financial history, a solid understanding of economics, and the right mindset to succeed.

## Mindset of Successful Crisis Investors

In every area of life, our mindset determines our success. During financial cycles, if investors become overwhelmed by their emotions and fill themselves with euphoria or debilitating fear, catastrophic losses or severe underperformance will result due to their lack of discipline and control. What if I gave you $100 million, or let's say $1 billion; would you be successful if you did not possess the right mindset or skill set? Of course, you would not!

## Concept #2

Successful crisis investors (or any investor for that matter) need to rid themselves of emotions and maintain focus on the intrinsic value of the asset or market. Prices of assets and markets do not reflect the intrinsic value; the prices of assets and markets are the reflection of market perception. Human beings can be controlled by their emotions. Investors are just human beings; investors similarly possess two critical biological emotions, namely fear and greed. Market movements are driven by the collective mass of investors, not a single investor. This collective mass of investors I will refer to as "the herd," and I am talking about the general emotions of the majority of the investment population.

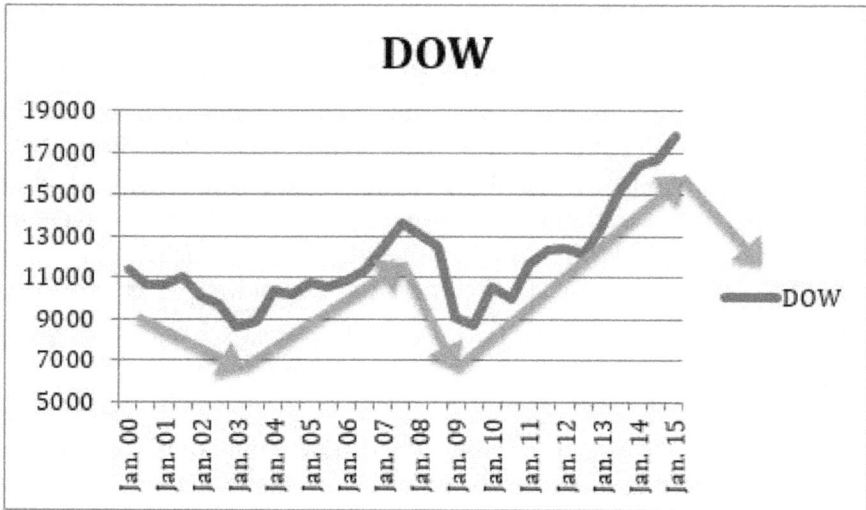

## DOW

(Data Source http://measuringworth.com/DJA/result.php)

Recall the quote by Rick Rule for Concept #1: "Bull markets are the authors of bear markets, and bear markets are the authors of bull markets."

Bull markets are driven when there are more buyers than sellers in the market. A bull market drives the price beyond what the intrinsic value can sustain, creating fewer buyers than sellers. The price then begins to reverse, and the herd starts to panic, creating more sellers than buyers causing a radical decline in the price. Historically, the price not only reverts to the intrinsic value but it typically overshoots to an undervalued territory.

A bull market authors the bear market by the market becoming overvalued, then the market reverts towards undervaluation in a bear market. Likewise, a bear market authors a bull market by reaching severe undervaluation territory, then the market reverts towards the intrinsic value of the market. Bear markets reverse when the undervaluation is so great that it creates fewer sellers than buyers in the market, initiating higher prices in the asset. Prices are not a reflection of *valuation* but rather a reflection of the *supply and demand* of the asset, which is dictated by the sentiment of investors in the market.

# Concept #3

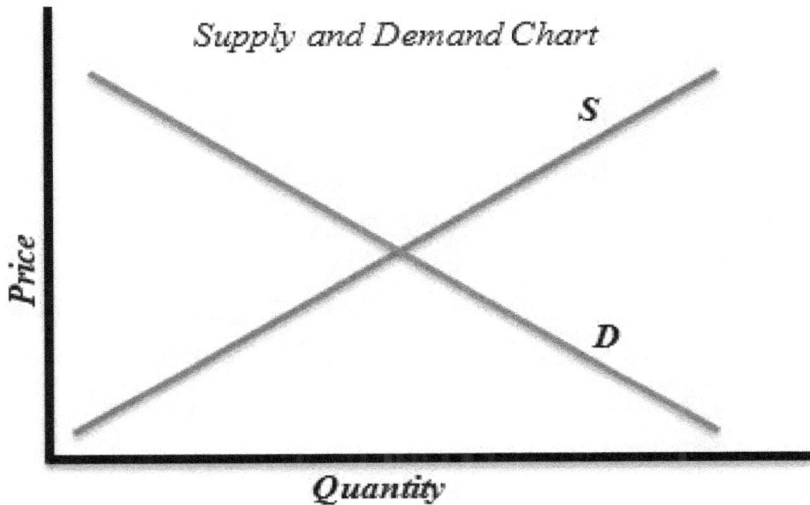

*Supply and Demand Chart*

**S**

**D**

Price

**Quantity**

Prices are a reflection of supply and demand, not intrinsic valuation. The law of supply and demand applies to assets such as stocks, bonds, real estate, businesses, commodities, etc. When there are more sellers than buyers, the market falls; when there are more buyers than sellers, the market rises. Utilize the chart above to understand supply, the demand line falls since a lower price increases the quantity demanded from buyers, and the supply line rise since a higher price stimulate sellers to produce more.

The law of supply and demand comes into effect as the price rises, demand decreases, and the supply of assets increases. Once the market reaches the tipping point, where supply meets and then exceeds the demand of buyers, prices start to fall. The herd begins to sell to take profits, stop any losses, and to meet margin calls. Supply surges from sellers trying to sell their assets to buyers; however, there are fewer buyers left, since the herd transitioned from buyers to sellers. This action drives prices radically down, causing a market crash. Because demand can only be stimulated by lower prices, the herd of investors sells their assets at low prices to find the buyers to purchase their assets. Falling prices decrease supply and increase demand. Eventually, the market will reach a point where demand meets then exceeds the supply, causing the prices to stabilize then rise. The cycle then repeats over and over again. All of this time the herd focused on the price, and not the intrinsic valuations. Crashes in price are caused by valuations straying too far from the intrinsic value.

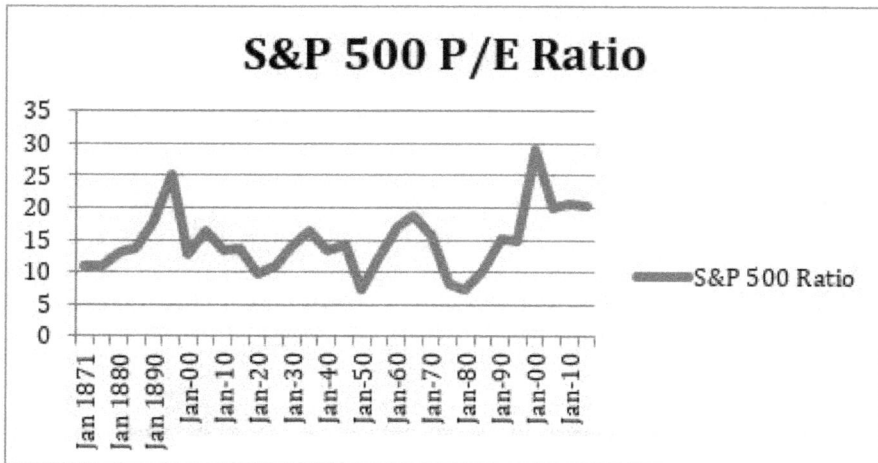

(Data Source http://www.multpl.com/table)

Intrinsic value is directly related to the income of the asset class, incomes of individuals, and the incomes of a nation or geographical location. The price of the asset may change, but the intrinsic value is based on the return on investment (ROI) or the income.

Successful investors are not swayed by the emotions of the herd, which is typically trapped in the cycle of fear and greed. Instead, successful investors direct their focus on finding the intrinsic value.

Markets and assets move from overvaluation to undervaluation: successful investors buy undervalued assets, let the herd drive the assets to overvaluation, and investors then sell to the euphoric herd. An investor can identify an overvalued asset or market by the income the asset generates. Observe the S&P P/E Ratio chart above; the price of the stock divided by the earnings is the P/E ratio. Prices and earnings change; nevertheless, we can take the historical mean to find the intrinsic value. The rule of thumb for the valuation of the stock or stock markets is anywhere from a P/E of 10 to 12. The return is 8% to 10%, which would take an investor 10 to 12 years to break even on their original investment. In the Dotcom bubble, the Dow Jones P/E peaked at 45! The rate of return was 2.2%, meaning it would take an investor 45 years to break even on his or her original investment. How many people would knowingly invest their money and wait 45 years to break even? Not many! Successful investors recognize that a market cannot sustain itself on incomes that do not support the current price.

In the decade of the 2000s, real estate prices, gold and silver prices, commodities prices, bond prices, and stock prices *all* went up. But if there is a limited amount of currency in the world, how can all of these markets go up in price? Especially when one market went into a bubble, it would have to draw currency away from the other markets, causing prices to fall in those markets. In the real world, central banks issue more currency every year, causing prices to rise.

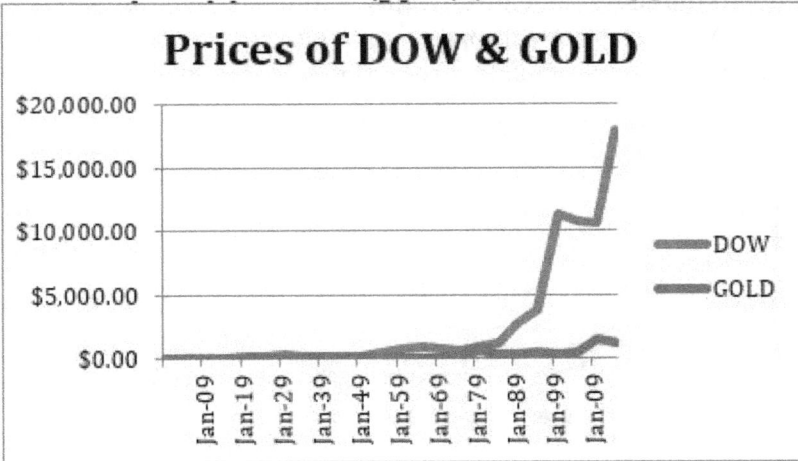

(Data Sources http://onlygold.com/Info/Historical-Gold-Prices.asp
http://measuringworth.com/DJA/result.php)

*How should an investor invest in these two assets?*

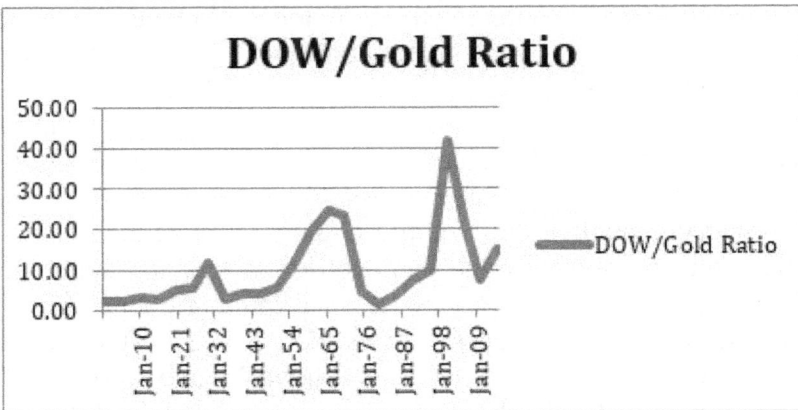

(Data Sources http://onlygold.com/Info/Historical-Gold-Prices.asp
http://measuringworth.com/DJA/result.php)

Investors need to understand that asset prices and market prices are abstractions to intrinsic value. Intrinsic value may be best measured by one asset class against another asset class or a market against another market.

## Concept #4

Capital flows from market to market. It never pools in one market for very long. Here is a brain exercise: If stocks outperformed real estate *forever,* then there would come a point in time where one share of the Dow could purchase the entire world. You and I both know that can't happen. Markets are trapped in this valuation channel of overvaluation to undervaluation reverting to overvaluation.

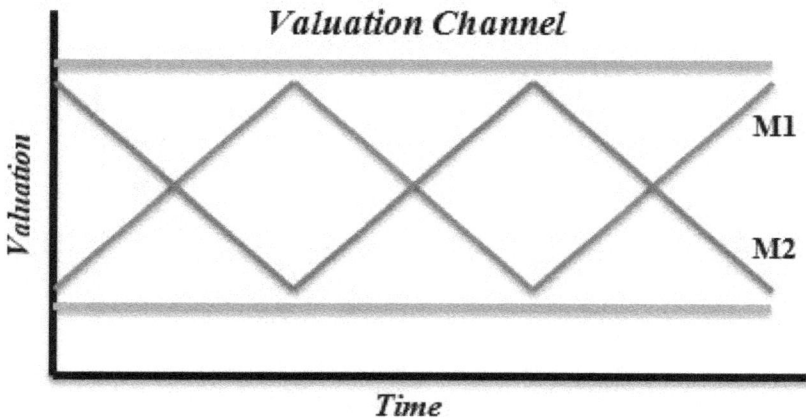

**Valuation Channel**

When one market is outperforming (capital flowing to) another market (capital flowing from), that market (M1) becomes overvalued while the other market (M2) becomes undervalued, and then the trends reverse. Capital flows where it is needed the most: capital is needed the most by undervalued markets, and needed the least by overvalued markets. The smart investors realize that they hold assets in an overvalued market; they sell those assets to move their capital to the undervalued market. Capital begins to flow into the undervalued market causing the cycle to reverse. Capital flowing from an overvalued market to an undervalued market creates a cycle. In a later chapter, I write in great detail about how I have applied Mike Maloney's Wealth Cycle Principle to my own financial future, and how you can as well.

---

## Success Is a Habitual Practice

*"We are what we repeatedly do. Excellence then, is not an act, but a habit."*
*-Aristotle.*

In my book, I give you many tools to succeed, but it's not up to me whether you succeed. That rests on your shoulders! Strive to become successful in your dream, whether it is a not-for-profit organization, a business, an invention, creating a nest egg for retirement, becoming financially free, or some other entrepreneurial activity that you desire to achieve. To achieve your dream, you need to develop successful habits and practice them every day.

Investors or individuals for that matter need to practice the skills of a successful investor: discipline, using logic not emotion, focusing on intrinsic value rather than price, identifying capital flows, and always remembering that bear markets are the authors of bull markets.

When the tumultuous times come, you will find success by providing goods and services that humanity desperately needs. When the fun times roll around, enjoy, but start preparing for the next crisis.

Always remember that crises produce great opportunities.

Question: How many people think that great crises are the best times to find or make great opportunities for themselves?

Answer: Very few people understand this fact. Throw away all of the insecurities and all of the negativity in your life, because now is the time to take control of your future! Do not fear what is outside of your control—corrupt governments, depressed economies, out of control bankers, world violence, or anything else that you cannot control. Work on all of the things that are inside of your control, starting with yourself. Empower yourself to become the best that you can be, and continual to improve yourself.

Do not fear what is outside of your control; instead, work on things that you can control. Establish the mindset of empowering yourself by acquiring marketable skills, properly utilizing your emotions, understanding how the business world operates, and having the courage to put yourself into situations to succeed. The best way to become successful is to be your own boss and become an entrepreneur.

# Chapter 2: Booms, Busts, and the Economic Cycle

Here's how the economy works: Individuals make transactions every day, businesses make transactions every day; the sum of these transactions form the economy. Fundamentally, the economy is the sum of all transactions conducted within a defined period of time. Crisis investors understand those transactions and how those transactions occur. These transactions construct the booms, busts, and economic cycle. The importance of this chapter cannot be stated strongly enough.

What goes wrong to cause an economy to decline? What causes the catastrophes to occur? It's the natural cycles that ebb and flow in the economy are essentially the cause. These natural cycles are caused by the human mind, human perception, human emotion, and the human element. People try to correct these imbalances by governmental action, legislation, coercion, or a bureaucratic dictate. They all, of course, fail; and history proves this true. In my opinion, these interventions in the economy make everything worse.

For example, take the Argentine Banking Crisis in the early 2000s. The country had gone deeply into debt and began to inflate its way out by printing currency. Not only that, the Argentine currency was backed by the U.S. dollar. Bank runs ensued, resulting in banking restrictions, where depositors could withdrawal a small amount of money every week to pay bills. The government was printing pesos to buy dollars to back their banking system, and to pay down debt. This action caused a devaluation of the Argentinian Peso against the U.S. Dollar, essentially robbed everyone who held Argentinian Pesos by destroying their purchasing power.[ii]

The truth is that the Argentinian government should have let those banks go belly up, and the people who deposited their money in the bank should have lost their deposits. The country would have had a downturn, but it would not have led to hyperinflation and depression.

My logical reason why governments make the problem worse is because they are trying to use the human element and behavior to correct other human elements and behaviors; therefore, such measures are doomed to fail because human beings are flawed.

*"You cannot solve the problem with the same consciousness that created the problem. You must see the world anew."*
*-Albert Einstein.*

In such cases, the solution I propose is to do *nothing*. Let nature take its course, but I will hold myself accountable for the actions that I take as an investor. I will empower myself, by financially educating myself, taking actions in my life to allow me to prosper, and grow my financial capital base. I hope you dear reader choose to do the same.

People want the government or some financial planner to solve their financial woes for them. You need to take the responsibility for your financial future, and financially educate yourself about the world of financial history, economic history, and most importantly monetary history. So, the beginning of the first lesson is to understand the credit cycle, since credit is used in many transactions.

## Credit Cycles

What is credit? Here is roughly the dictionary definition: Credit is the ability for customers to obtain goods and services from other individuals, businesses, or institutions on the premise that payment will be made in the future.

Everybody has an understanding of credit since most of us use credit in our daily lives. When you or I go to the store and purchase something on credit using our credit card, we are increasing the seller's income. When you or I borrow money, we are not increasing our income we are increasing our debt. Instead, we are creating debt, and spending that currency into the economy. Credit card companies just type numbers into the computer stating you owe them money. Literally, they create the credit currency out of thin air and charge you interest on it.

Whenever a credit card is charged, the amount due to the seller is paid by the credit card company. When someone pays the credit balance on their credit card, his or her personal bank account from which the payment was made is debited, and the credit card account is credited. If someone fails to pay off the credit card balance, the credit card company has to credit their cash account and debit the credit card account balance to make the account zero.

Look at your bank statement and your credit card statement to have a better understanding of what the debits and credits are.

Then there are loans that commercial banks make that expand the currency supply and create money.

*"Commercial banks create checkbook money whenever they grant a loan, simply by adding new deposit dollars in accounts on their books in exchange for a borrower's IOU."*
*-Federal Reserve Bank of New York, "I Bet You Thought", p.19*

The seller of the item gets dollars deposited to his checking account. The credit dollars that you create will increase a person's income, which the seller then uses to purchase other items, or if he or she decides to use credit, it increases the other seller's income.

This process leverages itself over and over again until it can't. The reason being is that eventually you have to *under-consume* to repay those fictional numbers back to the credit card company or the bank. This process means people spend less, which negatively affects others' incomes, and then the cycle reverses and a credit contraction begins to take hold in the economy.

Credit contracts in these ways: first, in order to save, people pay down debt and spend less; second, people default on their payments, meaning banks suffer losses causing them to lend less; and third, the currency supply contracts due to the credit numbers "currency" being written off and "destroyed." When incomes fall due to a credit contraction in the economy, it causes credit worthiness to decline because of the resulting loss in income. A good illustration of how this happens is the Ray Dalio video called, "How the Economic Machine Works by Ray Dalio."[iii] The link for the video will be written in the resources section of this book.

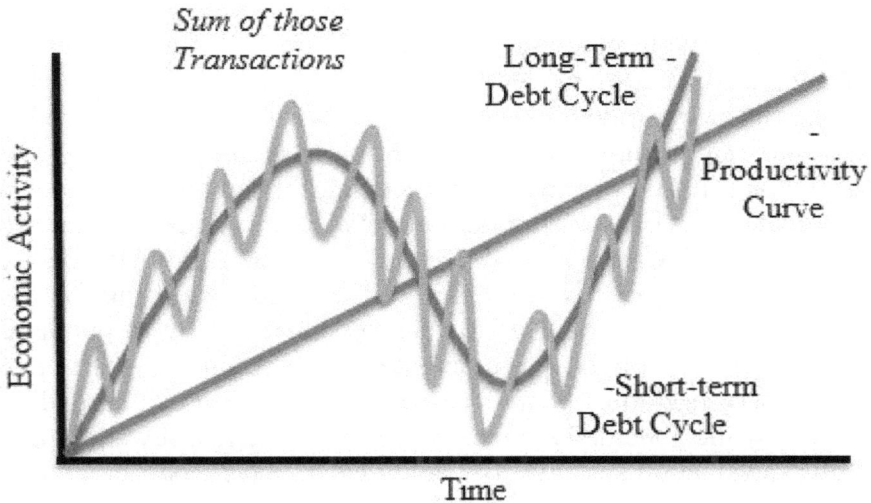

Most people believe that credit contraction is the problem, and they are wrong. It is the *solution* to the problem. The problem was the credit expansion in the first place, which created the unstable system in the economy, denoting the fact that a future economic catastrophe is looming in the future. Warren Buffett had an interesting saying in an interview: "Be fearful when others are greedy, and greedy when others are fearful."[iv] I relate this to my thought of paying down debt or "deleveraging" when others are getting into debt or "leveraging," and when people are deleveraging, you should start leveraging your capital in a sustainable way. The solution to this problem is to encourage people to save and discourage people from getting into enormous amounts of debt or speculation. A proven factor is high-interest rates, in reference to the 10-Year Treasury should have a real yield above 4%, and strict lending standards to discourage easy money.

Lending standards is a subjective term, so let me clarify. When you're buying a house the standard should be: a high credit rating, credit history, and credit worthiness, together with a large down payment (over 20%), result in the monthly payment taking a small portion of your income (housing, in my opinion, should be less than 25%), and a short duration (longest loan period is a 15-year mortgage). Unfortunately, we do not live in that type of world. No, we live in the type of world with No Income, No Job, and No Assets (NINJA loans), adjustable rate mortgages, 0% to 3% down payments, monthly payments for housing of 40% of their income, duration of loans typically 30 years now being increased to 40 years, and rampant speculation by Wall Street and individuals. Lending standards should abide by the risk-reward model.

The risk/reward model states that the higher the risk, the greater the reward. To promote longer-term business stability by banks and other lending institutions, banks and lending institutions should have high lending standards and pursue minimal risk for minimal return. However, the risk/reward model is just a model. Nevertheless, a person can find very low risk and high reward depending on the valuation of those assets. (In a later chapter I discuss how to purchase these assets.) Regrettably, the intervention in the economy by interest rate "influencing," quantitative easing programs, and other policy measures by the Federal Reserve have distorted the risk-reward model and other evaluation systems. The credit cycle plays a part in lending because lending standards affect certain aspects of the credit cycle.

Once credit begins to contract, incomes fall, the economy declines, businesses begin to close their doors, and the economy falls into a recession. The credit contraction is just a signal that the financial catastrophe is about to happen. Now, the credit cycle does not always result in a financial crisis or a banking crisis. If banks are sufficiently capitalized, then they will do just fine. The ones who are in crisis are the businesses, individuals, and investors who purchased assets on credit with valuations that do not support the underlying asset.

Credit or the access to credit with people willing to bid up evaluations on whatever asset or widget will cause the asset or widget to become overvalued. An overvalued asset does not revert to the mean, but will overshoot it because people now must under-consume to pay off the debt or liquidate the asset, causing downward pressure on the asset. The valuation of the asset mimics the overall credit cycle. Also, credit is just the tool for individuals to cause distortions, manias, or bubbles. It is the psychology of people that is the ultimate factor in valuations both in a collective sense and in an individual sense as well.

Credit
Expansion

Credit
Contraction

Credit
Recovery

Credit
Restructuring

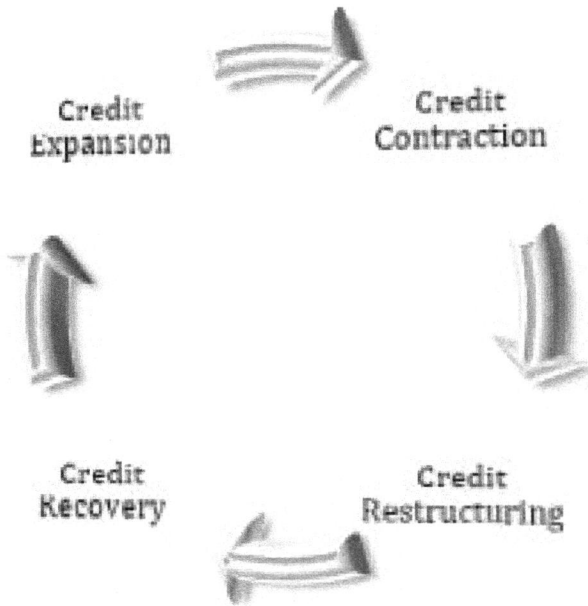

If an individual watches the credit cycle and understands the ebbs and flows of credit to certain assets, markets, or widgets; they will see a warning indicator and an opportunity to invest in an asset that is attracting capital. Observe the current human psychology and sociology of the markets, and understand the fear and greed mentality that plays in the market. This perspective will give you a tool and a warning sign of where potential catastrophes may occur in the future, and where the depressed markets are in an economy.

## Business Cycles

Business cycles follow credit cycles in the economy as a result of the use of credit in the economy. Credit, as stated before, increases the income in society, and increases part of the money supply referred to as M2 by the Federal Reserve. When businesses see an increase in sales and their capacity is reached, they start thinking of expansion. They will begin to expand their business either through capital or debt. Businesses will begin to hire new employees, their overhead will typically increase, and they will have added cost because of the debt service expense.

Businesses' incomes may increase; however, incomes are variable, whereas a business's expenses, such as the debt service, the larger electricity bill, the larger water bill, and other expenses, are *fixed*. When the credit in the system begins to contract, incomes fall as a result. When incomes of businesses fall subsequently, people now have to under-consume since they over-consumed during the boom.

Businesses then begin to try to shed expenses, such as their labor costs. If you, the owner, have decreasing sales, why do you need a large staff? Staff reductions typically result, followed by selling the assets that had been purchased during the expansion. Those assets may have produced income, but during the contraction, those assets may incur losses for the business. Those assets are then typically sold. The assets of businesses come onto the market, causing prices to go down due to the increase in supply. Since fewer people are expanding, demand for assets decrease. The law of supply and demand comes into effect, causing prices to fall.

Labor markets are also greatly affected by the business cycle. During an expansion phase of the economy, people are hired due to the increased demand for labor. The supply of labor decreases, making it more difficult for businesses to find prospective employees to interview and hire. Prices for labor increase due to the law of supply and demand.

When the credit contraction occurs followed by a downturn in the business cycle, businesses begin to lay off employees, meaning the supply of labor increases, and the demand for labor decreases. Of course—you guessed it—the law of supply and demand takes effect and the price of labor falls.

All of these markets, such as the asset market, the business market, and the labor market, will fall to, or beyond, the productivity curve. The economy will not spiral down to the Stone Age, and people's wages will not fall to $1 or zero dollars, because how many businesses want to hire people for free? Prices and wages will fall below the equilibrium, spurring demand and decreasing supply, causing prices to rise. The law of supply and demand then balances out into equilibrium, finding the price of labor where wages spur demand for labor from businesses.

Incomes stabilize, debts are paid down, and the real assets are still there, just the valuations along with ownership change. People then begin to rebuild on a strong foundation that is congruent with the productivity curve. Economic growth resumes, businesses expand and open, technological development progresses, and the labor markets return to normalcy with wages following the productivity curve.

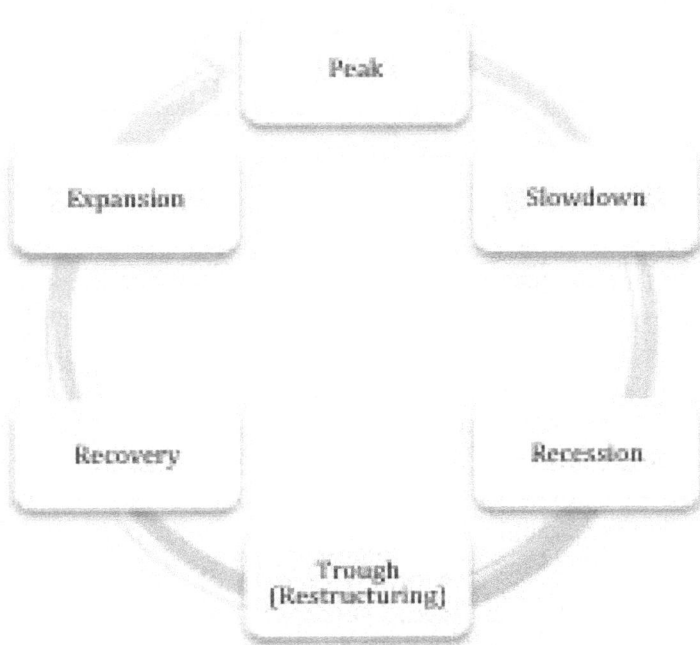

To summarize the business cycle: the credit cycle induces the business cycle by stimulating demand through the increase of credit. The increase of credit directly affects individuals' incomes as well as businesses' incomes. Businesses begin to expand by purchasing new businesses, mergers, and acquisitions, increasing staff, and typically getting further in debt. The credit contraction occurs due to individuals and businesses having to under-consume to pay down debt and increase their capital base in the form of savings. The business cycle begins its downturn with businesses cutting expenses since their incomes and revenues decreased, layoffs ensue, assets are put on the market, and the law of supply and demand comes into effect with prices falling as the result of market forces.

## Economic Cycles

In this segment of economic cycles, we will discuss these topics: resources such as land, labor, capital, and entrepreneurship, understanding the allocation of these resources, mal-investment and misallocation of resources, and the Kondratieff wave. Once I have presented these topics to you, I will tie them all together along with the credit cycle and the business cycle to show the full picture of the economic cycle.

I started off first with the credit cycle and the business cycle, and it is easier for most people to grasp these large concepts as opposed to the very intricate interactions in the economy. The interactions between land, labor, capital, and entrepreneurship can be awfully complex, but I hope that I can clearly explain the convoluted economic theories that cause the confusion. I always try to boil it down to the five fundamental principles.

The first resource is land, a very easy resource to begin with. We all need land to live on, to grow food, and to produce our goods by building factories on the land and extracting resources from the land to build the factory. Then we need the raw materials from the land to shape into goods for people. We then take those goods to market. The shops or shopping centers need land for consumers to go to their stores to select the certain goods they want or need.

**Land** is the physical foundation for all physical and even digital materials to be created, either through the extraction of raw resources or the buildings to produce or provide the value for the goods.

Real estate is broken down into these categories: commercial, residential, and rural real estate. Land is just land, but it takes people to transform the land to provide value for others.

**Labor** is the time and energy of people to transform the raw materials into goods or maintain the goods through services. It is essential to every business. Labor can be directly related to the actual product, or it can be indirectly related to overhead or other personnel expenses. The energy and time of people to create value from raw materials creates wealth, or a synonym for wealth, capital.

**Capital** is the second most important part of the equation. At its most fundamental, capital is the right and the ability to acquire ownership of a product or service. Nowadays, capital most often takes the form of currency, but in the old days, it could be gold, silver, beads, fur pelts, or rice. Land can be a form of capital because you can swap your land for something else like cash. We also recognize intellectual capital, like a secret recipe for a beverage that consumers are willing to pay for.

Once capital is created, it has to be maintained. When a business goes bust, the capital simply does not vanish into thin air. It simply transfers from one individual or group of individuals to another individual or group of individuals. Capital includes the plant, equipment, tools, patents, contracts, brands, and machinery to generate wealth. The labor and the management together are before a business begins to create capital, someone must organize capital to begin the venture.

**Entrepreneurship** brings everything together: capital, labor, and land to bring upward movement to society. When it comes down to it, someone needs to take the risks, the long hours, work ethic, communication skills, and all of the other resources to create value for people. These individuals are the magical ingredients that bring all of the economic resources together to create value for society. Without someone having the courage to pursue his or her dream and create value for others, no wealth would exist. It is the responsibility of the entrepreneur to effectively engage all of these resources and allocate them properly.

In a perfect world every resource is properly allocated by entrepreneurs, investors, and business owners; however, you and I live in the real world. We understand that this does not happen. Resources are allocated properly 95% of the time. The other 5% of the time, resources are misallocated, and investments are what Austrian economists have called "mal-investments." When resources are misallocated, and investments are mal-invested, there will be a looming catastrophe whether it be in finance, business, or in any other market. It is typically in a credit expansion when entrepreneurs, businesses, and investors misread the market expansion as a sustainable recovery. During the credit contraction when incomes fall, entrepreneurs, businesses, and investors find that their cash flows and incomes will fall. Incomes fall below what the expenses of the business or asset are. Defaults and bankruptcies occur with those assets and businesses being sold for valuations that are in line with value, or are sold undervalued to cut an investor's, business's, or entrepreneur's losses.

Allocation of capital and resources are determined by market demand. If there is a demand for the product or service and prices rise, supply will increase to meet demand and bring the price down. Let's say demand is stimulated by the use of credit, and people over-consume to purchase more products and services from businesses. Businesses expand to produce more to increase the supply to meet demand. What would cause the demand to decrease, and cause prices to fall?

What stimulated the increases in demand? Credit stimulated the increase in demand. People borrowed to consume more than their earnings could support and the businesses produced more to fulfill the increase in demand. When consumers have to consume less to pay down those debts, demand decreases, resulting in prices falling, and then supply decreases to remain in equilibrium with the decrease in demand.

The expansion phase was where the misallocation of resources occurred due to the overconsumption and overproduction of goods. Those misallocations of resources, time, and capital are transferred to people who better manage capital and resources. This process is called *liquidation*; selling those assets and businesses, and writing down or off bad debts. It is a natural phase of the business cycle to correct the imbalances. In the business cycle, we call this phase with everything that is taking place a *downturn*, while in the economic sphere, we call this a *recession*.

As an entrepreneur, business owner, or investor, you do not want to be the one to misallocate resources or make a mal-investment. The easiest way to do this is to stay away from markets that are expanding too fast on credit, and then purchase the assets and businesses that have gone bust in a credit contraction and business downturn, and then turn them around to ride the next expansion phase.

We see cycles that span years, but what about the economic cycles that take decades to complete?

A Soviet economist named Nikolai Kondratieff researched the capitalist system of economics. He was very distinguished in the Soviet Union before and after the Russian Revolution of 1917. Kondratieff had quite a few publications; one of his papers that he published was *The World Economy and its Conjectures During and After the War*.[v] He stated that capitalist economies were characterized by successions of expansion and contraction in the economy, which contradicted Marx's idea of the imminent collapse of capitalism back in the late 1800s.

In 1925, he published *The Major Economic Cycles*[vi], which in his time became very popular in Western Europe, and was almost immediately translated into German. The ideas of John Maynard Keynes eclipsed his ideas in the West in the 1920s. A member of the People's Commissariat of Agriculture and a proponent of the Soviet New Economic Policy (NEP) supported by Vladimir Lenin, Kondratieff was influential with writings about agriculture and planning methodology. Lenin's administration was friendly towards Kondratieff in respect to his ideas in agriculture.

However, when Lenin died, Stalin came to power. Communist ideologues reported Kondratieff on his pro-capitalistic publications to the authorities and tied him to the "Peasant Labor Party" (a fictional party made up by the People's Commissariat for Internal Affairs (abbreviated NKVD, which was closely associated with the secret police.

In July of 1930, Kondratieff was sentenced to eight years in prison, and he published more of his economic writings and literature during his imprisonment. In 1938, during Stalin's "Great Purge," Stalin's objectives were to clean out dissent to his power and the Communist Party. In September of that year, Kondratieff's great research, economic thinking, and many groundbreaking publications earned him execution by firing squad.

The work Kondratieff published in the 1920s and the 1930s informed the economic community that the economy operates in cycles. He postulated that each economic wave or cycle would complete roughly every forty to sixty years. We have gone through one complete cycle since his death in 1938. The economic cycles he was describing correlated to interest rates and bond price, or in my terms, the credit cycle.

All of these cycles are greatly effect by human endeavors and experiences. The cycles Kondratieff mapped were a little over 50 years, or in those days a human lifetime. Today, his cycle takes much longer to complete, and it is the belief of some that this is due to the increase in human life expectancy. Kondratieff's cycle now takes nearly eighty years or a human lifetime. Economies are influenced by human interactions. These cycles are caused by the generational interaction with the economy.

One generation will take on huge amounts of debt due to the mindset that the good days will never end. Suddenly, a depression erupts scarring their children's generation. Once this "scarred" generation dies off; their succeeding generation forgets the stories of their parents. They begin to take on more debt, this debt accumulation creates the next financial calamity, and the cycle repeats.

He broke his cycles down into seasons of Spring, Summer, Autumn, and Winter. Spring is characterized by the following: a fear of relapsing into a depression and fragile confidence in the economy, gradual inflation, slow increase in credit, falling unemployment, and productivity accelerates. Spring is the season of great economic expansion that encompasses real economic activity and growth. However, exponential growth will reach its limits causing social upheaval and a necessary restructuring of the economy.

Summer is the season where this upheaval and restructuring occur in the economy. There is a shortage of key resources, both natural and human. An economy is supported by the amount of natural and human resources at its disposal. The weak economy and weak global economy lead to war. Theses wars add more inflation to the economy since most governments will issue more currency to pay for the war. As a result of a larger monetary base and falling economic activity, inflation dramatically rises since there are more currency units chasing fewer goods. Inflation in conjunction with a stagnating economy is known as stagflation. Although the stagnating economy is short lived for a few years to five years, it has the effect of changing humans' perceptions and beliefs due to their recent economic experience.

Autumn is a deflationary growth or a disinflationary growth phase of the cycle (a plateau). Inflation falls and growth is characterized by industry, development of new ideas and technology, technological innovation, there are strong feelings of affluence, and those feelings become euphoric. Euphoria causes people to crave consumption and produces a rapid rise in debt. Eventually, wealth consumption consumes the saved capital created by prior generations. Consequently, demand grows beyond the abilities of the economy to satisfy it. The economy then slips into a deflationary depression due to the credit contraction with the realization that there were too many claim checks and not enough real wealth.

Winter is the depression phase of the cycle. The irrational exuberance of the autumn cycle (plateau) is realized, which is a good thing. An unbalanced economic system is unsustainable and destructive for the real economy. Kondratieff regarded the depression as a positive cleansing period allowing the economy to readjust from the mal-investments, over-indebtedness, and excess. The economy starts from a strong foundation for future prosperity.

I am going to present to you a brief example of a Kondratieff cycle starting with the winter cycle of the Great Depression that started in 1929, recall that autumn was the Roaring 20s. The winter depression was characterized by deflation, a great credit contraction occurred, banks runs ensued, and the economy stagnated for many years. This winter cycle ended in 1949 with the onset of the spring cycle.

Spring lasted from 1949 to 1966. Many historians refer to this as America's Golden Age with living standards improving, wages rising, productivity increasing, falling unemployment, and had inflation in the economy. People still remembered the struggles of the Great Depression, and many had fears of the economy reverting into a depression. Since this cautious attitude was prevalent, people had very strict lending standards, and many individuals did not want to take on debt since they made the costly mistake of having debt during a depression. However, as time goes on and the memory of the depression fades, people start to want things beyond their mean and what the economy could support. Growth surpasses what the economy can provide.

The last summer cycle began in 1966 and lasted to 1982. You might remember the Oil Crisis of 1973, which was for the most part created by OPEC. However, United States oil production peaked in the early 1970s, which exacerbated the oil crisis. Yet, oil production may pass its peak due to the Fracking Miracle. The United States was dependent on oil imports. Energy is vital for the economy: I elaborate more in depth in a later chapter. The Dow Jones peak on February 9th, 1966 was 995 points, and December 31st, 1982 the Dow was 1042 points. A 5% return over a 16-year period and this discounts the inflation of the 70s. Many resources were misallocated; such as land, labor, capital, as well as oil. Nevertheless, a limit was reached, during the plateau of the autumn cycle.

Autumn's phase started in 1982 and ended in 2000. Life was great, the economy expanded characterized by the advent of the technology industry, living standards improved, the world stabilized, and there was disinflation. In the autumn cycle, growth is characterized by disinflation. Consumption drove much of the economy funded through debt creation. There was a sentiment of euphoria in the stock market, and the dotcom bubble burst. Deflation set in after the 2000 stock market crash. Winter is here, but it is not here to stay.

In my opinion and observation, these cycles occur due to human behavior, human emotion, and the human element. A somewhat irrational emotional state occurs when fear or euphoria sets in. So, why not protect yourself from this irrational exuberance or irrational trepidation, and possibly profit from it as well. The overall tools for trade, such as money, currency, debt, and credit, are just merely tools, and the charts and graphs can be represented as the indicators when those tools are being misused.

We discussed how the credit cycle, the business cycle, and the economic cycle were intertwined. We also learned the cause and effect relationships of the credit expansions and contractions in the business cycle and economic cycle. Please remember that these cycles will continue, and do not panic when there is a downturn. The greatest fortunes to ever be created were in the depths of recessions or depressions. In a later chapter, I will show you the people who achieved much during these tumultuous economic times. Restructuring occurs during credit contractions, downturns, and recessions: just make sure you are astute enough with your capital and start acquiring assets. Do not be the person selling their assets, defaulting, or declaring bankruptcy because you did not realize the signs of the credit expansion followed by the credit contraction.

# Chapter 3: Credit and Monetary Cycles

Credit and money play a vital role in the economy; these items also play a part in how I boil economics down to the five basic fundamentals. The law of supply and demand, the four economic resources, human behavior and emotions, and how we exchange value by utilizing money and credit, Chapter 3 plays an imperative function of the understanding of the later chapters in the book. Credit, IOUs, and how the fractional reserve system creates credit, the inherent instabilities, and risks created by these aspects of the economy: money vs. currency, the creation of currency, the balance of payments, and World Monetary System are covered in this chapter.

## Credit

Credit is the ability of someone to obtain goods and services before payment, and the willingness to pay for those goods and services in the future. Credit is based on trust and the ability to repay. Our credit worthiness depends on a few factors: our history of repaying on time, the size of debt services we can sustain, and the ability to collect collateral if the debt is not repaid. When you enter a credit transaction, you enter into a written contract stating whom you owe and how much you owe. That piece of paper or digital record is called an I Owe You (IOU). IOUs can be written in numerous ways and numerous financial instruments.

Transactions are typically funded either utilizing money (currency) or credit. Investors, in this case acting as lenders, want to earn more money using their money. Borrowers want to use someone else's money to purchase a home, a car, consumer goods, or financial assets. The borrower and the lender engage in a financial transaction to create credit. Lenders will lend to the borrower with the promise by the borrower to repay the principal plus interest to the lender. The promise is written as an IOU and credit is created. While credit isn't complex, it has a plethora of names, such as debt, derivative contracts, obligation, loans, financing, and there is a list of synonyms. A concept that you must always remember in this transaction is that the borrower's debt is a *liability,* and the lender's bond, mortgage, or other credit instruments (the borrower's debt) is an *asset.* Whenever a financial transaction occurs an asset is created (a claim check on future wealth or income) and a liability is created (which has the possibility to be defaulted upon).

In the future when the debt is repaid, the asset and the liability both disappear: a company retires the debt, and the lender's bond (asset) and the borrower's debt (liability) have been resolved, and that IOU's promise is fulfilled thereby ending the IOU. Borrowers spend this newly created credit in their transactions; one person's spending is another person's income. An increase in credit will create an increase in spending, causing a rise in incomes; incomes play a part in determining a borrower's credit worthiness.

Credit worthiness is factored into several parts: income, assets, and credit history all play a part in determining an individual's credit worthiness. As credit is issued, incomes increase, making an individual more creditworthy, which allows an individual or group of individuals to borrow more, reinforcing itself until credit income diverges too far from the real assets and real income (productivity curve). Defaults result, causing the economy to contract. Borrowers defaulting on lenders typically initiate a financial crisis, wiping out the lender's asset, and losing their principle and their interest owed. A financial crisis occurs when there are too many "claim checks" issued, in this case, debt, where borrowers cannot repay the amounts owed either through their incomes or by liquidating the real assets to pay off the principles. To ensure recovery of their money, lenders bear the responsibility of not lending too much to borrowers.

When lenders extend too much credit to borrowers with their future earnings as collateral or issue too many IOUs on the underlying assets, these actions will eventually result in a crisis. When there are too many claim checks and human beings realize that fact, people will panic to get their wealth out of the system, subsequently triggering a crisis. Too many bonds were issued, too much credit card debt, too much student loan debt, too many car loans, too many derivatives, too many gold certificates—and the list goes on.

One cause of financial panics, in particular, bank runs or bank panics, is the fraction reserve system.

A fractional reserve system is a form of banking system that allows banks to create credit and monetize the debts of individuals. Referring to the Federal Reserve Bank of New York: "Commercial banks create checkbook money whenever they grant a loan, simply by adding new deposit dollars in accounts on their books in exchange for a borrower's IOU." - Federal Reserve Bank of New York, "I Bet You Thought."[vii]

Literally, they create money whenever a loan is granted. I know the question you have wanted to ask me is this: How is it done? It is a very intricate answer. If you are a visual learner or listening learner, then please watch Mike Maloney's YouTube video "The Biggest Scam in the History of Mankind."[viii]

Here is the answer.

When you or I deposit our currency in the bank, let's say $100, the bank types in credit dollars into our account. They are then required to hold a reserve ratio, let's say 10%, of that cash in the vault; this is referred to as vault cash. Vault cash is there in case you want some of your cash. The other 90%, or $90, is loaned to other people.

A borrower comes to the bank and takes out a loan to purchase an item. For example, he or she borrows $90 to buy a widget. The seller of that widget then goes to deposit the $90 in the bank. The bank types into the computer the credit dollars of $90 and lends 90% of that, which is $81. As of now, how many credit dollars are there in existence? Correct, $190, and when the seller deposits the $81 it will be $271 credit dollars in existence, even though we still have only $100 in real cash. This process repeats over and over until the $100 creates $900 credit dollars in existence. Now, what causes the bank run? When people start to demand real cash as opposed to using the credit dollars in the system. It says on your bank statement $100 when it's actually $10. People run to the bank believing that loans the bank lent out are bad, and they will not be able to recover their cash back. The bank may have good loans, but it does not have the cash to cover the credit dollars on your bank statement.

## Fractional Reserve Banking System

Among my list of systems to present are the banking and financial systems. The banking system operates with some continuity in the financial system as well as utilizing the system called the fractional reserve banking system. This system has been around since biblical times, and yes there are religious texts in the Bible as well as other religious texts that refer to the monetary system and the banking system. I could write a book on it, but in fact, someone already has

Jonathan Cahn's book *The Mystery of the Shemitah.*[ix] If I wrote a book, I would have more of a financial context backed by religious text. Cahn's book is more in the religious context backed by financial events. Nonetheless, it's a very interesting book, and I would recommend it.

Ever since people started to bank and save their money (at the time gold and silver) with banks, bankers have tried to figure out how to make their business more profitable. Originally, someone (call him Ishmael) would store his gold coin at the bank, and in return Ishmael received a demand note that was payable on demand to the person who held the note. Ishmael would spend his demand note to buy goods and services, and meanwhile, the banker would either loan out the gold coin that Ishmael had deposited or issue more demand notes to loan out, backed by Ishmael's gold coin.

When the banker would loan out Ishmael's gold coin, the borrower would purchase an item from a seller, and the seller would deposit Ishmael's gold coin back into the bank. For the purpose of this example, let's say it's the same bank because the whole banking system acts as one large bank from a financial perspective. The banker would issue another demand note to the seller, and store Ishmael's gold coin in his vault.

Pausing for a moment, we still have one gold coin, but we now have two claim checks! What if this process repeated three, four, or a dozen times? Correct, we would have three, four, or a dozen demand notes on that same gold coin. What would happen if there were a bank run? Correct, the banker would not be able to deliver the gold coin. If there were five demand notes for one gold coin; then one out of five people would get their gold back, or everyone would get 1/5th of their gold back.

This is just one way; the other way is to create more demand notes for gold.

A banker would issue more demand notes than he had gold on hand, for the purpose of earning more in interest payments. Let's say he had a reserve ratio of 10 percent. The banker would write up 10 demand notes on one gold coin, loaning the demand notes to the borrower at interest. This action is a form of leverage to make more profits for the banker. Borrowers would spend these demand notes in society, and sellers would accept on the trust that the demand note was backed by the actual gold coin in the bank. When a borrower earned gold or a demand note, the debt was paid off. A gold coin would add to the reserves of the bank, in this example, 10 demand notes on one gold coin would make 10 demand notes on two gold coins. If the loan was paid off by a demand note it would wipe out the debt and the demand note, so nine demand notes are in circulation for one gold coin. The interest paid to the banker would materialize as a profit that he or she could spend in the economy.

Modern banking practices the fractional reserve system, the same practices have been done since ancient times. However, today our money is currency instead of gold, and our claim check "demand notes" are digital instead of paper. Here is how the fractional reserve system operates today with the use of currency and digital currency.

Governments require banks to meet a reserve requirement. These reserve requirements differ from nation to nation. For this example, we will just use a 10% reserve ratio. When you or I deposit $100 in the bank, the bank then has to keep 10% of that $100, or keep $10 in vault cash to be stored to pay you if you want that money back. Then the bank credits $90 digital dollars to your account and takes the $90 to be loaned out. $90 is lent out to a borrower and is deposited into the seller's account. Now we have $190 worth of claims on just $100, and this process repeats itself until we have 10 times more digital claim checks than the currency in existence. So, the system will eventually have $1,000 digital dollars for every $100 real dollars in physical cash.

Since there are more claim checks in existence than the underlying asset, it is an unstable system. In the event of a bank run and people panic, if there is only $100 in existence and $1,000 worth of digital claim checks, depositors would only receive 10% of the money in their bank accounts, or receive a 90% haircut on their account.

This system works great until it doesn't.

The bank runs of the Great Depression were caused by the federal government issuing too many demand notes (Federal Reserve Notes, claim checks) on the gold and silver, causing people to run to the bank to get their gold and silver money out of the banks. Today, replace the gold and silver with the paper currency or U.S. dollar, and replace the demand notes with the digital currency that is a claim check for the physical paper dollars, and that is the nature of the system. In this system, it has a claim check (digital currency) on a claim check (paper currency), since all currency is a claim check on wealth.

Our system is similar to the system that caused the Great Depression, except this time it is with paper currency instead of gold and silver, and the claim checks are not the paper notes but digits in our account or digital currency. Today, there are too many digital claim checks on too few physical U.S. dollars.

The Federal Reserve publishes the statistics on base money (M1) and the claims on M1 by their measurements of (M2) and (M3). M1 is $3 trillion from the Federal Reserve website: others state that it is $4 trillion, and the Fed's accounting is faulty. Let's go with $3 trillion, and (M2) is currently $12 trillion. Meaning there are four times more claim checks in existences than currency to back those claims, and, therefore, everyone will receive a 75% loss in his or her deposits. M3 is a broader version of M2 encompassing more claim checks. The Fed stated that it was too expensive to keep track of, and it is useless due to M2. However, you can still use all of the Fed monetary aggregates to come up with M3. A site called shadowstats.com keeps tracks of M3, and states M3 is roughly $17.5 trillion, stating that a depositor could potentially lose 80% or more of their deposits held at the bank.

Credit card companies do not use a fractional reserve system. Instead, they type into the computer or their ledger that you owe $X. On the spot, they create the credit out of thin air and then charge you interest on the credit card charge. They will credit your account with them. When you pay them back, the credit card company debits the account, and the money they collect from the interest is theirs. If you do not pay them back, it affects their books, because they have to credit their cash to pay off the credit dollars by debiting the account. So, yes, a credit card company could go bankrupt. If they do not pay off the credit account, the government considers the action to be fraudulent, and will pursue criminal actions against the credit card company.

## IOUs

An IOU is simply a claim check on wealth or a product, or future wealth and production. The claim check is not real wealth in itself. Real wealth, such as real estate, has a claim check called the deed. If you have a note on the real estate, the bank has the deed until you pay off the claim check, called a mortgage. The car is the real wealth while the title is the claim check on the car, and the car loan is a claim check on the future payments to pay off the car. In higher finance, claim checks such as stocks, bonds, options, collateralized debt obligations (CDOs), credit default swaps (CDSs), mortgage-backed securities (MBSs), a whole slew of acronyms for financial instruments, currency swaps, derivatives, and much more are backed with an underlying asset or a re-hypothecated asset. All of this makes a person's head spin, and individuals need to understand that these are all forms of *claim checks*.

The real wealth or assets that underline stocks are the companies. The underlying wealth or promise to pay is the real wealth that underlies bonds. MBSs are backed by the mortgages and the real wealth underlying the mortgages is the real estate and the borrower's ability to pay. Derivatives derive their wealth from whatever source they write in the contract (granted some derivatives derive a claim check on another claim check, and that claim check is backed by a real asset). The fiat currency of a country is backed by the economy. If you watch or listen to the financial media, you will hear about how the U.S. economy is affecting the dollar and the implications that a strong dollar or a weak dollar has on the U.S. economy.

Nowadays, IOUs are numbers that we type into digital accounts to keep track of who owes what to whom. Bonds are a great example of an IOU. A business sells their bonds on the market with the promise to pay interest on those IOUs. The business repays the principal plus the interest to the bondholder. Credit cards keep track of consumers' IOUs; the company credits your account and debits the merchant's account. A check is an IOU from an individual saying that they owe the seller X amount and that they will make good on their payment when the bank credits the seller's account. The United States dollar is an IOU. Look at the top of the dollar; it will say, "Federal Reserve Note."

A mortgage is an IOU and is also referred to as a note. Your car loan is an IOU; those instantly approved credit deals you see on television for furniture, appliances, TVs, and any other item you have a monthly bill for are IOUs as well. In all of these instances, you obtain the item and pay later. What a wonderful world we live in where we can obtain the item, and the seller has faith that we will pay them back! I am not facetious about this at all!

I hope I have made credit and IOUs clear for you so that I can move on to the higher-level concept: How the credit supply and the money supply are interlinked with each other. The first part is very difficult to explain in a book, but if you are a visual person I suggest you watch these two YouTube videos by Mike Maloney called "The Biggest Scam In the History of Mankind" and "Money vs. Currency: Hidden Secrets of Money Ep. 1."[x]

## Money vs. Currency

I am going to use a quote from one of the greatest bankers of all time to dispute the claim that gold and silver are not money:

*"Gold is money, everything else is credit."*
*-J.P. Morgan*

Even though he did not use the word silver, I believe we can insert the words "and silver." It is my humble opinion that gold and silver are money and will be money for the next 5,000 years, just as they have been for the past 5,000 years. Gold and silver are the money, the "currency," and Federal Reserve notes were notes on gold or silver. The currency was merely a claim check on actual gold and silver held by the bank.

Money is a tool used to store your economic energy to deploy sometime in the future. Economic energy is created by the wealth you create for individuals and society. Your true wealth is your time and your freedom; money is merely a representation of your time and your freedom.

| Elements of Money | Elements of Currency |
|---|---|
| *Medium of Exchange* | *Medium of Exchange* |
| *A Unit of Account* | *A Unit of Account* |
| *Portable* | *Portable* |
| *Durable* | *Durable* |
| *Divisible* | *Divisible* |
| *Fungible* | *Fungible* |
| *A Store of Value* | *X* |

Currency is an IOU or a claim check on future production or real wealth. Over time currencies lose their value, because governments inflate the currency and print more currency into existence. When you or I receive dollars, it is not payment for value itself. It is a statement that you are now owed whatever value denominated on that currency. Going to a store to purchase a good or service is the actual payment for the good or service you provide for someone else. This whole system has to rely on faith and trust. Printed on dollar bills is "In God We Trust," but it isn't God we're putting our trust in.

Who are we putting our trust in?

It is the Federal Reserve. The nation and, by extent, the world are putting their trust in the Federal Open Market Committee (FOMC). The head of the Federal Reserve is currently chairwoman Janet Yellen. We are trusting her not to print too many dollars and cause runaway inflation like the Argentine Central Bank did in the early 2000s, or what the German government did to the mark during the Weimar Republic of the 1920s.

Here's something to think about: In the entire world's history, all fiat currencies have failed. However, the 100% failure rate does not necessarily imply that the fiat currency will *fail* in your lifetime, but it will certainly *lose purchasing power* during your lifetime.

Why is that?

Fiat currency is a claim check on wealth. It is merely an IOU; take a look right now at a one-dollar bill. As you read the top of the bill, it will state that it is a Federal Reserve Note. Rhetorical question, but what is a "note?" Correct, my dear reader, it is an IOU; just like a car note is an IOU.

Now I have another question: what is the physical wealth underlying that claim? A tricky question, because it is *implicitly* implied, not *explicitly*. The implicitly implied wealth is your (the individual's) future income and the assets of society that is real wealth underlying the claim check.

Why is it that currency systems inevitably fail, you ask? Great question! Claim checks are IOUs and IOUs can always be defaulted upon; however, defaulting on a currency is different in the action (the how) than a bond.

When a corporation defaults on a bond, they announce that they cannot pay it. In contrast, the issuer of currency is typically a government, and they are the ones who default on currency. Governments issue bonds just like a corporation; they also issue the currency that was used to buy those same bonds and the currency that will be used to repay those bonds. Whenever a corporation defaults, it is because they have no currency. Whenever a government has no fiat currency, they will just print more currency to repay the bondholders.

Granted, a government could choose an outright explicit default. Instead, nearly all governments have chosen to default implicitly by printing more currency. Printing more currency causes the currency to devalue; governments can ease their debt burdens and pay off their creditors. Another question that needs an answer is this: Who is defaulted upon when the currency fails? Society as a whole suffers, through rising prices, while in an explicit default it is only the bondholders who lose. Currency's basis is founded on faith in trust that it will maintain a stable supply for the economy as a whole; nevertheless, when a government hyper-inflates the currency supply, they break their promise. A broken promise results in a loss of faith and that loss of faith destroys the currency as a medium of exchange. So, what is money?

Currency contains all the qualities that money must have except for one: a store of value. Money must contain the quality of a store of value. A store of value must in itself be payment of itself, or a store of value necessarily implies that it is payment of real wealth. Another way to put it, money is not an IOU, it is exchanging wealth for wealth. Money for most societies has been gold and silver; some use copper, some use nickel, some use salt, and some have even used seashells. The true definition of money is this: it is real wealth.

Now that I have presented to you what money and currency is, the knowledge that everyone needs to possess is this: How is currency created?

## How Money "Currency" Is Created

It's imperative for any investor to understand the creation of money, or in today's case the creation of currency by the central banks of the world and their respective governments. How currency is created is one the most important subjects in today's economic thinking. I will very briefly go into how currency is created; because Mike Maloney's "Hidden Secret of Money Ep. 4: The Biggest Scam in the History of Mankind"[xi] can visually and orally describe how currency is created.

*"It is well enough that people of the nation do not understand our banking and monetary system, for if they did, I believe there would be a revolution before tomorrow morning."*

First, the Federal Reserve creates the currency either by typing digits into their accounts or printing more dollars. The U.S. government issues bonds; quantitative easing (QE) was the direct purchase of these bonds by the Federal Reserve. Typically, the primary buyers, which are the large financial institutions, buy the bonds from the government and sell them to the public or the Federal Reserve. What happened is that the Fed created an IOU called a Federal Reserve note, and the United States government created an IOU called a bond. All it is, are two financial institutions swapping IOUs. This newly printed currency funds the deficit. They spend it on welfare programs, the military, or public works. The government employees and contractors then deposit the newly created currency into their banks, which the banks lend out and create more credit dollars by way of the fractional reserve banking system.

The banks leverage the newly created money in the banking system to create more profits for the banks, and the government, who collects taxes from profits, and from the earnings of the people who deposited their currency in the bank. Then you and I work for this currency to provide real value for the currency: before these institutions were just trading IOUs, and no real wealth was created. We work for this currency to have an income to sustain ourselves. The government then taxes our work to pay for their employees, programs, contractors, politicians, special interest group funding (either directly or indirectly), etc., and some of our taxes pay the interest on the debt to the Federal Reserve and our creditors.

Now, what is the Federal Reserve?

I explain to people that the Federal Reserve is a publicly charted cartel owned by private banks.[xii] Go to the Federal Reserve's website:

http://www.federalreserve.gov/faqs/about_14986.htm

Once you have read it through, possibly a few times, you'll understand the Fed's answer. It comes down to the very end where the shareholders earn a 6% dividend on their shares. However, the Fed states that it is not a private institution, and it is not a profit-making institution. I disagree with their statement, since all private companies have shareholders or stockholders, and public institutions have none. Also, it is a profit making institution since it has to pay dividends by law to the shareholders. The only way to pay dividends is from past profits or present profits. Of course, it doesn't matter if you are profitable or not, when you can print the nation's currency as a private institution publicly charted by the United States government.

So, I get depressed talking about the subject, and I know others are angry with this as well. However, people such as Dr. Ron Paul and his son Senator Rand Paul are making efforts to audit the Fed or even end the Fed. Other grassroots organizations and others in Congress are pushing to audit the Fed. I am not making any endorsements; but simply stating who has been leading the effort to conduct the first audit for the first time in its history, as the privately owned central bank we call the Federal Reserve.

Okay, enough with this topic, let's move on to the dollar standard. If you are interested in learning about the operation of the Federal Reserve, go to their website, search the internet for content, watch Mike Maloney's YouTube video, and look at some of the references in the back. The economy has economic cycles, business cycles, and credit cycles; money has its own monetary cycle.

## World Monetary Cycles

First let us dive into world monetary cycles. Yes, there are even world monetary cycles. Roughly every 40 to 60 years, the world has a new monetary cycle. A definitive monetary cycle began in 1873 when Germany created the classical gold standard. The classical gold standard was where one unit of currency was backed by an equivalent amount of gold in the nation's treasury. In the United States, a $20 note or $20 dollar bill was backed by an actual $20 gold piece. If an American went to the bank and slapped down the $20 note or claim check, that American would receive the equivalent value in real gold. The gold was what gave the U.S. dollar value; otherwise, there was no reason to store gold in the vault (Ft. Knox). Gold gave confidence to the dollar and other countries' currencies.

When World War I started, all of the combatant nations except the U.S. froze redemptions and began printing currency to pay for the war. You could not go and trade your currency, whether pounds, marks, or francs, for gold. Between the World Wars, there was a world monetary system called the gold exchange standard, where the national currency was only partially backed by gold. During the war, the U.S. printed more dollars to pay for the war as well, but the U.S.

did not freeze redemption rights. Everybody loved dollars, and this is where the saying started that the dollar was as good as gold.

Under the Federal Reserve Act of 1913[xiii] the Federal Reserve could issue a $50 note backed by a $20 Gold Piece, meaning the dollar was only backed 40% by gold. The gold exchange standard was a very flawed system, because of the instability in the system, due to a high threat of default. Sixty percent of dollars could be defaulted upon since they weren't backed by gold. Not to mention it is fraudulent to print more receipts than gold in the vault to back the currency. After the 1929 stock market crash, the American people became very concerned about the stability of the financial institutions to make good on their notes for gold. Bank runs and bank panics became rampant in the early 1930s. Bank defaults and bankruptcy became a huge economic problem and caused capital formation to be absent for the remainder of the Great Depression.

When World War II erupted in Europe, the Allies started to print and inflate the currency supply to pay for the war. Gold was one way that European nations such as the U.K. and France paid for the goods and war material imported from the U.S. The United States had primarily stayed out of the First World War and stayed out of the Second World War for two years. Europe paid for goods and war material mostly with gold. By the end of the Second World War, the U.S. had nearly two-thirds of the world's monetary gold. The gold exchange standard would not work because other nations had very little gold.

In 1944, the Bretton Woods agreement solved the problem, and the world went on another world monetary system. The world currencies were backed by the dollar, and the dollar was anchored to gold. Gold gave confidence to the dollar, and the dollar gave confidence to the world's currencies.

This system would prove very stable if the United States government kept a 100% gold backing.

However, the United States government did no such thing.

Instead, the government ran budget deficits, and they exploded in the 1960s. We spent money to fund NASA, the War on Poverty, the war in Vietnam, and President Johnson's Great Society. There is nothing wrong with spending money on scientific innovation, or trying to solve poverty. The problem was the budget deficits and printing currency, which went hand-in-hand with spending money on these programs. Monetizing budget deficits causes inflation of the currency, and the symptoms are rising prices, which hurt the poor class the most since living costs rise faster than wages.

Since the U.S. printed more claim checks (receipts) than gold in existence, other countries began to worry that their gold wasn't there, or the U.S. would default on its promise to pay in gold. The president of France, Charles De Gaulle, started to demand payment on the dollars he submitted to the Federal Reserve, and gold started to flow out of the U.S. The United States lost half of its gold reserves from 1959 to 1971.

On August 15th, 1971 President Nixon "temporarily" suspended the convertibility of the dollar into gold. For the second time in U.S. history, the United States government defaulted on the promise to pay gold. Since 1971, the world monetary system has been the dollar standard. The dollar standard was formed out of the crisis of the default. A man by the name of Henry Kissinger backed the dollar by the international trade of oil. The gold dollar now became the petrodollar, and oil producing nations only accepted payment in dollars, not gold. The United States government convinced the rest of the world to quit using gold and replace it with a fiat currency.

Let's review the succession of world monetary systems.

Start in 1873 with the gold standard, where the IOU being the currency was backed 100% by gold.

World War I erupted and the world transitioned into the gold exchange standard where the currency was only partially backed by gold.

During World War II the Bretton Woods agreement stated that all of the world's currencies were backed by the U.S. dollar and the dollar was backed by gold.

In 1971, the U.S. government defaulted on the payment of gold, constructing the next era of world monetary systems, and finally the dollar standard.

The United States has had many monetary systems, and learning the monetary history of the United States is very important, especially for Americans.

# Chapter 4: America's Story of Money

Many of us have been taught in history class the origin of America and the founding principles of America. We learned about the history of Jefferson, Franklin, and Washington's efforts in the American Revolution, and the founding documents of America.

A story that goes untold and is seldom taught in history class is the story of America's money and wealth. What America's money is and how it came to be is probably one of the most stunning feats in the history of this great nation. Money is the principle trust that holds people and a nation together "In God We Trust."

There are many reasons the American Revolution occurred: taxation without representation, no elections, no rights for British American citizens, forced quartering of troops, all of the numerous draconian acts, and no sovereignty. Sovereignty over America: a representative government, freedoms, human rights, and personal sovereignty to own money, gold and silver, were important reasons for the American Revolution.

*"I prefer dangerous freedom over peaceful slavery."*
*-Thomas Jefferson*

Great Britain's policy of mercantilism made the colonies subservient and made the colonists pay their taxes and buy goods from Great Britain with a form of specie (coin money, as opposed to paper currency). All specie then flowed from the colonies to the mother country, Great Britain. Great Britain also passed acts to limit the colonies' ability to own gold and silver. Money (gold and silver) became very scarce in the colonies to the point that colonists began issuing paper currency. Colonial script became prevalent in the American colonies for payment of goods and services.

The Crown and Parliament saw colonial script as a threat to their power. Since the currency was issued debt free, paper currency made trade more efficient, as opposed to the alternative of barter, and more economic growth occurred. Britain's Parliament then issued the Currency Acts[xiv] of 1751, 1764, and 1773, which were designed to regulate and suppress America's paper currency. Failures occurred due to hyperinflation: bank failures and failures of commodity-backed paper currency. Some of the paper currencies were backed by tobacco, which was very problematic since tobacco rots and deteriorates quickly. Paper currencies allowed growth, but not as efficiently as gold and silver due to their stable supply.

The American Revolution was as much a tax revolt as it was for Americans to own wealth and coin money. When the American Revolution started, the Continental Congress was completely and utterly broke. The Continental Congress issued continental currency to pay for the war effort and issued so many notes that the currency was destroyed by hyperinflation.

This had disastrous effects on the U.S. economy, and people lost faith and confidence in the continental dollar. Americans tried as quickly as possible to dispose of the currency by purchasing items to protect them from the rampant inflation. Since the velocity was increased as well as the currency supply, these actions only added to the hyperinflation. Any American, who tried to save in continental dollars, had their savings destroyed by hyperinflation.

Savings are the basis for preservation of capital, and when the capital stock of the nation is destroyed, economic recessions and depressions resulted. Another damaging effect was that it wiped out many people in the middle class, and the middle class of the country shrunk. It made the Americans who held on to gold, silver, farmland, timberland, resource-based businesses, and other forms of real wealth very wealthy from the hyperinflation. Americans who had claim checks on the bonds, currency, or other forms of claim checks were wiped out from the loss of purchasing power. The phrase "Not worth a continental" was termed by the first American hyperinflation.

After the war, the founding fathers wrote into the new Constitution Article I Sections 8 and 10, which gave the Congress the power to coin money and emit securities, "make any Thing but gold and silver Coin a Tender in Payment of Debts"[xv] but not the power to print fiat currency. This was a result of the founding fathers' recent memory of the hyperinflation of the continental currency, and seeing the destructive nature fiat currencies had on the middle class. America's money was henceforth defined in gold and silver. The Coinage Act of 1792[xvi] defined the United States dollar as 24.1 grams of silver.

America's greatest purchase and investment was the Louisiana Purchase in 1803. The Louisiana Purchase covered 529,920,000 acres of land that would eventually encompass 15 states, effectively doubling the size of the United States. Napoleon sold the French territory for 60 million francs and 20 million francs in debt forgiveness.[xvii] In terms of United States dollars, Louisiana was purchased for $15 million, or roughly three cents per acre. 24.1 grams or .85 ounces of silver defined the United States dollar. $15 million multiplied by .85 ounces of silver would equal 12.75 million ounces of silver. 12.75 million ounces of silver bought the Louisiana Territory encompassing 529,920,000 acres of land. 529,920,000 acres divided by 12.75 million ounces of silver equals 41.56 acres of land for one ounce of silver. Today that would be the equivalent of buying 41 acres of land for fifteen dollars.

This purchase was one of the greatest investments made by the American people.

America's industry boomed and grew under the gold and silver standard from the time period of 1792 to 1861. Unfortunately, America was torn apart by the Civil War, in which half of the nation's wealth was destroyed. Abraham Lincoln and the United States Congress had to pay for the war, and they printed debt-free currency. This fiat currency later became known as greenbacks for the green ink that was used to print the notes.

During the Revolutionary War, the states acquired debts, and these debts were consolidated then passed on to The First Bank of the United States. These debts were paid off, and America was debt free in 1836. The United States government had a credible bond market since it incurred debt and paid it off. The Union's credit worthiness gave them a distinct advantage over the Confederacy since it had great access to the debt market in Europe. It also meant that the Union did not have to print as much currency to pay for the war while the Confederacy had to figure out a way to persuade European investors that the Confederacy was legitimate and had the ability to repay the investors with interest.

European nations such as Great Britain were very dependent on Southern agricultural products, namely cotton. The European textile industry was dependent on the flow of cheap American cotton coming from the Southern states. A solution that the Confederates came up with was to back the bonds by cotton.

Jefferson Davis and the Confederates also printed debt-free currency to pay for the Confederates' war effort and issued bonds backed by cotton. The Confederacy raised the necessary funds to sustain the war effort. As long as the South could break through the North's blockade and ship the cotton to Western Europe to make good on their bonds, they would be fine financially. Everything was going to plan in 1861 and 1862; however, their plan would eventually fail. Some historians state that the major turning point of the war was the defeat of General Lee's Confederate Army at the Battle of Gettysburg. I, however, believe the turning point of the Civil War was the Battle of New Orleans, nearly one year before the Battle of Gettysburg.

The Mississippi River was the major shipping lane for cotton to reach the Gulf Coast. The cotton was then shipped to Europe to make good on the promise to pay cotton on the bonds. If New Orleans was lost to the Union, then the shipments of cotton would decline significantly, possibly resulting in the loss of confidence that the bonds would be paid. When New Orleans fell the steady flow of cotton from the South became a trickle. European investors panicked, the loss of cotton to the textile mill meant layoffs, and European economies fell into recession. The Confederacy could not raise the funds it needed in the European financial markets, causing the Confederacy to print more currency to pay for the war. The more currency the Confederacy printed, the less it was worth, and eventually people lost confidence in the Confederate dollar, resulting in the second hyperinflation in U.S. history.

The Union Currency lost half of its value when the war ended due to the expansion of the greenback. United States debt dramatically increased throughout the duration of the war. The Confederate dollar went into hyperinflation during the war and then went to zero after the South declared defeat. Both sides suffered dearly from the Civil War, with half of the nation's wealth destroyed. A half a million men died, causing a very large loss in the economy and social structure of society. The United States government began its reforms, paying down the debt, and trying to enact policies to improve the economy. Possibly the worst time to be alive in America was during and after the Civil War.

In the 1870s, America was still a war-torn country. Even though America was unified in 1865, it was very much a divided nation politically, socially, and economically. One policy that the United States established was to contract the currency supply of the greenback, which created a deflation in the economy. Demonetizing silver was another policy adopted by the U.S. government; this demonetization contributed to the deflation seen in the economy. This act became known as the Crime of 1873[xviii]. This action was a factor that caused the Long Depression of 1873.

America went back to a gold standard but demonetized silver from the monetary system. This caused the worst deflation in economic history; farmers could not repay their debts, causing massive defaults, and resulting in periodic bank runs during the 1870s. Banks issued their own currency, called bank notes, which were redeemable for money (gold and silver). Many banks issued currencies failed during the 1870s to 1907. Banks were lobbying Congress to create a central bank. After the Financial Panic of 1907, bankers advocated Congress to create the Federal Reserve. In 1913, the Federal Reserve was created and printed Federal Reserve notes (FRN) redeemable in gold. World War I unfolded in 1914 and the Federal Reserve printed currency to pay for the U.S. effort. Inflation broke out, and mal-investments were made, particularly in the stock market. Since the Federal Reserve printed more notes than they had gold, the possibility of bank runs for gold increased.

Under the Federal Reserve Act of 1913, the Federal Reserve could issue a $50 note backed by a $20 gold piece, implying the dollar was only backed 40% by gold. The gold exchange standard was a very flawed system, due to the threat of default that arose from 60% of dollars not being backed by gold. Not to mention that it can be considered fraudulent to print more receipts than there is gold in the vault to back the currency. After the 1929 stock market crash, the American people became very concerned about the stability of the financial institutions to make good on their notes for gold. Bank runs and bank panics became rampant in the early 1930s, and bank defaults and bankruptcy became a huge economic problem.

The response from Washington D.C. and Wall Street could have been to declare a default on the promise to pay gold, back the dollar 100% by gold, foreclose banks, and jail those who perpetuated the fraud—executives of banks and Federal officials. They all should have gone to jail. It is fraudulent to state that a $50 note was backed by $50 worth of gold when in reality that $50 note was backed by a $20 gold coin, so it wasn't 100% backed by gold.

If this had occurred, the financial system would have started with a clean slate, clean system, and government would have placed laws to prevent these frauds from ever happening again. Would there have been financial turmoil for a few years? Of course! However, we would have averted a decade-long Great Depression, and instead had a three-year Great Depression followed by a sustainable recovery. Unfortunately, the exact opposite happened.

In 1933, the newly elected President Roosevelt decided to declare a "bank holiday." Don't you just love the sound of that? It's a "holiday" (sarcasm). He issued an executive order to nationalize gold. U.S. citizens who owned physical gold in their possession had to turn in their gold to the nearest Federal Reserve Bank, where they'd be paid $20.67 per ounce. If anyone refused, a person could be fined $10,000 and be thrown in jail for ten years. This was the exact opposite to my solution of putting those in jail who caused the problem in the first place; instead, the president went after ordinary Americans.

The rationale behind the order was that if gold could not be legally owned, the American people could not legally redeem gold "money" from the banks. If the American people could not legally redeem their gold "money" from the banks, then the Federal Reserve, the banking system, and the government could not be restrained from printing more currency.

On May 1st, 1933, America's gold was sent to the vaults of Fort Knox and the Federal Reserve of New York. The president and the Treasury Department raised the price of gold from $20.67 per ounce to $35.00 per ounce. A theft of purchasing power occurred when the Treasury raised the price of gold. Everyone who had traded their gold for paper lost roughly 40% of their purchasing power. Americans could not take the $20.67 that they were given by the government and purchase an ounce of gold. They could only purchase .59 ounces of gold with the $20.67.[xix]

Everyone who did *not* trade in their gold—political and financial insiders, the Federal Reserve, the Treasury, and the United States government—gained 75% return on the gold they held. In the second greatest deflation in United States history, the gold price increased by 75 percent.

Keep in mind that they did not nationalize silver since it was not a threat to the monetary system, and silver was widely used for industrial purposes. Americans who held physical silver gained in purchasing power from the deflation, had no counter-party risk with the banks, and could still use silver as a medium of exchange. After the gold nationalization, Federal Reserve notes became the predominant currency, replacing the United States dollar.

The next major milestone in America's story of money was the Bretton Woods agreement in 1944. For the first time in American history and world history, a nation's currency backed nearly all of the other world's nations currency, and the dollar was backed by gold. International trade boomed and Americans at home enjoyed the largest peacetime expansion in U.S. history. Unfortunately, for the second time in United States history, the United States government along with the Federal Reserve printed more currency than gold in their vaults. Other nations realized this and started to demand their gold, resulting in a worldwide bank run on gold. The United States was the bank, and the other nations ran on the bank to demand their gold "money" back!

In August of 1971, President Richard Nixon closed the gold window and told other nations that the United States would not make good on its promise to redeem dollars for gold. The reason the U.S. government defaulted on its promise is because it had printed more claim checks than actual gold held in its vaults.

In a hurried effort, the world and the U.S. developed a new monetary system.

Nixon, along with Secretary of State Henry Kissinger, had to establish confidence in the dollar and try to maintain the dollar's world reserve currency status. As the nation's principal diplomat, Henry Kissinger negotiated with Saudi Arabia to sell oil in dollars. The United States would promise to maintain and defend the House of Saud and in return Saudi Arabia would sell their oil for dollars. The Organization of the Petroleum Exporting Nations (OPEC) went along with Saudi Arabia, and other countries, including Iran, negotiated the same deal with the U.S., promising to sell their oil in dollars. Since oil was sold and priced in dollars, the dollars held by other central banks would be held as a fiat currency to purchase oil off of the oil market, creating the demand for dollars to be still held as the world's fiat reserve currency.

Many currencies have failed in the United States. We have had two hyperinflations, bank runs, financial crises, and other catastrophes. Gold and silver have always been a store of wealth. Gold and silver are a form of savings, not an investment. Fiat currencies are for short-term savings while gold and silver are for long-term savings.

Are fiat currencies bad? Yes.

Are we in a serious situation? No, life will go on just like it always has.

The questions are: do you understand what is happening, do you know what future world monetary system lies ahead, and do you know how to prepare?

# Chapter 5: Learning From Past Financial Calamities

Manias, bubbles, panics, crises, hyperinflations—catastrophe is always around the corner! Before I begin to help you better protect yourself from financial calamities, and, more importantly, show how you could profit from these financial calamities, we first need to go over the history of manias, panics, bubbles, crashes, crisis, and other financial calamities. Without the foundation of financial history, and learning from past financial mistakes made by other investors, we are doomed to repeat those mistakes.

*"Those who do not remember the past are condemned to repeat it."*
*-George Santayana*

## The Tulip Mania

A mania is caused by the public bidding up a non-financial item to extremes, and people willing to trade incredible value for an item that has little to no value. A modern day example of this would be the Pet Rock craze that happened in the 1960s. Granted, it was not a mania, but it showed how people would pay outrageous amounts of money for something that was worth nothing. These manias usually end in a fantastic crash of the price of the item. Manias are typically not harmful to society because they do not affect asset prices. They only hurt people who were foolish enough to participate in the bubble. The individuals who benefit are the ones selling the item or the ones who buy early to sell to the gullible crowd. Bubbles include financial assets or instruments that cause enormous problems for the economy, often leading to a panic or crisis.

One of the very first recorded manias occurred in Denmark. In the early 1600s, tulips were introduced to Europe. Among the wealthy they quickly became a coveted luxury item. As their popularity grew in Denmark, the mania spread to other markets in France. French speculators took part in the market along with professional growers and the wealthy in Denmark.

In 1636, the mania started to inflate. The Dutch opened one of the first futures markets. Growers and buyers could negotiate contracts to buy and sell tulip bulbs to be delivered for next season's production. These contracts were called futures contracts. Tulips also became the fourth leading export from the Netherlands, and the bubble for tulips grew rapidly. The mania was so out of control that a single tulip bulb called the Semper Augustus sold for ten times the annual salary of the typical skilled tradesmen; today that would be the equivalent of a tulip bulb selling for $500,000. In the winter of 1636-1637, the tulip mania peaked. Speculators, wealthy individuals, growers, and the public were in a frenzy, sometimes trading the same tulip bulb a dozen times a day.

The future contracts were to be fulfilled in the month of February 1637. However, suppliers never delivered the tulip bulbs, and those contracts were never fulfilled. This was due in part to the collapse of tulip prices that occurred in February, and the trading of these bulbs halted. Some historians believe that an outbreak of the bubonic plague could have contributed to the collapse in tulip prices. Others believe that the Tulip Mania ended when people finally realized that these were just bulbs after all and had very little value compared to what they were trading for at the height of the mania.

## The Mississippi Bubble

One of the greatest bubbles in the 18th century occurred in France in the early 1700s. The Mississippi Bubble began and fell apart dramatically; this was the first bubble on record that used a paper currency system to purchase the speculative asset class, and the first bubble to have a central bank actively issuing currency.

The architect behind the bubble was a convicted murderer and mastermind gambler named John Law. He murdered a man in England and fled to France to escape the hangman's noose.

In May 1716, John Law created the Banque Generale Privee or General Private Bank. The government's treasury bills and government-accepted notes backed the bank's capital. Most of the bank's capital was leveraged by France's large debt. John Law consolidated that same debt into the Banque Generale Privee. John Law's bank was permitted to issue paper money, another fiat currency.

In August of 1717, he bought the Mississippi Company. That same year he created a joint-stock trading company called the Compagnie d'Occident (The Mississippi Company). The company was granted a monopoly of the West Indies and North America by the French government. In 1718, Law transformed his bank into the Banque Royale (Royal Bank), meaning the French King Louis XV guaranteed the paper money and notes. John Law also had Compagnie des Indes Orientales and another rival company called the Compagnie Perpetuelle des Indes merge with the Mississippi Company. On May 25th, 1719, John Law had a monopoly of all French commerce on the seas. Literally, the French government encouraged and backed a man to create a trade monopoly.

Of course, all of this corruption can only lead to disaster. Law exaggerated the wealth of Louisiana and the Mississippi Company. He created a very effective marketing scheme leading to wild speculation in the stock. Markets, assets, or products need to capture the imagination of investors, speculators, and the public. Cheap credit or money printing needs to be available to kick it into the euphoric phase of the bubble.

John Law would watch the price of the stock go up and down. When the stock did not perform as he wished, he would walk up two floors in the same building where shares were issued to print more currency and issue new notes, spurring the stock higher. The Banque Royale distributed its "profits" in bank-issued notes. The scheme was immoral and corrupt since the bank was issuing more notes than coinage existed. The new paper money was causing incredible inflation in the economy and propagated more speculation in stocks, agriculture, and other assets.

When a currency or paper money begins to be debased, whether it is Roman or Greek coins being debased with base metals, printing ever more paper money, or in the case of the modern world just typing digital currency into a computer, the result is the same. Rampant speculation, inflation, and increasing economic instability result from an unstable currency supply created by central bankers or financiers who misuse the system for their benefit.

In 1720, the Banque Royale and the Mississippi Company merged into one company. Phillippe II, Duke of Orleans, appointed John Law to be comptroller of finance. Everything seemed to be fine, even better than anyone could have possibly imagined.

Then suddenly, near the end of 1720, everything quickly changed. Holders of the bank's paper money went to the bank and demanded specie (gold and silver coins). Soon, word spread that the bank had issued more currency than gold and silver on deposit. This sparked a bank run. The bank closed, refusing to redeem its notes for gold and silver, and the Mississippi Company stock began to plummet. The bubble had burst into a dismal failure, and panicked investors began to sell.

John Law, as quickly as he came, fled to Venice where he lived off of his gambling and later died. The French government issued a new currency and halved the value of the old currency, meaning it took two old currency units to equal the new currency. Investors who had invested in the Mississippi Company lost over 90% of their investment and then lost another 50% due to the devaluation of the currency. So if an investor bought shares at the top of the bubble and sold on the bottom, they would have lost 95% of their purchasing power, while an investor who had sold at the top and held bank notes only lost half of their purchasing power. The only way to have profited would have been to purchase shares at the beginning, sell the shares at the top for a ten-fold gain, and then trade the bank notes for gold or silver, which would then have doubled in purchasing power. If someone did that, they would have seen a twenty-fold gain on their investment as opposed to losing 95 percent.

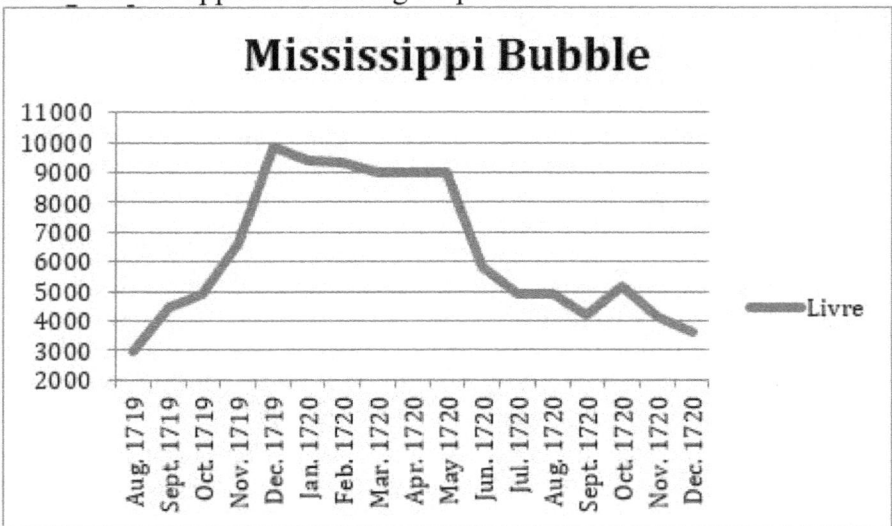

(Data Source: http://www.cato.org/publications/commentary/2009-charts)

For me, this event clearly reveals how valuable silver and gold are as a store of value. Silver and gold cannot be defrauded, and cannot go to zero since they have intrinsic value. Everyone who participated in the Mississippi Bubble and got out in time to buy real tangible wealth made enormous fortunes. Real wealth such as farmland, timberland, businesses, factories, merchant ships, gold, and silver protected individuals from this fraud and wealth destruction. Those who did not take physical possession of the gold and silver by turning their receipts or bank notes were caught up in the panic.

## Panics and Bank Runs

Panics and bank runs are the "boogeymen" of financial history. Of course, they seem a distant memory in the minds of many Americans. I am going to focus on the bank runs and panics that occurred during the 18th century of American history.

A few bankers who wanted to drive up the price of United States debt securities and bonds created the Panic of 1792. These prominent bankers, such as William Duer and Alexander Macomb, speculated in the debt markets of the newly formed United States. A bubble was created in the United States bond market by the rampant speculation of bankers and other banking institutions that borrowed to speculate in the market. Like all bubbles, it burst, and the prices of bonds fell, and the yield on the Treasury increased. Those bankers and banks defaulted on the loans, causing the bank runs. Many people believed that the banks would not be able to keep their promise to redeem species on the depositors' deposits. In fact, the banks did default on their promise, causing much financial hardship among the middle classes.

The bursting of the land speculation bubble in the United States instigated the Panic of 1796-1797. Speculation in American land started when people were trying to protect themselves from the rampant hyperinflation of the continental dollar. In conjunction with the Panic of 1792, it encouraged more people to purchase land, as land was seen as a "safe" asset. A few speculators, such as Robert Morris, John Nicholson, and James Greenleaf, took it even further by issuing their own notes. These notes were accepted because of Morris's financial status as the greatest financier in America at the time. They formed the North American Land Company in 1795, and by 1797 the company had issued $10 million worth of notes (roughly

$600 million in today's dollars). Like all paper pyramid schemes, it came to an end. In 1797, the notes were worth one-eighth their value.[xx]

Panics are simply bank runs caused by a bubble, default, or in some cases a loss of confidence in the banking industry for printing more claim checks (referred to as demand notes) than actual coinage stored in their vaults. Depositors rush to the bank to demand their deposits of gold and silver, causing the bank to collapse when they do not have enough gold and silver to meet demand. In today's case, the paper dollars have replaced the gold and silver while the digital currency has replaced the bank notes issued. Crises can result when the panic spreads into other financial institutions and disrupts the economy to where the economy is in a recession or downright depression.

## The Roots of the Great Depression

The Great Depression is the most widely known and written about topic in U.S. economic and financial history. Unlike most economists who believe the cause of the Great Depression was the stock market bubble and succeeding crash of the market in 1929, in my research, I found a stunning factor in the year 1913 that contributed to the crash sixteen years later: the creation of the Federal Reserve and the Internal Revenue Service (IRS).

The year 1913 saw two major bureaucracies formed that directly affected the national economy. The Federal Reserve, first influenced interest rates, bank lending standards, capital reserves for banks, at the time indirectly influenced the treasuries market, and the Federal Reserve was granted control of the money supply. How couldn't a privately owned central bank that was publicly chartered by the U.S. government and was passed in secret on Christmas Eve have a negative effect on the economy? It wasn't the Fed's intention to create the Great Depression, but it was the actions taken by the Federal Reserve in response to World War I that laid the foundation for the Great Depression.

The First World War was the source of much of the turmoil that occurred in the early part of the 20th century. When the United States declared war on the Central Powers and joined the Allies, our nation needed to fund the war. War bonds did help fund the war, but it was the Federal Reserve's policy of expanding the money supply by writing "checks" to its member banks to purchase war bonds. A check and balance structure was needed to keep the Federal Reserve honest. Where the Federal Reserve could not print too much money to fund reckless government spending, and limit the creation of new Federal Reserve notes (printing more claim checks on gold and silver). The United States government decided to create a debt ceiling to cap the debt to make sure the nation's politicians did not take the U.S. into financial ruin. There is just one problem with their remedy: the same spendthrift politicians who passed the law to install the debt ceiling could raise the debt ceiling.

As the war in Europe progressed, the Federal Reserve printed more notes, but they did not suspend redemption rights, in contrast to the other nations that participated in the war. America never left the gold standard during the Great War, while other nations abandoned the gold standard, in particular, Weimar Germany, which saw a hyperinflation in the early 1920s. This monetary policy created the term "The dollar is as good as gold." The Federal Reserve Act required a 40% backing of gold, and the Federal Reserve printed to that ratio.

The possibility of bank runs and bank panics was laid in the early 1920s but not realized until the end of the decade.

When the war ended in 1918, Europe was devastated. The U.S. soon had a depression of its own—the Depression of 1920-21. This depression was more catastrophic in its first year than in the first year of the Great Depression, which began in 1929. Unemployment soared to double digits; homelessness surged, and other distortions were seen as a result of the Great War. Why was it that the Depression of 1920-21 only lasted eighteen months as opposed to the Great Depression of 1929 that lasted for nearly eighteen years? A president named Warren G. Harding promised the nation a return to normalcy before The Great War ever happened.

President Harding shrunk government spending and deficit spending, shrunk the size of government, returned to peacetime policies, repealed acts that were introduced in the war, and did not intervene in the affairs of Americans or the free market. Instead, he believed that the American people were the best ones to sort out the problems and rebuild the nation after the war. The United States government took no form of action in the form of economic aid or stimulus. One of the positive policy measures the Fed took was to raise interest rates from 3.7% to 5.5% to control the post-war inflation.

As we learned in Chapter 2 when interest rates rise it discourages borrowing and speculation while encouraging savings and capital formation. The law of supply and demand of money says that people value money more when it is worth more, either in purchasing power or interest bearing accounts above three percent. In short, during the Depression of 1920-21, the U.S. government did nothing: no bailouts, no stimulus, no TARP, no HARP, and no deficit spending. The federal government was responsible for the fiscal policy of paying down debt, cutting taxes, cutting spending, and running a budget surplus. Monetary policies such as raising interest rates to encourage savings and capital formation; removing incentives for speculation, overconsumption, mal-investments, and gives the economic system a structural reform and a cleansing cycle by exposing and removing bad debts and investments. I have to give credit where credit is due: The Federal Reserve conducted proper monetary policy for the Depression of 1920-21. Interest rate hikes were made by the Fed to stop inflation, and they had little regard for unemployment, even though unemployment was worse in the first year of the Depression of 1920-21 than the first year of the Great Depression.

One of the problems that lay dormant during the greatest decade-long boom in American history was that there were more claim checks or Federal Reserve notes in circulation than actual gold held in the vaults.

During the 1920s, several factors contributed to the huge economic boom:

1. The restructuring that occurred in the 1920s.

2. The savings that laid the foundation for capital formation.

3. The federal government's inert state of allowing the economy and people to make choices.

These next points were contributing factors to the boom and bust:

4. The access to consumer credit. For example, General Motors had established itself as a major competitor to Ford, and GM allowed Americans to purchase cars on consumer credit. Henry Ford did not believe in consumer credit, and it was his belief that it was a form of usury. He relented until 1927 due to other executives pressuring him and seeing GM's increasing market share of the car industry.

5. The easing of lending standards by banks and other financial institutions.

6. The accumulating margin debts by investors to speculate in the stock market.

7. The lowering of interest rates from the Federal Reserve, which as you know encourages speculation and discourages savings and capital formation.

So what exactly caused the Great Depression?

1. Too many Federal Reserve notes in circulation, allowing for the possibility of a banking panic.

2. The access to credit and the easing of credit standards.

3. The lowering of interest rates encouraging speculation and discouraging capital formation.

4. The mass speculation that went on at Wall Street.

These factors are the warnings signs of economic recessions, and please make note of what *not* to do. You shouldn't take on massive amounts of debt just because you *can* take on massive amounts of debt. People need not speculate in markets! I mean do not make financial purchases that stray away from investing fundamentals.

## Who Survives a Depression?

During a depression, where do the successful people store their capital and how do they preserve their capital?

We have seen that throughout history, individuals who saved in physical gold and silver and invested in resource-based companies have been more successful than individuals who have held the claim checks. These individuals who saved and held primary wealth and secondary wealth outperformed individuals who held tertiary forms of wealth. In panics, depressions, and crashes, the people who hold tertiary forms of wealth—also referred to as claim checks—were wiped out.

Economic growth and development can only occur when the four economic resources are used and utilized properly. Those resources, of course, would be land, labor, capital, and entrepreneurship. When you have a free market, people can purchase land, if there is minimal government intervention, and develop the land for productive purposes. Then entrepreneurs need to hire the labor to produce the goods from the land, in the factory or distribute the goods or services in the marketplace. Hopefully, the government is not pricing your labor out of the market through taxes and regulations, and then you can hire people at the market price of the labor.

During economic downturns, capital needs to be reorganized through bankruptcies and defaults. Capital also needs to be formed. Capital formation can only occur through savings, and savings are a reflection of spending less than you earn.

Entrepreneurship is typically readily available. The problem entrepreneurship faces is when it is discouraged or punished, such as the 90% tax rate that the government imposed on wealthy people and the people who wanted to become wealthy.

When the government borrows, taxes, and spends too much, it requires capital to do so. There is less capital available for entrepreneurs and the American people to feed their families, support themselves, grow their business, or invest for retirement. Entrepreneurship and capital formation are discouraged through government regulation and taxation, which impedes economic growth and development.

With that being said, I would love effective regulators with an unlimited amount of funds to work tirelessly to eradicate fraud. Unfortunately, you and I live in the real world, and taxes are the way we allow the government to fund the regulators.

Taxes impede economic growth and development by removing capital and discouraging capital formation. In the world of economics, there are trade-offs, and I would rather have economic growth and development with fraud being *caught and punished* instead of being *prevented*. If you disagree with me and would prefer little economic growth and development as well as very little fraud, I do respect that view. However, I do not want to live in a developing country with very little fraud. What ended the Great Depression was when the government was rolled backed, and free market capitalism allowed capital formation for economic growth.

The economic growth and capital formation did not occur *because* of World War II, but it *in spite* of World War II.

You and I could dive into the subject of the Great Depression, but this is not a book about the Great Depression. This book is about finding success in difficult economic situations, and I know as of now I have been simplistic in how to become successful. If we do not ground ourselves in the historical context, we cannot create a game plan for our success.

# 1970s Recessions, Inflation, and Gold Bubble

Most baby boomers will remember the 1970s recessions, 1973 oil shock, double-digit inflation, and the gold bubble were the first financial and economic calamities and disasters that the baby boomer generation encountered. A few reasons the recessions of the 1970s occurred is for the same reasons why we had the Great Depression in the 1930s: the United States government printed more notes than gold held in the vaults. Other countries such as France under Charles De Gaulle began demanding gold on their Federal Reserve notes. Gold began to flow out of the vaults in New York, and back to the countries demanding gold. In 1971, Nixon defaulted on the promise to pay gold, and with the aid of Henry Kissinger, backed the dollar's value on the oil trade with deals made in the oil producing nations of the Middle East. They made the dollar the first fiat currency that backed the rest of the world's currency, replaced gold with the U.S. dollar, and placed the world monetary system on the dollar standard.

Inflation roared because of the deficit spending by the United States government, and this deficit spending was funded through currency creation to pay for the deficits. The price of gold surged in response to the devaluation of the U.S. dollar. Going back to the law of supply and demand, when the supply of dollars increases, the value of the dollar decreases; subsequently the price of gold rises, since it takes more Federal Reserve notes to purchase gold due to the devaluation.

Free markets try to find equilibrium, and this is what they did back in the 1970s when people bought gold to preserve their purchasing power. The amount of currency the United States government created caused the response of the price of gold to rise. When Paul Volcker became chairman of the Fed, his mission was to kill inflation. He did that in two ways: slowing the rate of currency creation and raising interest rates to 20 percent. Raising interest rates above the inflation rate gave people an incentive to save in dollars, causing those dollars to become more valuable while high-interest rates discouraged speculation in all markets including the gold and silver market, which had gone parabolic. The gold bubble burst, inflation slowed, savings increased, and capital formation began to allow economic growth in the 1980s and 1990s.

## Dotcom Bubble

Here are the main factors that gave way to the Dotcom Bubble. Fundamentally, the Dotcom Bubble was a mania spurred by cheap credit and speculation. Interest rates had been falling since 1981 and in the late '90s, interest rates were between six and eight percent. Due to falling rates, in the minds of many speculators and investors, borrowing to purchase stocks had become "cheap." Credit was available, but not in copious amounts. The main factor for the bubble was the mania that spurred the public to borrow to speculate in the stock market while emerging technology stocks captured the imagination of the investing public.

Massive losses in wealth occurred when people realized that the technology companies were overvalued, and some were a sham since they didn't earn any money. Nevertheless, people will still buy "assets" that have no intrinsic value, and that is why you stay away from those valueless assets in a bubble. No one can time the inevitable collapse, so it's smart just to stay away. The Dotcom Bubble burst, and we had the recession of 2003. It was the response to this bubble and recession, by the Federal Reserve and the government, that caused the Financial Crisis of 2008.

## The Housing Bubble and Financial Crisis of 2008

To increase home ownership, Federal Reserve Chairman Alan Greenspan lowered interest rates and the United States government started to deregulate the banks, such as repealing Glass-Steagall in 1999,[xxi] to allow lower lending standards. The banks resisted initially. The U.S. government then gave them an implicit guarantee on sub-prime mortgages. Lowering interest rates to historic lows produced rampant speculation on Wall Street, investors, and the public while discouraging savings and capital formation. On top of that, they lowered lending standards, and the federal government permitted non-financially astute or non-financially capable people to borrow to purchase homes and speculate in the real estate market.

Then we had the moral hazard of the United States government guaranteeing home loans.

Moral hazard is the lack of incentive to minimize and protect oneself from risk, since one does not have to accept the consequences of their action(s). It's when an individual or an institution does not have to bear potential losses even though they acquire the gain. Typically, due to the human element, people will take riskier actions to increase gain since they do not have to bear the consequence of the financial loss.

Banks knew that too many bad loans were on their books, so they did whatever they could to get these loans off their books. One way was to securitize these sub-prime mortgages in financial instruments such as mortgage-backed securities (MBS). The banks would insure these mortgages, and then the banks structured tranches of mortgages in these securities. (A tranche is one of a number of related securities offered as part of the same transaction.) Investors could purchase which tranche they wanted to invest depending on their risk tolerance. Never mind that the securities were backed by worthless mortgages.

The availability of credit, historically low-interest rates, abhorrent lending standards, and the government creating a moral hazard: these aspects allowed the Housing Bubble to come into existence. With any good bubble, it needs to capture the imagination and emotion of the investing public to move the markets in a parabolic fashion. Home sweet home! Look at all of the emotional attachment and excitement someone has for their home. In a nutshell, society just needs emotion, excitement, and the access to credit to move an asset, an item, or a market into overvalued bubble territory.

In 2008, we watched in horror what happened to the markets. Financial markets seized because no one wanted the securities (merely another form of a paper claim check). Investors did not want the counterparty risk involved with the financial system, and we had an electronic run on the banks. (Counterparty risk is the risk to each party of a contract that the counterparty will not live up to its contractual obligations.)

Please watch this video of Rep. Paul Kanjorski on C-Span stating that we were having an electronic bank run and a bank panic: 2-minute video: https://youtu.be/Sxz6gYIiFHc[xxii] or an alternative link https://www.youtube.com/watch?v=Sxz6gYIiFHc&feature=youtu.be or 6-min. video: https://www.youtube.com/watch?v=pD8viQ_DhS4

Instead, investors wanted their money or their paper Federal Reserve notes. Investors, institutions, and individuals around the world were drawing on their money market accounts and depositing the digital dollars in their bank accounts. What I would infer would have occurred after that was for people to go down to the banks to physically withdraw their paper currency out of the banks. Essentially, many people wanted to cash out all at once. Bankruptcies and defaults of major companies, such as Lehman Brothers, terrified people: because of the implications of counterparty risk, and the valuations of the underlying assets. A rapid stock market crash transpired due to the overvaluations of the stock market; margin calls on speculators. People needed cash to cover their positions, to stop losses, and to try to save their capital from the bubble annihilation.

I like to say that history does not repeat; rather it rhymes from one catastrophe to another. In my research, I found individuals who have the contrarian view that the public or the herd charging into the bubble will protect themselves and can profit if they take the appropriate actions to do so. Individuals who save their capital in non-counterparty assets, who have real wealth, service low debt to no debt, stay away from the financial manias and get-rich-quick schemes, understand how the economy functions, and then position themselves financially to take advantage of the next economic growth phase, will prosper.

I will show you historical examples of individuals who have done exactly that, and created multi-billion dollar empires.

# Chapter 6: Self-Made Entrepreneurs

How many times have you been trapped in a fear loop? Fearing what will lie ahead, what may happen, that the world will end, and simply being paralyzed by fear. Don't paralyze yourself with fear, and don't panic when there are financial disasters in life. Instead, pursue your aspirations in life and be a blessing to others. Remember that the most perilous times are the most opportune times to make fortunes, and that the greatest opportunities are found in the greatest economic catastrophes. Great individuals have faced the same types of financial difficulties you have and have accomplished great feats.

I know the future may seem bleak. You may think you cannot accomplish your retirement goals, business goals, or personal finance goals. I am here to tell you that you can, regardless the difficulty. First of all, you need the mindset for success. If you *believe* you will fail, you *will* fail. If you *believe* you can achieve, you *will* succeed. Think you *can* as oppose to you *can't*. Mindset determines all, and how well you can control your emotions will have a significant correlation to your success.

Here are just a few of my favorite self-made entrepreneurs. I'm sure you'll be as inspired by their stories as I am.

*"I had to make my own living and my own opportunity. But I made it! Don't sit down and wait for the opportunities to come. Get up and make them."*
*-Madam C.J. Walker*

## Madam C.J. Walker

If you couldn't tell, I love history! I am one of those people who learn from other people's failures and successes. The first self-made entrepreneur I want to discuss with you was not one who began her business out of a crisis but had to succeed through difficult circumstances. In 1919, Madam C.J. Walker, born Sarah Breedlove, became America's first self-made female millionaire—and she also happened to be the daughter of slaves. Sarah Breedlove was the first child in her family to be born in freedom in 1867 after the Emancipation Proclamation Act. In her early childhood, Miss

Breedlove had many sorrows. Her two parents passed away at the age of seven, and she was adopted by an abusive in law.

In 1881, at the age of fourteen, to escape her abusive guardian she married her first husband, Moses McWilliams. Six years later Moses passed away, and she found herself widowed with a two-year-old daughter named Lelia. Determined to give Lelia a formal education, she went to work as a washerwoman earning less than a dollar a day. This first step was the start of her becoming one of America's greatest entrepreneurs.

When she acquired a scalp disorder from the lye used in the soaps employed in her job as a washerwoman, Breedlove researched hair care. She initially acquired her knowledge about hair care from her brothers who were barbers in St. Louis. Then at the 1904 World's Fair, she became a saleswoman for Annie Turnbo Malone, a leading African-American entrepreneur, selling hair care and beauty products.

Having learned the hair care business from Annie Malone, she moved to Denver, Colorado to begin her own business in the hair care industry. There she met her husband Charles Joseph Walker and adopted the name Madam C.J. Walker. Charles Joseph Walker was a newspaper advertising salesman. He was tasked with selling the advertising slots to companies to advertise in the newspaper. With the help of Charles Walker's skill at salesmanship and promotion, Madam C.J. Walker became a star saleswoman.

She promoted her business and expanded into the Deep South. Madam C.J. Walker hired and trained "beauty culturists" to learn and practice the art of selling her hair care products. In 1910, Madam C.J. Walker established her headquarters in Indianapolis, Indiana, with a factory, hair salon, and beauty school to train her "beauty culturists" to sell her hair care products. Her business grew throughout the United States and into Cuba, Jamaica, Haiti, Panama, and Costa Rica. By the year 1917, she was asked in an interview whether or not she was a millionaire. She replied, "I am not yet a millionaire, but hope to be in some time." At her death in 1919, she was the wealthiest woman in the United States.

I want you to ponder for a moment on the enormity of the accomplishment! Madam C.J. Walker started in 1904 in her profession in the beauty industry, started her business in 1906, and was a millionaire by 1919! Within a fifteen-year time span, she became a millionaire in the hair care industry that generated most of its business in the South. In today's dollars, she would have become a billionaire in a fifteen-year time span. Don't tell me that you can't do a tenth of that or even one percent of what she did! I know you could, and I believe you do too! A person doesn't have to become a large business magnate, but could you open up a small business for yourself.

Madam C.J. Walker's accomplishments did not just come from the great business and vast fortune she created. She was a great philanthropist, donating large sums of money to the National Association for the Advancement of Colored People (NAACP), orphanages, churches, and charities. Mrs. Walker also had to fight during some of the greatest panics in U.S. history. The Panic of 1907 caused a crippling of capital in the U.S. and plunged the U.S. into a recession. I wonder how she managed to get her beauty care business through that panic and recession—but a tough mindset has the right mentality to raise the capital, be resourceful, and demonstrate an incredible work ethic.

A few things I want you to take away before we move onto our next entrepreneur.

First, Madam C.J. Walker had the drive and the inspiration to succeed, and her greatest motivation was her daughter.

Second, she found herself people who could help her succeed in her vision. She had her brothers, a mentor Annie Malone, and her husband who specialized in promotion.

Lastly, she had a plan, and she described that plan and vision to her "beauty culturists."

Next we are going to look at a product that was launched in 1908 by one of America's most famous industrialist, Henry Ford.

*"Failure is simply the opportunity to begin again, this time more intelligently."*
*-Henry Ford*

## Henry Ford

Henry Ford is most widely known for founding the Ford Motor Company. Due to the innovations he and his company contributed to American capitalism, he's one of my favorite businessmen in world history.

We'll begin with his childhood experiences and early career that shaped him into the business magnate that he would later become. In 1876, one of the early tragedies in Ford's life was losing his mother when he was thirteen years old. Ford's father gave him a watch when he was very young, and by the age of fifteen, he was dismantling and reassembling watches for friends, family, and neighbors, and became known for repairing watches. The mechanical functions interested Ford and led to his passion for engineering. Ford left home at the age of sixteen to become a machinist for James F. Fowler and Bros., and later he was hired by the Detroit Dry Dock Co.

In 1882, Ford came back to the family farm to work and maintain the farm. A Westinghouse portable steam engine was operated and maintained by Ford on the farm, giving him the experience that led to being hired by Westinghouse to service portable steam engines. Note that during his early years, Henry Ford was acquiring marketable skills that he could use both as an employee and later as an industrialist. During his tenure at Westinghouse, Ford also enrolled at Bryant and Stratton Business College in Detroit to study another marketable skill, bookkeeping.

Ford became an engineer for the Edison Illuminating Company in 1891, and in the next two years, he was promoted to Chief Engineer. With the increase in pay and some time to devote to experimentation, Ford began to work on his self-powered "quadricycle" vehicle. By 1896, he had finished his prototype of the quadricycle and presented his invention to Thomas Edison. Edison approved of his prototype and Ford's other automobile experiments. Encouraged by Edison, Ford built the second automobile and completed it in 1898. Ford decided to go into business to produce his automobiles; he needed only to raise the capital to do so.

William H. Murphy, a lumber mill tycoon, backed Ford and provided the necessary capital to start his company. Ford resigned from the Edison Illuminating Company, and on August 5th, 1899 created the Detroit Automobile Company with William H. Murphy. Unfortunately, for Ford and Murphy, the venture proved to be unsuccessful, and the company was dissolved in early 1901. However, this setback did not discourage Ford.

In October of 1901, he designed, built, and raced another automobile. (Remember, these were the days when automobiles were made entirely by hand, piece by piece.) A month after he raced his automobile, the success spurred Murphy and other stockholders who had invested in the Detroit Automobile Company to start up the Henry Ford Company. Henry Ford later left the company in 1902 after a disagreement with Murphy over the hiring of a consultant named Henry M. Leland. The company subsequently changed its name to the Cadillac Automobile Company.

Ford later built another racing automobile with three times the horsepower of the previous version. Henry Ford needed to find the capital and the partners to create a new automobile company. An old acquaintance, a coal dealer named Alexander Malcomson, partnered with Ford to start Ford and Malcomson Ltd. They leased a factory and contracted with a machine shop that was owned by the Dodge Brothers.

A crisis arose when the company could not make the first payment to the Dodge Brothers. Malcomson acted quickly by bringing in new investors—Malcomson's uncle John S. Gray, Malcomson's secretary John Couzens, two of Malcomson's lawyers—John W. Anderson and Horace Rackham—and the Dodge Brothers. The company reorganized and renamed itself the Ford Motor Company in 1903. Malcomson had persuaded John and Horace Dodge to accept a portion of the company and help fund the business by using their machines. John S. Gray, Malcomson's uncle, was a well-known industrialist in the confectionery industry. His secretary, John Couzens, would later become a United States senator from Michigan. The Dodge Brothers would later leave the Ford Motor Company to start the Dodge Brothers Company.

The year after the Panic of 1907, Ford introduced the Model T. The Model T was revolutionary for an automobile: it had the steering wheel on the left-hand side, the entire engine and transmission were enclosed, the four cylinders were cast in an iron block, and it had a suspension that utilized springs. It was easy to drive and cost only $825, or roughly $22,000 in today's dollars. Ford continued to make improvements in the Model T and the manufacturing process to eventually bring the cost down to $360, or about $7,000 in today's terms. Ford reduced the cost by improving the concept of the assembly line and perfecting mass production. To reduce the employee turnover rate, thereby reducing the cost of production, Ford introduced the $5-a-day pay for his factory workers and reduced the workweek to 40 hours. This action increased the profitability by reducing costs, and it also had an unintended consequence of increasing revenue because the pay increase gave factory workers the ability to purchase his automobiles, causing his sales to increase. Eventually, Model T production reached over 15 million before the Model A replaced it. Ford made many contributions to the American automobile industry. Publicity was the way the Ford established awareness and helped deliver his product to the consumer. He made sure that every newspaper carried stories or ads of his automobiles in Detroit. Ford created a network of dealers that promoted his cars to other independent dealers across the country. Local motoring clubs sprang up to help people understand and find the enjoyments of driving.

Henry Ford made many contributions to the automobile industry, helped raised the living standards of many Americans, improved the systems for assembly lines and mass production, and created one of the greatest automobile companies that the world has ever seen. He acquired marketable skills that he used in business, whether it was the management side or the labor side. Failure never fazed him, and even though his first two companies failed he carried on. He made plans and then had to alter his plans; he created teams of individuals to back him, and later found the right partners.

The last thing to add is that Henry Ford was allegedly semi-literate, and it is my view that he might have been dyslexic, which impeded his writing and reading abilities. Even with that major obstacle to overcome, and all of the economic crises in the early 1900s, Ford became a great success. Forbes estimates his net worth to be approximately $190 billion in today's dollars, which would be more than 2.5 times the size of Bill Gates's net worth.

I have shown two cases of success; now I will show you a great success story that transpired in the depths of the Great Depression

*"Success seems to be connected with action. Successful people keep moving. They make mistakes, but they don't quit."*
*-Conrad Hilton*

## Conrad Hilton

The world's greatest hotelier that has ever lived created an empire that still bears his name. Conrad Hilton was born in New Mexico to a very devoted Catholic mother, and a father who owned and operated a general store. His father taught him at an early age about hard work, determination, managing people, and how to run a business. Conrad also learned important negotiation skills from his father.

However, he and his father had conflicts when operating and expanding the business. Disagreements over the business and Conrad's belief that his father would never treat him as an equal partner caused him to leave the family business. Against his father's wishes, Conrad ran for and won a state representative seat in New Mexico's first-ever statewide election held for its legislature. Conrad only served a single two-year term and then left politics. He felt politics was slow, tiresome, unproductive, and too political!

Now Conrad needed to either find a venture or reluctantly return to his father's general-store business. In the summer of 1916, he became manager of The Hilton Trio, an entertainment group composed of his sisters. The venture proved unsuccessful, and the group barely broke even. Hilton believed that the group was going to find great success because they were the only entertainment group in New Mexico and, therefore, people would flock to see them. A small failure was the fate of the venture: Conrad Hilton was forced to make a decision to either work for his father or pursue another business.

Conrad decided to open up a bank in San Antonio, New Mexico. His father advised him not to start a bank because the town was too small to service. The largest obstacle Conrad couldn't overcome was people trusting him to hold their money. Since Conrad was only twenty-nine years old, he seemed inexperienced, and he had not built a reputation for himself other than the son of a general store owner. Due, perhaps, to the memory of the Panic of 1907, people did not trust him—or any bank—with their money. The bank closed within a year, and Conrad was again faced with the choice of either working for his father or trying to strike it out on his own.

In 1917, the United States entered World War I and Conrad found his next venture in the U.S. Army. He enlisted and was sent to France. Conrad wanted to fight on the front lines, but his experience working for his father's general store business caused the Army to utilize his skills in the supply line.

A few days after Armistice Day, Conrad received a telegraph message from his mother. It read, "Father dead, please come quick, Mother." Conrad returned home, but not soon enough. Returning to late, Conrad did not get to pay his respects to the man he loved, respected, and admired.

Conrad took over the general store, but he knew bad times were coming. The mines that had supported the local towns were running out of minerals and metals. He looked across the border to Texas, where black gold—oil—was making millionaires overnight. In the spring of 1919, with his life savings of $5,000 pinned to the inside of his coat, he traveled to Texas. Conrad was planning on purchasing a bank in Cisco, Texas to take advantage of the oil boom. But the bank owner raised the price on the bank when Conrad submitted his offer. Conrad retreated to the Mobley Hotel. There he saw the hotel was booked to capacity; rooms were renting by the hour, and the hotel manager was still turning people away.

Hilton decided right then and there to buy the Mobley Hotel. He saw the enormous opportunity of owning this hotel in an oil boomtown. He approached the owner of the Mobley and asked him whether or not he was considering selling the hotel. By sheer coincidence, the owner was considering going into the wildcatting business and wanted out of the hotel business. The owner would sell the hotel to Hilton for $40,000 if he could gather the rest of funds to purchase the hotel.

He was able to gather a group of investors to purchase the Mobley Hotel. The Mobley brought in $2,000 a week in profit. Hilton wasn't satisfied with the Mobley's performance, so he converted part of the hotel lobby to more rooms, and added a bar and a buffet-style restaurant to serve better his customer base of oil field workers. The strategy increased the revenue and profit margins for the Mobley. The Mobley was running smoothly and bringing in plenty of money. Hilton set his goals on expanding and purchasing more hotels in Texas towns.

Soon he acquired hotels in Waco, San Angelo, Dallas, Marlin, Wichita Falls, Abilene, and Lubbock. At bargain basement prices Hilton would buy dilapidated hotels that were losing money and then renovate them. By 1925, his hotel business owned eight hotels, and he was earning over $100,000 a year. By the late 1920s, Hilton had built his first hotel in Albuquerque and was constructing a high rise in Dallas. He seemed well on his way to becoming a millionaire until the Great Depression struck. Out of all the businesses to be in during the Great Depression, a hotel business was not one I would want to have owned or operated. The Depression couldn't have come at the worst time; as he was finishing the high rise, and Conrad had deeply gone into debt.

He lost all of his hotels except for one—the El Paso Hotel. Hilton worked harder than ever and was determined not to declare bankruptcy. At the time, Hilton had a negative net worth of $500,000 and was struggling. A bellboy even loaned Conrad $300 to help him operate his business and support his family. According to the *Wall Street Journal,*[xxiii] his attorneys wanted him to file for bankruptcy just like all of his competitors were filing, but he refused to give in. Conrad tightened his belt and became more financially sound.

By expanding slowly and buying back four more hotels, Hilton emerged out of the Great Depression debt-free and with five out of his eight hotels. Many of his competitors had filed bankruptcy, or had managed to keep one out of eight hotels following the Great Depression. Since Conrad did not file for bankruptcy, he had a huge image boost that added to his reputation. He was the only hotelier who emerged from this debacle relatively whole; giving him a competitive advantage over his competition because people wanted to do business with him since he was the only one who did not declare bankruptcy.

This event was just the start of the billion-dollar Hilton empire.

Conrad Hilton believed the strongest economic recovery would come on the West Coast. In the early 1940s, he was looking to purchase a hotel in California. Then World War II started with the bombing of Pearl Harbor. Many investors would think this was another calamity, but Hilton saw it as an opportunity. Many Americans on the West Coast feared a Japanese invasion. People were selling their real estate to move out of state, allowing Hilton to buy The Town House at a great bargain. He then purchased hotels in New York City, at the time the toughest place to own and operate a hotel. Hilton purchased the famous Waldorf-Astoria and began setting his sights outside of the U.S., creating the world's first international hotel chain.

Entrepreneurs such as Conrad Hilton set ambitious goals, were not afraid of trying new things, took calculated risks, had setbacks, and pushed through difficult times. Throughout his entire life, Conrad had a strong work ethic. He did not surrender when the economy took a horrible downturn; he kept focused, made better decisions, and had resilience in the face of all of the challenges.

So, what do these three extraordinary people have in common?

✓Passion and aspiration to build a better future for themselves, and their families, including a drive to fulfill their dream.

✓All of them had mentors, whether it was brothers, husbands, fathers, or great inventors. They all had someone to help them improve upon their marketable skills, or help them develop their business skills.

✓They networked with individuals who shared similar interests and goals, forming dream teams for boards of their company, or investing partners who had an invested interest in the business success, found and made deals, or produced a business plan.

✓They found the financing to finance their deals or business.

✓They got their name out there and built a reputation for their business and themselves.

So, what is the formula for success, and turning a financial crisis into a profitable opportunity? As an investor educating oneself on how financial crises form and how they unfold is extremely important, I will cover this first then move forward with how to turn a crisis into a profitable opportunity.

# Chapter 7: Identifying Future Financial Calamities

For an investor, identifying future financial calamities is the most important part of the blueprint. An investor's ability to identify and avoid the calamity, profit from it, and then position him or herself for the subsequent boom is the key. Granted, there is an overabundance of charts, graphs, tables, etc., of data we can look at to indicate a potential calamity. However, there are too many to go over, and the indicators are not always right. Then comes the timing problem of those indicators.

One way I can identify a future financial calamity by collecting the data on how many claim checks there are on the real wealth.

## Too Many Claim Checks and Not Enough Real Assets

You may recall from Chapter 5 the historical event of John Law's Mississippi Bubble. It was created by too many claim checks on the real underlying assets that backed those claim checks. The government debt was a claim check; however, it did not have any real assets to back it, only taxes the government collected. Bank notes issued by the government bank were simply claim checks on gold and silver. The French claim on North America was the real asset that backed the stocks that were issued by the Mississippi Company.

All of these claim checks are only sustainable if real assets or payments back them, and if an entity or an individual issues more claim checks than real assets in existence, we have a future financial calamity in the making.

Why do people tend to issue more claim checks than real assets? The answer is to make more money by selling something they don't have! They are defrauding investors, speculators, and money managers who purchased these claim checks. This type of fraud is typically done by the John Laws, Bernie Madoffs, Charles Ponzi, and other scammers who sell you counterfeit notes or documents then run off with the money. Just like with Madoff, you may open up an "account" with them to manage your money only then to find out that they made off with your hard earned cash in a Ponzi scheme.[xxiv]

These types of schemes are easy to detect. If it seems too good to be true, then it is. A man went to the Security and Exchange Commission authorities for eight years with proof that Madoff was running a Ponzi scheme, and the SEC still gave Madoff the stamp of approval.

A solution to prevent these types of personal financial calamities from happening to you is to take control of your financial future, your finances, and your financial assets. This kind of a solution echoes one of my main points in the book: Take control of your future! When an individual has personal control over their assets and reduces counterparty risk, it either reduces or eliminates the risk of being financially scammed. If you do want to hand off your finances to a certified financial planner (CFP), then vet him or her thoroughly and, if you can, diversify your assets among various financial planners.

Doesn't that increase my counterparty risk if I have multiple CFPs managing my money? Good question! No, it does not. If an investor has $500,000 of wealth in someone else's hands their risk is $500,000. If an investor has $500,000 divided amongst ten CFPs, then only one CFP can defraud that investor of $50,000 as oppose to all ten CFPs being fraudsters and defrauding that investor of the total $500,000.

It's similar in principle to diversifying your portfolio in a market to minimize being exposed to just one company. I would do the same thing when it comes to brokers as well, particularly in the paper markets. An interesting example to research is the MF Global scandal[xxv] where MF Global's segregated customer accounts "magically" disappeared, and then reappeared once the bankruptcy trustee conducted the necessary work to find the missing funds. Fortunately, for most of the MF Global victims, they will become whole again.

Then how do we identify future financial calamities when it comes to the economy, manias, bubbles, crises, panics, and bank runs?

Look at the claim checks; but this can be more complex to identify than boiling it down to the basic fundamental principle. Recollect Chapters 2 and 3, and the credit cycles in the economy that cause the booms and busts; what you need to focus on is the expansion of credit and where credit is expanding in the economy. In the early 2000s, many analysts who were predicting the housing bubble saw the increase in debt. Debt is merely a claim check on wealth, whether the claim check is collateralized such as the real estate or your future income to pay the mortgage off.

When there is too much debt in a society, incomes cannot service debt. Defaults on the debt will ensue, with the collateral being sold on the market. The law of supply and demand then comes into action. When there are an extreme number of defaults, large amounts of collateral are seized then sold into the market to recover the money. There is a rapid increase in supply; and when there is an increase in supply, prices fall while demand falls due to the contraction of credit by lenders fearing that they will not be able to recover their principal on their loans.

Prices collapse, causing a crisis or a bank panic similar to the one we saw in 2008.

Now let's take out real estate to insert the real asset of choice. It can be anything: businesses, business assets, car loans, boat loans, construction equipment, and anything you can think of. However, collateralized loans are not the only forms of debt issued. There are other forms of debts issued, such as consumer credit and bonds.

Since there is no collateral, consumer credit has higher interest payments and costs more to use. The most common forms of consumer credit are credit cards, credit for furniture and appliances, and other big item purchases. When a default happens, it is the lender who takes the hit. When lenders take a hit, they either raise credit standards or contract lending; and enough of this will negatively influence the economy. Bonds are even more important to the economy since bonds typically finance capital expenditures.

Bonds issued by a corporation are nearly always used to finance capital expenditures for the corporation. A corporation will issue a bond to sell to an investor, whether an individual, hedge fund, money manager, or even governments, who will purchase the bond to collect the coupon payments to then eventually receive their principal back. The goal of the corporation is to increase revenues to pay off their creditors; if they cannot, then they will file for bankruptcy. When a corporation defaults on its bonds, the assets of the company are sold off to pay off its creditors. If there are any assets left to the owners of the corporation or company, they will divide the assets among themselves. If there are not enough assets to cover the creditors, then the owners receive nothing, and the creditors have to take the losses.

Governments issue their own bonds to individuals, the public, businesses, and other governments, who purchase the bonds to collect the coupon payments and then receive their principal returned. Bonds typically fund roads, public works, welfare spending, and, unfortunately, are sometimes used to finance a war. The government's ability to pay derives from the taxes it collects from the nation's businesses and people. The health of the economy directly affects the ability of the government to repay its bonds. When a government defaults, it is catastrophic to the national economy.

Imagine investors losing money, welfare programs not funded, troops not paid, the currency collapsing, roads not built, and government employees are not showing up to work. That's the scenario if it's an outright default and collapse similar to the one that was seen when the Soviet Union collapsed during the 1990s. A horrific result of this was the life expectancy dropped to fifty-four due to suicides, homicides, alcoholism, and the government-run healthcare system collapsing.

If a bankrupt government restructures its debt, the economy will be in turmoil, but it will not collapse. A recent example of this is in Greece in 2012.

Now with that all being said, let's examine the industry that focuses on debt.

Banking is the industry that deals with debt. When banks issue too much credit placing debtors into an excessive debt load position. They cannot pay off the debt due to the debt load; bankruptcy and defaults will occur, and losses will mount. Since the bank loans out primarily other people's money—also known as depositor's money—people fear the loss of their deposit and realize the counterparty risk. When a financial firm collapses because it issued too much debt claim checks on its capital or on its deposits, people begin to fear that their money is not there in the bank and people will run to the bank to collect their money from their savings and checking accounts. The bank tries to recall the loans, sell assets, and pay off as many people it can.

Banks and financial institutions re-hypothecate the assets or the claims on assets to create more claims, meaning that there are too many claims and not enough assets. They leverage themselves to increase their revenues and profits, and they typically will keep leveraging until they hit the legal limit or until they collapse.

However, there are financial institutions that do not do this type of financial insanity—just like there are plenty of individuals who do not mortgage everything, use a credit card to their maximum limit, and party like the good times will never end. History shows it only takes a few financial institutions to collapse the entire financial system, as we saw in the Financial Crisis of 2008.

Everything I described above comprises an unstable system. To identify an unstable system just look at a few things. How many claim checks are there, and can the incomes and the underlying assets support the debt? Remember that the asset valuations change. So comparing assets with each other allows the individual investor to more accurately determine whether or not the assets are fairly valued.

## Analyzing Unstable Systems

Let's talk about unstable systems. Unstable systems form in the economy when there is too much debt, too much leverage, and too many claim checks for the system to sustain. When a system becomes unstable, unless the system can rebalance itself a financial calamity will occur in the future. A rebalance will occur when there is a change in the income or a change in the intrinsic value of the asset. A rebalance can also occur when debt is wiped out, the claim checks and people and institutions begin to deleverage, causing the valuations of those claim checks to revert past the mean to undervalued territory.

The optimum time for an investor to buy any asset is when it's undervalued.

Now, let me explain the basic fundamental system. The first two models are the fundamental claim check system models. There are other models that resemble economic systems; if you want to study systems, I recommend studying complexity theory. If you are interested in complexity theory, I suggest reading and viewing James G. Rickards—a regular commentator on finance, and the author of *The New York Times* bestseller *Currency Wars: The Making of the Next Global Crisis*, published in 2011, and *The Death of Money: The Coming Collapse of the International Monetary System*, published in 2014.[xxvi]

Stable System

Unstable System

Current Financial System

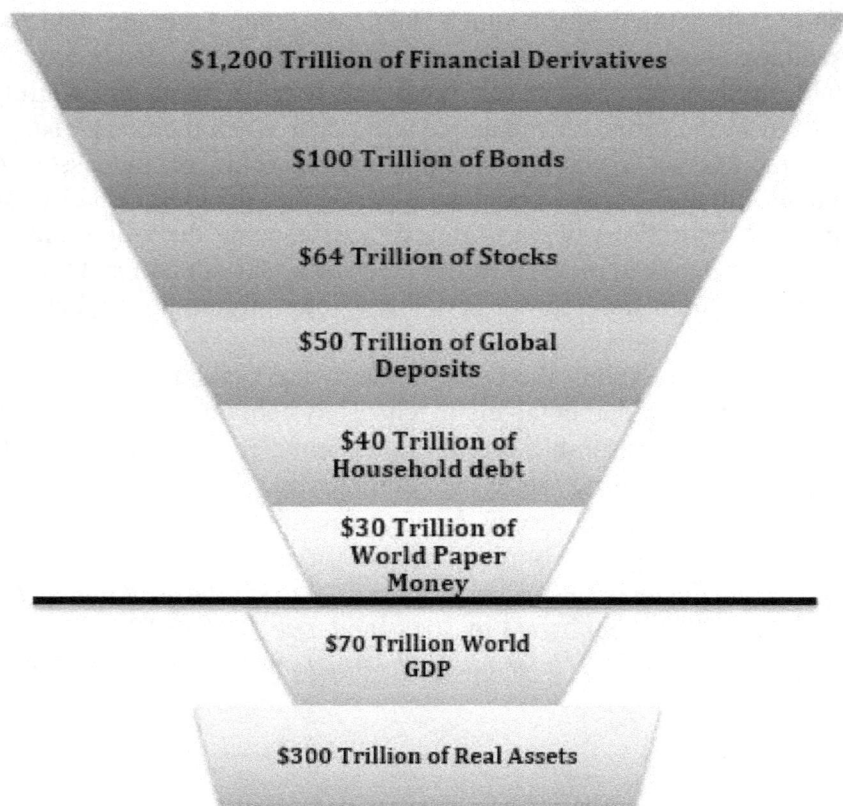

$1,200 Trillion of Financial Derivatives

$100 Trillion of Bonds

$64 Trillion of Stocks

$50 Trillion of Global Deposits

$40 Trillion of Household debt

$30 Trillion of World Paper Money

$70 Trillion World GDP

$300 Trillion of Real Assets

(Data Sources: Data Sources are provided in the Sources section of the book)

The model above shows the current world financial structure, which resembles an unstable system. Financial derivatives are causing the instability within the system. There are roughly $1500 trillion of claim checks on $370 trillion of real assets and income. However, assets and incomes can change, while debt and claim checks are fixed. If asset valuations decrease along with incomes, it creates more instability in the system. When the system hits a limit, the economic cycle reverses, revealing that too many claim checks were issued on the real assets, or what real incomes could not support.

I believe the world economy is in serious trouble. I do not worry about it so much because it is entirely out of my control. What I do control are my personal finances and preparing myself for the future financial calamities that could come.

Within this large system are other systems relating to real estate, bonds, stocks, derivatives, and all of the other markets.

Stock prices fall due to investors selling their stocks to acquire cash to pay down debt or avoid taking a loss. Comparing the unstable system model to the second chart, there is a direct resemblance to the amount of debt, claim checks, being greater than the underlying assets compared to the model. When a financial system is carrying too much debt with too few assets, a rebalancing of the system needs to occur. Income either has to *increase* to sustain the debt load, or income has to be *diverted* to pay down debt. When incomes have to be diverted to pay down debt, this will cause a slowdown somewhere in the economy.

To conclude, we need to remember a few important fundamental details when identifying future financial calamities:

1. Identify which market to analyze.

2. Research the data in regards to the debt claim checks and the underlying assets.

3. Find the real historical values of the asset class and compare them to other assets.

Unstable systems form when there are too many claims on the assets and not enough real assets to back up the claims. To limit losses, investors could purchase and have physical possession of the real assets, which prevents an investor from being defrauded. Diversify counterparty risk and diversify holdings among various CFPs, financial institutions, brokerages, and banks.

## Demographics

Because economies are made by human interactions, demographics play a vital role in the growth of the economy. Demographics drive both economic growth and economic contraction. For instance, the baby boomer generation has driven much economic growth, since their generation was much larger than the previous generation. This situation differs in other countries. In Japan, the demographics are collapsing, causing the economic stagnation that Japan has seen for the past two decades.

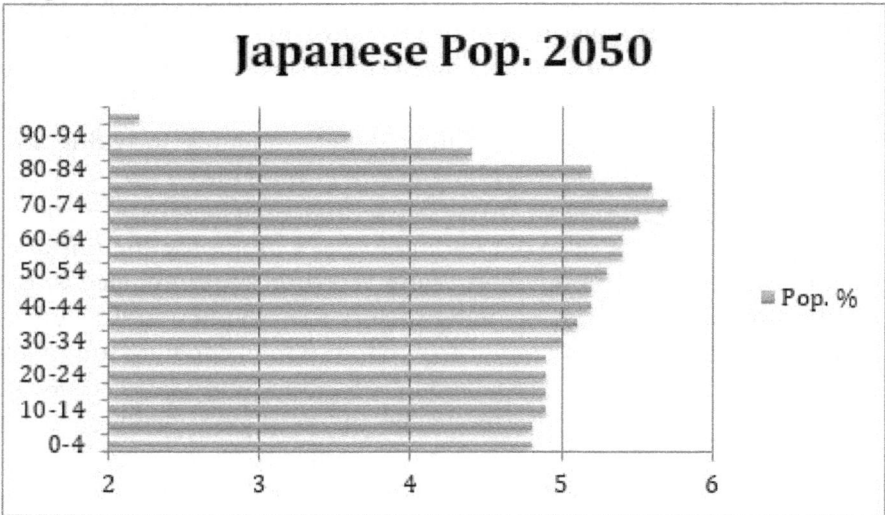

(Data Sources: https://en.wikipedia.org/wiki/Aging_of_Japan
http://www.pewresearch.org/fact-tank/2014/02/03/10-projections-for-the-global-population-in-2050/
http://www.stat.go.jp/english/data/jinsui/tsuki/index.htm)

Looking at Japan in the 1950s, the population formed a pyramid, with larger numbers of young people, which is a stable system. In the 2000s, the pyramid transformed into an obelisk shape. The projection for 2050 (above) takes the form of an inverted pyramid. An inverted pyramid for demographics makes Japan one of the most unstable economies in the world.

There are a few major factors affected by the demographic model: the welfare system, economic growth, and national debt repayment. All of these factors have systemic risk due to the structure of the financing for the national debt and the welfare system. When there is an older larger demographic followed by a younger smaller demographic, deflationary pressures build up in the economy; and since there are more sellers (older generation) than buyers (younger generation), prices fall. In this case, it is asset prices that fall when the older generation sells to retire. Government revenues fall while their welfare expenses increase, creating financial and economic problems for the nation as a whole. Now I could write crucial information that needs great detail about this topic; nevertheless, some already else has. Harry Dent focuses part of his investing strategy based on demographics of the country. Mike Maloney has also produced content on the subject and has produced content with Harry Dent as well.

Mike Maloney YouTube video: Rollercoaster Crash[xxvii]

https://www.youtube.com/watch?v=8GP87dgTqF8

The very end of the video there is a bonus link at the bottom of the video. I recommend clicking the bonus feature link and watching.

Analyzing a country's demographics will provide a financial road map, as investors need to understand how demographics will drive, slow, or contract an economy. I will continue with Japan later in this chapter.

## Forecasting Economies and Dealing with Probabilities

I have a great vexation with many of today's economists and their total disregard for utilizing probabilities in economic forecasting, and extrapolating continuous economic growth without any recession in the forecast. Economic growth develops through many changing variables consisting of independent, dependent, and codependent variables that are interconnected. "Trend forecasting" neglects the credit, business, and economic cycles while only utilizing short-term economic growth. This type of forecast does not reflect the productivity curve of the economy due to the use of credit and the expansion and contraction of credit.

I believe that economists will eventually throw out the old models and forecasting and shift towards analyzing systems, the possible outcomes of an unstable system rebalancing, and the probabilities of those outcomes.

Investors and analysts use probabilities to decide how likely an intended outcome is, along with the risks involved. Why is it that people who operate in the real markets must employ practical applications in the real world, yet academia and economists use only theoretical models and not applicable models? Apparent problems do arise in forecasting; for example, the Dotcom Bubble, the Housing Bubble, the Financial Crisis of 2008, and the other numerous crises, bubbles, and economic recessions that we have seen.

## Municipal Bond Bubble

We saw GM and Chrysler bailed out in 2008, and five years later the city of Detroit declared bankruptcy. I thought the President and the federal government promised that the 2008 bailout would *save* the Detroit economy and by extension the city! Politicians don't always keep their promises. I find it depressing that the top management of GM and Chrysler kept their jobs and made millions of dollars by allowing their companies to fail and then lobbying the government to bail them out. The men, women, and children of the city of Detroit are having their pensions defaulted upon, government services cut, and a slew of other financial problems burdening on them.

As of this writing, The Commonwealth of Puerto Rico is predicting a default in either January or May of 2016. For years, Puerto Rico borrowed to fund its social services programs, expand government services, and create public works. Government officials wanted to take advantage of the historic low-interest rates, and they also wanted to kick their fiscal problems down the road. In 2015, they met the end of the road and are expected to go through a painful restructuring and address the problem.

The Fed's historically low-interest rates and tax exemptions on municipal debt have caused investors to move further on the risk-reward curve, providing the financial incentive for municipalities to hang themselves financially.

Interest rates at all-time lows incentivize not only people but also governments to borrow more. Low-interest rates encourage speculation, overconsumption, and excessive borrowing, creating mal-investments. Cheap borrowing costs discourage savings, capital formation, and production; moreover, investors want a yield and tax-free income. Municipal debt allows investors to find better yield, with perceived low risk, and it is tax-free. Since borrowing is so cheap, municipal governments have been borrowing to build massive buildings and public works. Investors have been more than willing to invest in municipal bonds because they are desperate for yield and the tax benefits in owning municipal bonds.

Municipalities borrow money to build schools, build roads, build administration buildings, develop parks, and for other public work projects. Expenditures have been rising dramatically due to the added maintenance expenses for these public works and the increasing debt expense. These expenditures are fixed expense, while the variable costs such as administration salaries, firefighter salaries, police salaries, and teacher salaries can either be increased or decreased depending upon the financial condition of the municipality. Variable expenses typically are cut first, and the municipality will choose to cut teachers, extracurricular school activities, police, firefighters, and other staff to direct spending towards paying off the debt or spend towards maintenance costs.

My former school district took on incredible amounts of debt for expensive school buildings, and they have been recklessly spending millions of dollars on technology. Case in point: At $1,000 each, the school district bought iPads for teachers, administrators, and staff. The school district then proceeded with massive layoffs of teachers, taking the average class size of 22 students per teacher to 35 students per teacher. While those iPads temporarily boosted the technology at the school, those iPads bought five years ago are now obsolete. The school district has racked up a debt of $40,000 per current student. One day the citizens will be fed up, realizing that the school district has defaulted on their promise to meet the educational needs of the community. The citizens will then most likely choose to have the school district default on their promise to pay creditors back.

There are many similar situations in the domestic and international arena: where governments have borrowed excessively, and there is a battle concerning who will bear the blame and responsibility of the default.

## Greece and PIIGS

Greece has now had a third bailout package from the European Central Bank (ECB) and the International Monetary Fund (IMF) in roughly five years' time. The bailouts have not fixed Greece's problem of too much debt, too much spending, a very large welfare system, and too much government intervention in the economy. The ECB, IMF, and the Greek government are trying to kick the can down the road. However, this delays the inevitable crisis and restructuring to a later date, and makes the problems worse, leading to a larger crisis in the future.

I expect Greece to ask for a fourth bailout by 2018, and I believe the other PIIGS of Europe—Greece plus Portugal, Italy, Ireland, and Spain—will face similar crises. The culmination of these crises in these European countries will undermine economic growth and confidence.

Europe is facing massive problems, but the country that has the worst problems so far is Japan.

## Japan's Economic Crisis

During the current century, Japan has been economically stagnant for numerous reasons: declining demographics, immigration issues, political issues, debt issues, currency issues, and a slew of other problems. Japan's fiscal and monetary policies are creating great distortions in the economy. Stimulus packages and currency creation by the Bank of Japan (BOJ) is distorting the interest rates in Japan, the value of Japanese government bonds (JGBs), and the value of the yen. Japan's government and central bank have effectively been monetizing debt at ever-increasing rates. The monetization of Japan's debt has been outpacing the issuance of JGBs.

Economists, hedge fund managers, financial analysts, and others have been trying to answer the question: What would happen if the BOJ printed enough yen to own all of the JGBs? What would happen to the JGB market, and the yen?

I have a few ideas of what could happen, based on history.

Numerous countries that do not anchor their currency to gold, silver, or another real asset can print any amount of currency in existence. Fiat currency can either be backed by nothing or backed by debt. Debt-backed fiat currency needs more currency issued into existence to pay off the old debt that was issued that created that unit of currency (principle) and the interest. A debt-backed fiat currency can revert to a fiat currency backed by nothing if the central bank chooses to monetize all of the debt, the deficit spending, and charge frivolous interest rates such as .5% or even .01 percent. Nevertheless, if the central bank prints more currency to pay the interest, it makes the interest rate irrelevant.

I believe Japan's Central Bank will monetize all of the government's debt and monetize the government's deficit spending. A consequence of turning a debt-backed fiat currency to a fiat currency is the enormous devaluation that has to occur to monetize the entire debt. The enormous devaluation of the currency may result in hyperinflation, but it is not a guarantee.

In theory, the devaluation of currency would reflect the chosen interest rate. After the devaluation, a 2% interest rate on government debt would result in a 2% inflation rate. However, in the case of Japan, their social obligations would cause hyperinflation if the government decided to keep its promise of writing checks. Those checks will lose purchasing power, and will purchase very little real goods and services.

Japan, in my opinion, has the worst East Asian economy. Other countries in East Asia have growing economies that will see setbacks from time to time, but will continue to excel economically.

## China's Real Estate and Stock Market Bubbles, and Shadow Banking System

China has become the world's center of industrial manufacturing. The industrial revolution in China only took two to three decades, and they have experienced double-digit growth. Chinese individuals, families, and companies have accumulated massive amounts of savings. The typical Chinese earner saves 35% of his or her paycheck. These savings have been invested primarily in real estate, due to government policy and intervention in the economy. The Chinese people have experienced numerous currency collapses in the past decades, and Chinese citizens do not trust their government to manage the yuan properly. The Chinese people are effectively diversifying themselves out of the currency into any tangible asset possible.

The Chinese government allows investors to purchase gold and silver, and gold and silver exchanges have been created in Shanghai. The Chinese people and government are purchasing nearly half of the world's production of Gold.[xxviii] A dramatic rise in the price of gold and silver has been absent since other institutions, and Western central banks, have been selling their gold or leasing it into the market, creating the supply of gold to meet the Chinese demand.

China's gold purchases have not created a bubble in gold; however, the Chinese government allows ordinary citizens to invest in the stock market, and that has created an enormous bubble. Another contributing factor is the quantitative easing programs from various

Western governments creating easy money. Institutions and investors use this easy money to purchase assets such as Chinese stocks. Everyone wanted to get in at the same time, and now many want to get out. CRASH!

I could write volumes concerning China's current economic; however, I invite you, my dear reader, to do your own research on China. James G. Rickards has great insight. I also respect as well the McAlvany Financial Group[xxix] viewpoint as they have significant operations in East Asia. In chapter 11, I resume my coverage on China. However, due to the ever changing economic environment, I move part of this section from my predications chapter to this chapter. Since my predictions from Spring of 2015 are in part coming true.

## Globalization

The macroeconomic viewpoint has a generalized understanding of globalization, and how it is affecting the world and even your local metroplex. Factories and industries are being shut down, with those jobs outsourced and exported overseas. Cheap consumer products are being imported, and global social connectivity is increasing, along with a plethora of other actions. The world economy has seen globalization in the private sector progress at an incredible rate, and what were once diverse economies are now becoming more assimilated and homogeneous. First it was the private sector, and now governments are following suit.

Governments around the world have been following policy in unison, primarily following the direction of the United States. Governments have shifted their policies—fiscally, monetarily, and economically—to align with one another. In the world of investing, finances, and business, this has created problems even for countries' economies that did not depend on the global market and could have risen and fallen based on their own merits and own policies. Investors and businesspeople could flee from a recessionary country to an expansionary country, or they could flee from a kleptocratic government to a government still controlled by public sovereignty. Individuals could protect themselves by diversifying internationally; however, that has all changed.

Let's talk about the fiscal side first, and then move towards monetary, and finally political interventionism.

During this century, governments around the world have been taking out more debt and running large deficits. This continual acquisition of debt was sustained by the continual growth of the world economy. Fundamentally everything was fine, just as the growth in income could sustain the debts. In the Financial Crisis of 2008, this fundamental disappeared as the world GDP contracted and the subsequent "recovery" has been flat to slightly growing. However, governments around the world have been acquiring debt at a faster pace than the rise in GDP, creating instability in the economic system. The fiscal policy of running large budget deficits and taking on debt to "stimulate" the economy has failed in one sense: it has not created the growth to sustain the debt. Governments have also made future promises to retirees through Social Security (in the U.S.) and other welfare programs.

According to the Social Security trustees, there is $2.6 trillion in the Social Security trust fund, and according to the trustees and current U.S. Secretary of the Treasury Jack Lew, Social Security will be fully funded until 2036. Contradictory claims were made by President Barack Obama, stating that if the debt ceiling was not raised retirees would not receive their checks in the mail.[xxx] So, someone is lying; it is either the President or the supporters of the Social Security status quo. Many sources believe that the Social Security trust fund has been investing in government treasuries; or another way to put it, the U.S. government has been borrowing money out of the Social Security trust fund to spend. Estimates of the off-balance-sheet liabilities are the very least $70 trillion—and the government only takes in $3 trillion a year in taxes![xxxi]

Governments around the world have been following the same welfare policy and fiscal policy. Greece is just a microcosm of the European socialist problem in Europe, and the solution the Eurocrats propose is for Greece to take on more debt. As of this writing, Greece can take on more debt because they have people willing to loan them currency and the Greek politicians are more than willing to take on more debt. This will end when the other European nations finally end up in the same situation Greece is in, and the PIIGS of Europe reveal their major economic problems. Note that a relatively minor problem was seen in Greece, which consists of only 3.5% GDP of the European economy.

East Asian countries, such as Japan, are near the end of the road. There are very few places for people to hide internationally; investors are looking for the cleanest dirty shirt. Monetary policy has also been globalized; Japan's monetary policy of huge stimulus packages financed by money printing began when Japan imploded in the late 1980s. Look at the United States policy regarding interest rates and quantitative easing (money printing); the ECB, the UK Central Bank, the Australian Central Bank, the Chinese Central Bank, the central banks in South America, and many other central banks around the world are following the same monetary policy. For the first time in human history, we have negative interest rates! People are lending to spendthrift governments that promise to pay them back less than they loaned to the government. In consequence, since interest rates are at historic lows, everyone wants to borrow (the law of supply and demand), and debt is exploding on the municipal, state, and federal government level.

Accrued debts are causing budgetary strains, but the strains will be exacerbated when interest rates rise. Monetary policies conducted by the world's central banks are permitting the financing of unviable debt-ridden, cash-strapped governments and overburdened taxpayers. Eventually, governments will have to, and have already started to, default—either the people, social and defensive services, or the bondholders. When it comes, the day of reckoning will be remembered forever for the destruction of claim check wealth and the rise of real wealth. The world will see a transfer of purchasing power from those who hold paper claim checks to those who hold tangible wealth. An investor who identifies the unstable system and positions himself or herself appropriately will not only protect themselves but create generational wealth.

I have discussed how crises are brought upon by unstable systems. Unstable systems are developed by the issuance of more claim checks than the real wealth in existence. Investors are wise to purchase real assets and take physical possession to protect their wealth from being lost in the destruction of these claim checks in an event of a crisis.

I am looking forward to the eventual transition from the dollar standard to a new world monetary system, and to turning future financial calamities into profitable opportunities.

# Chapter 8: My Fundamentals for Wealth Creation

Wealth is derived from the creation of value. Your wealth is your time and your freedom; money is just a reflection of the value you create for society. Money is merely a tool to store your economic energy to deploy at a later point. In this chapter, I will discuss these topics: why I do not follow modern portfolio theory, Mike Maloney's Wealth Cycles Principle, how to protect your wealth, my wealth pyramid, and how to position for the coming boom. My motto for you is, "Think for yourself!"

## Why I Do Not Follow Modern Portfolio Theory

Modern portfolio theory is a hypothesis put forth by Harry Markowitz in his paper "Portfolio Selection," published in 1952 by the *Journal of Finance*. It's an investment theory based on the idea that risk-averse investors can construct portfolios to optimize or maximize expected return based on a given level of market risk, emphasizing that risk is an inherent part of higher reward.

Now for the majority of the time, the modern portfolio theory is fine—an investor diversifying his or her portfolio among the various markets, between various stocks, and the same with bonds. In my opinion, if I were going to follow a portfolio theory I would follow Harry Browne's "permanent portfolio."[xxxii] However, the modern portfolio theory, in my opinion, has its flaws, and many other theories do have their flaws too. With that being said, in my opinion, for someone who does not understand the financial markets, or for whom managing money is not their cup of tea, I completely understand. I would find a credible CFP with a good track record. All CFPs are not created equal, so you must do your research. Also, if you do consider a theory that is perfectly fine, I hope that you use a theory as opposed to picking stocks due to friends, market analysts, or even day trading.

*"Money management has been a profession involving a lot of fakery - people saying they can beat the market, and they really can't."*
*- Robert J. Shiller[xxxiii]*

---

Modern portfolio theory's major flaw it does not consider counterparty risk, systemic risk, or market-to-market purchasing power. Let me define counterparty risk: the risk in any financial relationship that the *other* party does not fulfill its obligations. Nearly all the financial instruments an investment advisor will point you towards will have some form of counterparty risk, either with him or with a financial institution.

The reason is that CFPs and other financial professions need to make money through their services they provide. When anybody sets up an account with a CFP or a broker, there is counterparty risk involved. The risk can be low or high. Professionals perform their job appropriately, and they just don't run off with your money!

Now there are many trustworthy people in the financial industry whom you can trust. I have no problem handing over some of my money to a financial advisor or setting up a brokerage account. Before I write a check, I thoroughly conduct my research on the firm, broker, or CFP.

I believe that my own destiny is in my own hands, and that destiny requires me to manage my own personal finance and investments. A major point in this book is that you need to take charge of your future and think for yourself. I use Mike Maloney's Wealth Cycles Principle[xxxiv], and because of these reasons, I have control over my finances. His system creates generational wealth, focuses on purchasing power, not the dollar, and it is backed by history evidence. I'm a passive investor as well as an active investor. My dear reader, you are most likely a passive investor, which is great! I prefer to be an active investor. An active investor is someone who starts businesses with their own capital or purchases other businesses. You will get both perspectives. The reason I am an active investor rather than a passive investor is because it is more profitable; however, it requires time, work, and typically greater risks are involved—meaning greater rewards.

*"Control your own destiny or someone else will."*
*-Jack Welch*

# Mike Maloney's Wealth Cycles Principle

The U.S. dollar is a floating abstraction, a characteristic it shares with all of the world's fiat currencies because fiat currencies are claim checks on wealth and not real wealth itself. The Wealth Cycles Principle focuses on acquiring more *real wealth*, and as entrepreneurs, business person, or individual investors, this is our goal. Putting it simply, the Wealth Cycles Principle is measuring a market against a market or an asset class against another asset class, identifying the long-term trends, investing in these long-term trends, and generating value during the economic boom time for the market or asset.

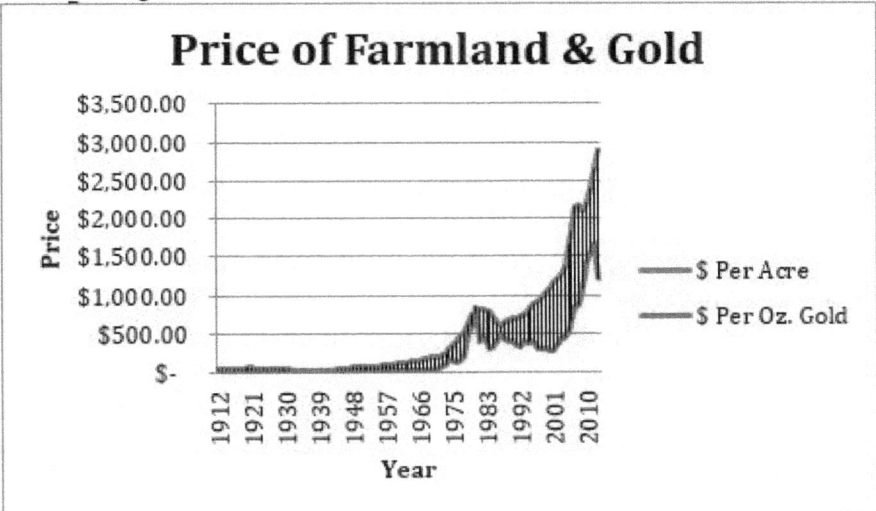

**Price of Farmland & Gold**

(Data Sources: http://extension.missouri.edu/p/G404
http://www.nma.org/pdf/gold/his_gold_prices.pdf)


*"The best investment you can make in your lifetime is your financial education."*
*- Mike Maloney*

# Oz. of Gold per Acre

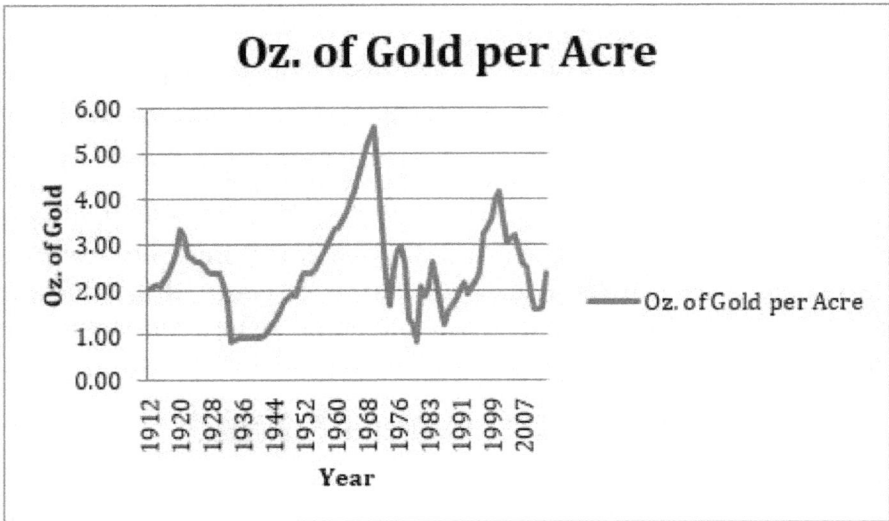

(Data Sources: http://extension.missouri.edu/p/G404
http://www.nma.org/pdf/gold/his_gold_prices.pdf)

I have two graphs above, one showing the dollar terms of the asset classes and the other the actual purchasing power of gold. Let me clarify the second graph: what I have done is just replace the dollar sign with an ounce sign or the abbreviation "oz." There is an old saying that you should buy low and sell high; it's the same principle here. You want to buy farmland with gold below the 2.00 oz per acre mark and sell it when it gets above the 3.00 oz per acre or more. Right now in 2015, farmland is above $3,000 per acre and gold is roughly $1,200, or 2.5 oz. per acre. Meaning that farmland is historically overvalued by 45%, the mean being 2.0 oz. per acre. If I were in a situation right now where I had unproductive land with no cash flow, I would sell the unproductive land and buy some gold. With that being said, this is just what I would do. If I had productive land generating *income*, I would not sell. Instead, I would be saving some of that cash in gold.

Let's take a look at silver, which is a fascinating story.

# Price of Farmland and Silver

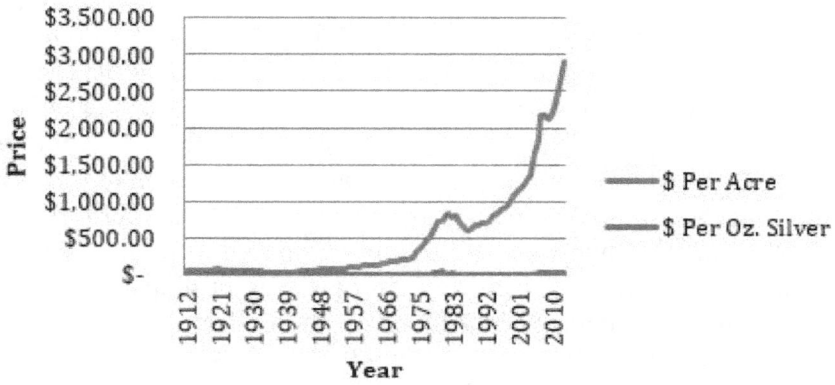

(Data Sources: http://extension.missouri.edu/p/G404
http://seekingalpha.com/article/422081-324-years-of-the-gold-to-silver-ratio-and-195-silver)

# Oz. of Silver Per Acre

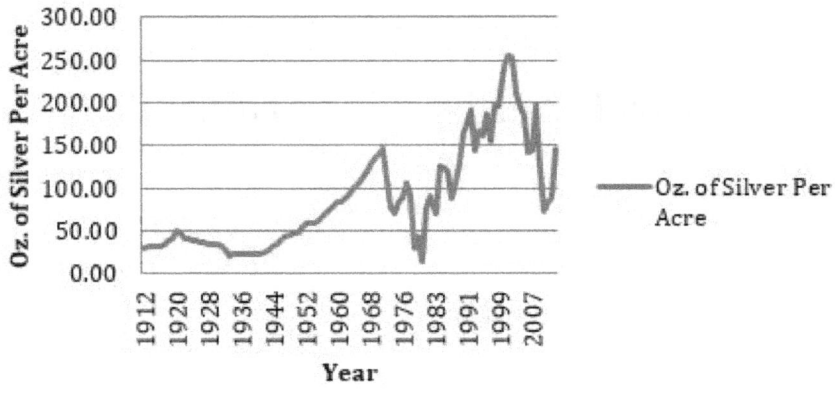

(Data Sources: http://extension.missouri.edu/p/G404
http://seekingalpha.com/article/422081-324-years-of-the-gold-to-silver-ratio-and-195-silver)

Again I'll show you the price that goes parabolic to show you the distinction of using the wealth cycle principle. In the future, I'll just show the charts that are used in the wealth cycles principle. Silver is even more undervalued, or as the chart above shows farmland is overvalued compared to silver.

As of this writing, silver is trading around $15 to $16 an ounce, while the average price per acre of farmland is roughly $3,000. Thus, the current price is roughly 200 oz. of silver for one acre of farmland. The historical price to purchase an acre of farmland for silver is 30 oz. of silver for one acre. In the 1980s, with silver's high of $50, the ratio went to 15 oz. of silver for one acre of farmland. If you lived in Texas at the time, the ratio was 7 oz. of silver to purchase on acre of Texas farmland. Imagine purchasing 7 oz. of silver right now for $105, and then an investor trading it for an acre of Texas farmland that is now nearly $1,800 per acre. Do not focus on the dollar terms, because of inflation or deflation. Instead, focus on the purchasing power gained.

If I bought 120 oz. of silver approximately for $1,800; history then repeats itself: I would be able to buy 17 or 18 acres of Texas farmland as opposed to one acre right now. An investor could gain 17x or 18x in real wealth; whether it was a deflationary environment or an inflationary environment, it does not matter. The wealth cycles principle only focuses on the real purchasing power.

Let's compare the purchasing power of farmland compared to the Dow Jones.

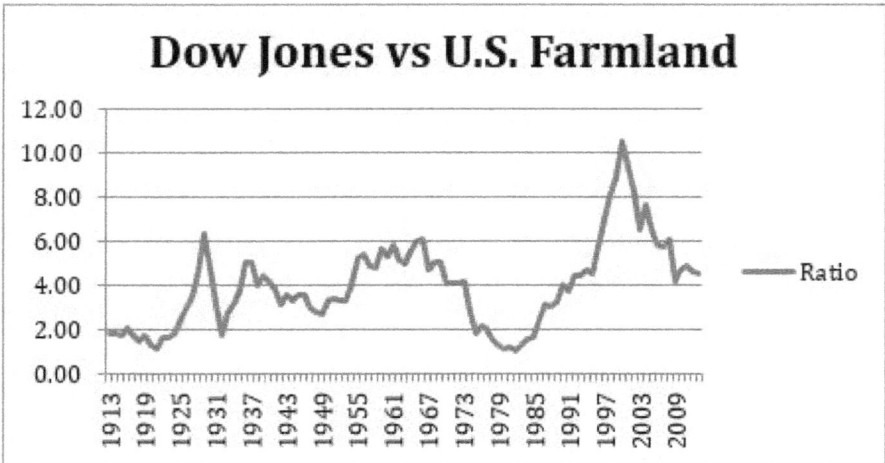

(Data Sources: http://extension.missouri.edu/p/G404
http://www.ritholtz.com/blog/2012/07/dow-jones-industrial-average-since-1900/)

In the previous chart, we used gold as the measuring stick stating how many ounces of gold would it take to purchase an acre of farmland. With the chart above, it is how many acres of farmland would it take to purchase one share of the Dow Jones. The historical mean is around three acres of farmland to purchase one share of the Dow Jones. Currently, the Dow Jones is trading around 18,000, and an acre of farmland is around $3,000 making the current ratio around six acres to purchase the Dow. Whenever the ratio trades above 5.00 or 6.00, it nearly always has a correction. The lowest point was in 1982 when the ratio hit 1.00. Now when markets or assets become overvalued, they do not just revert to the mean, they have to overshoot.

In 1929, the ratio went above 6.00 and fell to 2.00. In 1966, the ratio flashed across the 6.00 mark and fell to 1.00, and then in 2001 the ratio hit its largest mark at 10.55 to fall to 4.5, with us now at 6.00. I believe we are just in a dead cat bounce about to hit historic lows. The time to buy stocks was in the 1980s, and the time to sell stocks to purchase farmland was in the late 90s and early 2000s.

Here is my final chart. At first, it doesn't seem frightening at all, but it has unequivocal importance to your financial situation.

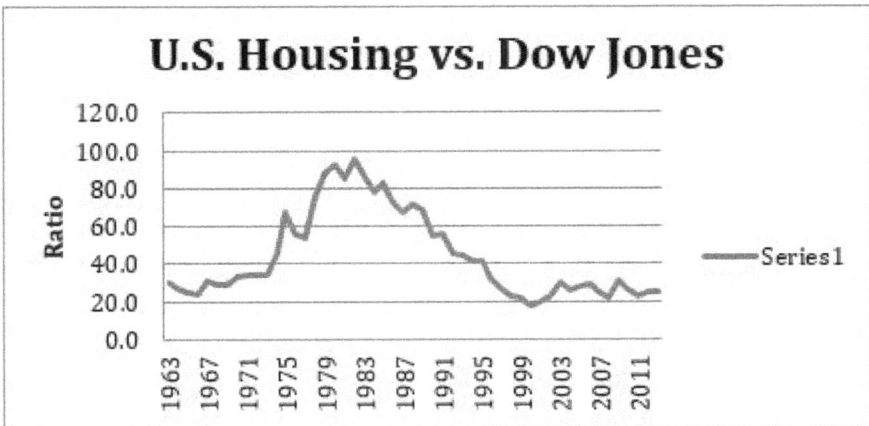

U.S. Housing vs. Dow Jones

(Data Sources: http://www.ritholtz.com/blog/2012/07/dow-jones-industrial-average-since-1900/
https://www.census.gov/const/uspricemon.pdf)

Before 2000, housing and equities traded independently of each other; since then they have had a similar correlation in direction and performance. The chart above is how many shares of the Dow Jones it takes to purchase the average American house. During the housing bubble of the 1980s, the ratio skyrocketed to 100, meaning it required roughly 100 shares of the Dow to purchase a house. Housing has been sliding ever since until 2000. Something interesting happened before 2000, and that was the repeal of the Glass-Steagall Act. Glass-Steagall prevented commercial banks from investing their capital in the financial markets. This act also prevented financial institutions from investing on the commercial side of banking, and loaning or purchasing mortgages to invest in.

A financial institution had to decide whether or not they were a commercial bank or a financial institution and invest accordingly to the Glass-Steagall Act. This act was passed in 1933 after the Great Depression, and if I had to make an educated guess as to how the chart above would look like before the Great Depression. I would make a guess that housing and the Dow Jones correlated with each other before 1933 then diverged after the Glass-Steagall Act was passed, with the banking and financial institutions buying, selling, and trading paper contracts on mortgages. Today this intermingling is done in the derivatives market with CDOs, CDs, MBS, and other paper.

Housing and equities are the two asset classes in which the majority of Americans have their wealth positioned. If the housing market does poorly, so does their stock portfolio. Causing a great financial strain on individuals, family, and the economy, these are the implications created by the intermingled industries of finance and real estate. The generation that saw the Great Depression understood and wrote into law to keep these two industries separate to prevent the risky behavior in the banking industry.

In summary of the wealth cycles principles, I will purchase undervalued assets using this valuation system (and there are plenty of other charts and valuation tools for wealth cycles). I will create value in these undervalued asset markets; and then I'll start businesses and companies to produce value in an undervalued market that is on its way up.

Regarding the self-made entrepreneurs, many entrepreneurs simply positioned themselves to be at the right place at the right time. I believe they had a sense of these wealth cycles, and if they had the knowledge, it would only reflect proof that it works. This strategy is a generational point of view of how to invest and to create generational wealth.

I do not invest by the day, week, month, or year. I invest by the decade. I have given you some insight into the world of wealth cycles, but investors need more information regarding personal finance and wealth protection.

## How to Protect Your Wealth

There are threats to your wealth including political, financial, counterparty risk, and systemic threats. Yes, even politics is now involved when it comes to your personal finances, wealth, and economic freedom. Due to the over-politicized world, politics has seeped into the financial industry, markets, and our money supply. Most financial books will tell you just to diversify into other political jurisdictions and open up foreign bank accounts. I do believe that is a good idea. However, there are better alternatives than just opening up foreign bank accounts in Switzerland, Singapore, or in New Zealand. Currently, the U.S. government has now bullied banking institutions in other countries to divulge your personal banking information to them under the guise of preventing or finding tax frauds.

So, when an individual opens a foreign bank account, they need to be aware of the risks, and particularly of how the U.S. government may perceive and interpret what individuals are trying to do, which is preventing the U.S. government from seizing their assets in a financial crisis to satisfy their political ends. I will one day eventually start diversifying my assets among certain political jurisdictions. I'll do this for two reasons:

First, I want to diversify politically to prevent one group of politicians of confiscating my wealth either through taxation or outright nationalization like Americans saw in the 1930s, similarly to what the Argentinians saw in 2002, the Cypriots saw in 2012, or other world citizens have seen in their country.

Second, I want to diversify globally into other markets, not just the United States.

Starting a foreign business to take advantage of globalization is also a great way to diversify politically. If I had a business in the U.S., I would find ways to export products or services to other foreign markets. This strategy protects businesses in the political aspect of not being subject to one group of politicians, and it helps protect businesses from being directly correlated to just the U.S. market.

Diversifying amongst various political jurisdictions is not the only way of protecting yourself. To completely protect yourself from all governments, an individual can hold real tangible assets that do not bear the market of any government. The best assets are gold and silver. These two assets functions as a form of savings, not an investment, since they are a store of wealth.

Any and all other industrial metals such as platinum, palladium, copper, nickel, etc., are also stores of wealth. Consider carefully the supply and demand fundamentals before saving in any form of an industrial metal. Digital currency may be an option; however, currently alternative digital currencies are in speculative phases, and have systemic and possibly counterparty risks.

Raw land is another option for a form of savings. However, land carries political risk, since an investor cannot transfer land to another country. However, a citizens political elites of the home cannot confiscate land in another political jurisdiction.

Let's talk about the financial losses or risks your wealth can encounter. Rick Rule has a wonderful saying that the greatest risk to your wealth and success.

*"The greatest risk as an investor is conveniently located to the left of your right ear, and to the right of your left ear."*
*- Rick Rule*

Some of an investor's worst financial mistakes will occur from their own mind and mindset; this is a critical reason why financial education is so important. Financial education is a continual, lifelong process learned through experience and knowledge; studying from financial history in congruence with relating the information to today's economy will provide greater success in investing. If we look to very successful entrepreneurs and investors such as Conrad Hilton, or even Rick Rule, their greatest catastrophic losses ensued because they were over-leveraged. All at one point in their life, they had negative net worth for the simple reason that they took on too much debt.

Here's Warren Buffett's response to people who ask him about using debt.

*"If you're dumb, do not use debt; and if you're smart, then there is no reason to use it."*
*- Warren Buffett*

Debt can easily be acquired and extremely difficult to repay. I have a saying that when people are leveraging you should be deleveraging, and when others are deleveraging you should be leveraging. During the boom times, people take on more debt than they can support, and the boom times are the easiest times to pay down debt. When the bust comes, if you need to take on debt, then you have the option of taking on debt with no debt. When the boom times roll around, then pay off that debt.

Unfortunately, most people do the reverse: they take on more debt during the boom times and must struggle financially to pay it off during the busts.

A great way to become successful is to know when to leverage yourself if you need to. Because if you do acquire debt, you always have the financial risk of defaulting, having your cash-flow assets seized to pay off debt, and creating the counter-party risk that you may not pay back the bondholder or the debt holder.

Counterparty risk is the risk that occurs when a financial agreement is made with obligations on one or the other parties involved. Your bank accounts, mutual funds, and brokerage accounts all involve counterparty risk. When you or I deposit money at the bank, we are the unsecured creditor of the bank, meaning we receive no collateral to back the deposit in case the bank fails. Our deposit is actually a loan to the bank. Banks take our deposits to loan to other individuals, businesses, and institutions. When people default and the economy experiences a deleveraging, people default on the bank, and the bank defaults on the promise to pay the depositors. Until the advent of Federal Deposit Insurance, our deposits would go down with the bank.

If you hand money over to a CFP or a brokerage firm, you have the counterparty risk that the institution mismanages or steals your money.

A summary of diversification for protection: bank accounts, personal income, business income, land, business assets, gold and silver, and other assets amongst various political jurisdiction. Control your mindset, an individual should never take on too much debt.

## Derivatives

In the high finance world of Wall Street, central banks, international banks, insurance groups, hedge funds, and so on, they use financial agreements that are typically called derivatives.

Derivatives are purely a financial agreement between two or more parties who write a contract over a security, real wealth, or even future wealth. A derivative derives its value from the *market performance* of the underlying asset; whether the asset is a paper asset or a tangible asset, it does not matter. Before the Great Recession, many large financial institutions such as JP Morgan, Goldman Sachs, Lehman Brothers, Bear Stearns, AIG, etc., engaged in these financial instruments or agreements.

Firms create numerous derivative contracts to suit the financial goals in the business. They may use terms such as MBS, CDOs, CDs, options, puts, calls, and more to describe the derivative contract. When people fail, and there is counterparty risk involved with the many large financial institutions, banks, financial firms, central banks, and even governments, it may generate systemic risk to cause a crisis or collapse the financial, banking, or monetary system.

Systemic risk involves the parties pertaining to their financial agreements needing to be fulfilled to maintain the system. When one party or a group of parties defaults on the promise to fulfill contracts such as derivative contracts, it causes another party to default. We saw this in 2008 when Bear Stearns collapsed, and then Lehman Brothers collapsed also. The people and institutions who participated in these contracts found that one party defaulting caused them to default, creating a domino effect. Other parties within the system either begin to default, or they quit creating contracts, quit buying, and start selling. You will see the liquidity in the system dry up completely, and people panic and start to sell everything to get into cash or near-cash securities such as government bonds.

A crash can occur in the stock market and real estate market. People panic and bank runs ensue, and then the whole financial system freezes up. People cannot get their money out of the banks, as we saw in Cyprus in late 2012, or now we see in Greece. Greeks could only get 50 euros (roughly $67) a day out of the ATMs. Try living on $67 a day to pay all your bills, and then going to work to have your paycheck directly deposited into the bank that you want your money from; it is a frightening situation. Systemic risk exists whether it is in one institution, many institutions, or even a nation—they all have some form of systemic risk.

Protecting your wealth from systemic risk is the same as protecting yourself from counterparty risk. Pay off debts, get money out of the financial system, get money away from individuals, and take physical possession and responsibility for your wealth.

Now I'm not completely withdrawing my entire wealth out of the system. In certain situations, you need to keep wealth in, but this must be wealth you are willing to lose. My wealth pyramid shows how to manage risk and how to manage wealth.

## My Wealth Pyramid

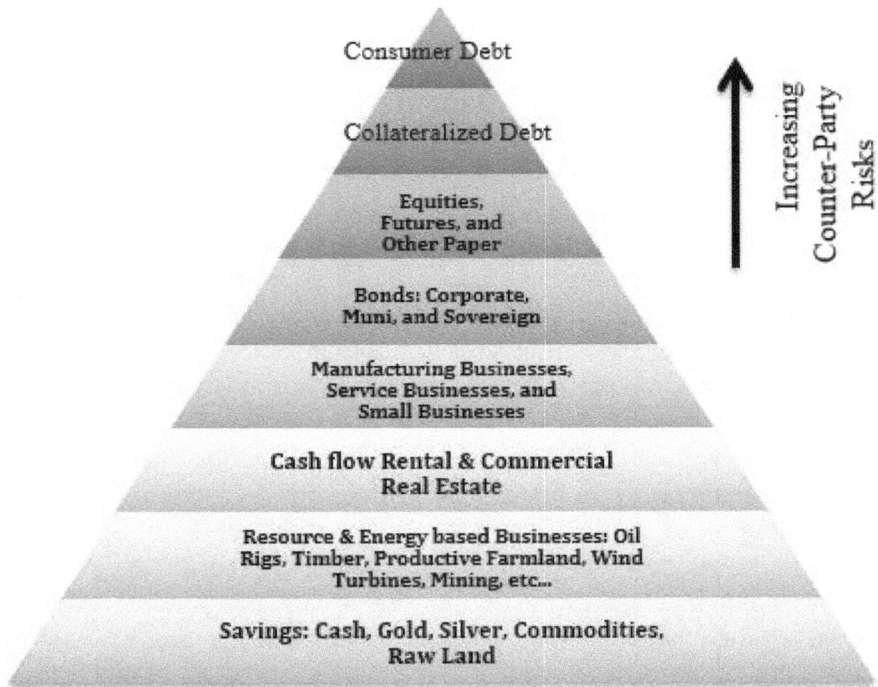

I am in my prime saving years. Personally, I need to accumulate as much capital and store it in a form of savings. Precious metals and industrial metals (PMs and IMs) hedge my cash position against inflation and the devaluation of the dollar and cash hedges my PM and IM positions from short-term deflation and dollar strength. Industrial metals are a double-edged sword concerning inflation and economic growth. During times of inflation, industrial metals will rise faster than inflation because producers purchase more to beat inflation, causing demand to increase. In economic growth periods, industrial metals perform well due to the increasing demand and utilization. However, industrial metals are very cyclical, and they will fall dramatically if there is an economic recession.

If I could, I would purchase raw land to diversify my savings even more! However, if I held certain cash flow assets in my wealth pyramid, I would not liquidate those assets. Instead, I would take the cash flow and save it in my savings level of the pyramid.

Resource and energy-based businesses and assets such as oil rigs or pumps, wind turbines, productive cash positive farms, etc., are the next level on the pyramid and the first level to consider producing cash flow. The reason I place them here is because they are the foundation for all the higher levels to function. We need energy and resources to supply are manufacturing businesses, service sector, and our information sector as well. The resources are natural resources, energy, and agriculture, which are the basis for human existences and survival.

The next level is shelter, or cash flow real estate. Stay away from empty buildings or empty homes, because a house is a consumer good, not an asset. The equity in your home is an asset, but that home must be maintained, meaning you pay expenses on real estate. Not having cash flow means money is taken out of your pocket to maintain that home.

Finally, we get to manufacturing businesses and service businesses that produce all of the value-added goods we enjoy. Nevertheless, they typically are the most vulnerable to economic downturns, so properly managing these businesses is critical.

The next levels are the claim check levels: bonds, equities, futures, and derivatives. These paper claim checks are assets but reflect their underlying assets or levels. Paper assets have counterparty risk, can be defrauded on or defaulted on, carrying greater risk compared to the assets below that are held out right.

Finally, the last two levels are debt. Collateralized debt is collateral of a house or a car. Consumer debt such as credit cards, credit at stores for furniture, appliances, etc., and personal loans carry greater risk to your wealth and well-being. They have the highest forms of counterparty risk because typically in a bankruptcy the assets below will be liquidated to pay off the debts.

I find it very unfortunate that the average American's wealth pyramid is an *inverted* pyramid.

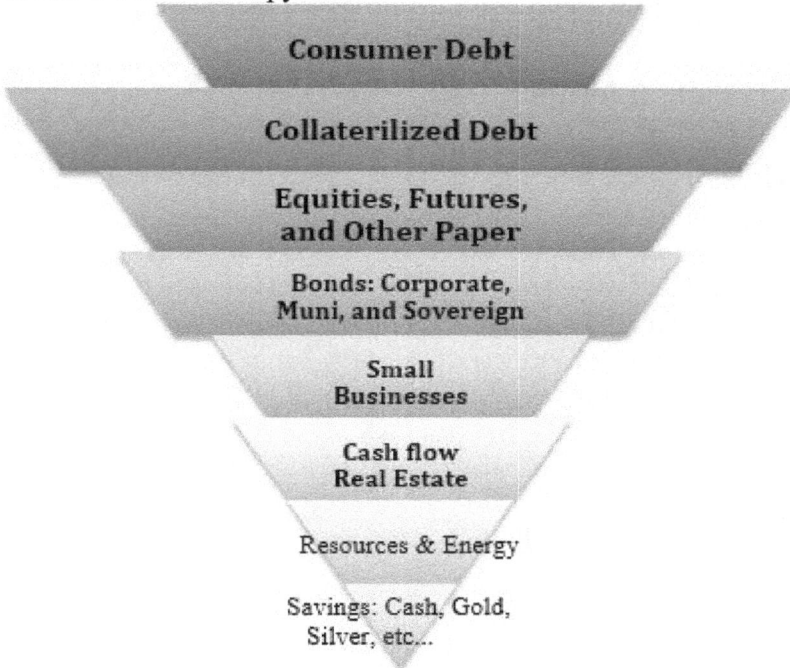

**Consumer Debt**

**Collaterilized Debt**

**Equities, Futures, and Other Paper**

**Bonds: Corporate, Muni, and Sovereign**

**Small Businesses**

**Cash flow Real Estate**

Resources & Energy

Savings: Cash, Gold, Silver, etc...

While a pyramid is the most stable geometric shape in the world, an inverted pyramid is the most *unstable* geometric shape in the world. Inverted pyramids tend to collapse catastrophically. Typically, when a person declares bankruptcy, the inverted pyramid looks extremely thick at the top while thin at the bottom.

To see what your wealth pyramid looks, write down all of your personal financial information including your liabilities and your assets. Now if you're starting out like me, or haven't acquired much wealth, that is fine. Most people can't be giant oil barons or agricultural giants. If you consult with your CFP or CPA to find equities that participate in the resource or energy sector, that's great. I understand that most people do not want to own outright a farm and operate it, or an oil pump. At least with equities you can have a claim check on natural resources or energy—it's better than nothing.

It's much easier to own bonds or stocks, but if you are willing to invest in cash flow real estate and small businesses you can. I will show you in my next chapter how to create companies and gather investors to invest in passive small businesses and real estates. The lower levels require outright ownership and responsibility, but not necessarily outright management of those assets; you can hire someone to do that for you.

## How to Position for the Coming Boom

My wealth pyramid allows me to pivot from one asset class to another. It depends on the valuations of those assets classes; purchasing the undervalued assets with cash flow is my goal. A boom occurs when an undervalued asset begins to attract investors, increases productivity, and then the market or asset moves into overvalued territory. In Chapters 9 & 10, I will show you how you could position yourself in these financially tumultuous times and turn them into profitable opportunities for yourself and your family.

# Chapter 9: A Blueprint for Long-Term Prosperity

So far I've talked about the mental mindset, financial education, historical context regarding crises and successful entrepreneurs, why crises form, capital preparation, and how to understand systems and utilizing systems to identify a possible future financial crisis. In this chapter, I will give you the blueprint for how to create generational wealth and a financially sustainable future. This blueprint was generated through my research into how other individuals built large business empires, and this process can be scaled up or down to fit your needs.

## Eight Points for My Personal Plan to Become Wealthy

1. Understand the credit, business, and economic cycles
2. Save and diversify your capital (savings)
3. Avoid financial calamities
4. Possibly profit from a calamity
5. Invest utilizing wealth cycles
6. Acquire marketable skills
7. Start, develop, and grow businesses currently in the growth phase of the "wealth cycle."
8. Exit out of an old growth phase and transition into another wealth cycle that is in a growth phase.

Marketable skills are the personal capital contribution to the world economy: whether it is accounting, bookkeeping, lawyering, doctoring, engineering, technology (IT), marketing, salesmanship, product development, customer servicing, and plenty of others. With that being said, the more marketable skills you acquire, the more productive you will be, resulting in promotions, better pay, and better benefits. If you work for someone else, make yourself an indispensable employee. Human capital has a limit to income, so understand that your profession has a ceiling for pay. This element is why it's important to find other avenues to earn income.

Individuals, in my opinion, should not solely depend upon their labor for income. It's by becoming an entrepreneur where an individual invents a product, provides a service, starts a business, or organizes the four economic resources. Entrepreneurs, investors, and individuals like you need to create a plan, a blueprint for success and then have marketable skills to execute the plan.

## The Blueprint

1. Identify undervalued assets and avoid the crisis.
2. Create a plan and/or business plan.
3. Assemble your dream team.
4. Launch the company and create value or find the deals.
5. Buy an existing business.
6. Develop your business.
7. Have a strong work ethic.
8. Be resourceful.
9. Create and deliver value where people need it most.

## 1. Identify Undervalued Assets and Avoid the Crisis

This is the most important step in the process. If you have a dream and passion, then pursue those in any circumstances. People who are lying on their deathbed often regret not taking the risks to accomplish their dreams and pursue their passion in life. If your goal is simply to increase your net worth and the type of work you are doing doesn't matter; then it's not going to affect how you use your capital other than for the most profitable enterprises.

*"A financial crisis is a great time for professional investors and a horrible time for average ones."*
*- Robert Kiyosaki*

The sure way to identify undervalued assets is how I showed you in my previous chapter concerning wealth cycles in regard to market-to-market evaluations, or asset-to-asset class evaluation with those charts. If you need to flip back to those charts, do so.

Gold has been money for 5,000 years, so I love to price assets and markets in terms of gold. All these charts are essentially replacing the dollar sign with gold. So, we sell when the Dow is high, and we buy when the Dow is low. The mean is anywhere between four to five ounces of gold to purchase the Dow is fair. Currently, the Dow is roughly 15 ounces, meaning the first graph shows that gold is undervalued, and the Dow is overvalued. Taking a 100-year perspective, we see that the Dow/gold ratio is in the trend line. The chart indicates there could be a massive correction down to or below 1.

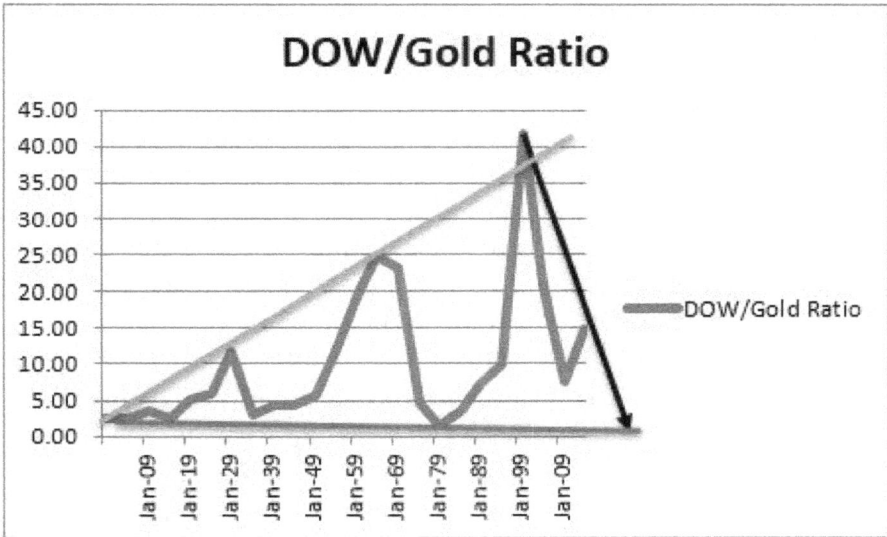

Due to all of the financial instability in the system, I believe we will have a massive correction. We will see gold outperform the Dow. How quick it comes, or when it comes, is anybody's guess. The probabilities are highly likely that an event will occur, and if you're reading this book due to a crisis—possibly the crisis I outline in this book—you already know about, or you're currently in.

There are many charts I can show you that identify undervalued asset classes in the world. Remember the four major assets—real estate, equities, bonds, and commodities—and then you can create your own charts by taking two of these assets and measuring them against each other.

There are many market indicators, and you can find them all online. They are typically free as well. Follow *Market Watch*[xxxv] and *Business Insider*[xxxvi], and there are a plethora of analysts with free information; just make sure to do your homework. In avoiding the crisis by building up your capital possibly in a similar fashion to the wealth pyramid, not only are you avoiding the crisis by holding tangible wealth, but it also gives you the ability to pivot when you have identified the crisis or when the crisis occurs.

Once you have done your homework and research on the future crisis and want to avoid it, what is your plan?

## 2. Create a Plan and/or Business Plan

Every individual needs some form of plan or strategy to get him or herself from their current state to their desire future state, or from A to B. The first step is finding something you are passionate about, and love to do. A similarity all successful individuals have is pursuing something they are passionate about. Once a person chooses their passion the next step is formulating your plan.

The plan needs to include your passion, your mission, your objectives, your mentors, your ideals, and your research. Always remember this, the plan is just a plan, and you need to spend a day or two on your plan. When you have formed a plan for an invention, a book, a movie production, your career, entrepreneurial activity, or your business, move ahead to developing a business plan. In the meanwhile, I believe it would be wise to find mentors and create a Dream Team.

## 3. Assemble Your Dream Team

We all need mentors, and if you're looking for personal financial advancement, then I suggest finding individuals who are wealthier than you. Go to conferences in your local area, go to golf clubs, join Toastmasters—you are going to have to find places where successful people congregate. Where I live I have met many successful people through the Boy Scouts; just put yourself out there to meet new people. Hopefully, you can find a similar interest or activity the two of you like, and just tell them that you would like someone as a mentor. It's all right to be honest with people. If they do not want to be a mentor it's best to find that out sooner rather than later, so ask early. Another great way to find mentors is to ask the person. It's all right to ask anyone to be your mentor; however, that "anyone" needs to be in the position you want to be in, is vastly more successful than you, and hopefully in a near geographical location preferably. A side note, your dream team needs to include a well-established accounting firm and legal firm.

Your dream team is the board of directors for the company that you want to set up. For those who are looking to set up their first company, or even your second or third, and you haven't made any plans to find mentors, then stop and find the mentors first. Find people who are in the position you want to be in X amount of years. You will greatly increase your chances of success if you have mentors as opposed to having none. Your dream team needs to consist of your mentors.

These mentors who are going to be your future board of directors will not invest any money, and do not ask them for any money, period! You have mentors for advice and guidance. They are not your bank. Instead, what you are going to do is offer one or two percent equity to each board member or mentor. Have at least three to five, but no more. In most countries outside of the Western world, entrepreneurs offer their board members nothing. However, I believe you will have more engaged mentors if you offer at least one percent stake. They are purely there for advice, not for sweat equity, money, or any other thing you think of. Your mentors are simply there for mentorship. Once you have your mentors, you need to complete your plan or business plan.

## 4. Launch the Company and Create Value or Find the Deals

People do not plan to fail; they fail to plan. Success always requires detail planning. How many people have pictured a financial life's plan, broken it down in yearly increments posited yearly plans and goals, drilling all the way down to the monthly budgets? Conversely, seventy percent of Americans live paycheck to paycheck.

First of all, create your financial plan that will take you to retirement or financial independence. For the first, what is the dollar amount needed? In the case of financial independence, how much recurring cash flow on a monthly basis?

Once you have set down that dollar amount, what is your plan for acquiring it? Will it be through rental or commercial real estate? Will it be acquiring restaurants, beauty salons, gas stations, grocery stores? Will you pursue becoming an author, inventor, designer, film producer, or another entrepreneurial activity to reach your goal? Find a passion, or a business you have an interest in. When you have something that you are passionate about you can create more value and enjoy the process.

Create value for people!

To reach this goal I suggest starting a business venture as we have discussed, when you have mentors and a business plan it's time to move forward to forming the business. There are a few ways to do this: form a sole proprietorship, a limited liability company (LLC), a limited partnership, a partnership, or incorporating. Since there is a dream team in this example, I will exclude sole proprietorship and focus on the LLC, partnership, and corporations. Legal advice is vital at this stage. Your advisor should be an experienced attorney focused on business ventures.

Remember, this book is simply a guide. *Please do your own research and seek professional advice from an accountant and an attorney!*

LLCs are my favorite tool for starting your business. They are less onerous to set up compared to incorporating a company, and they provide the same legal protections as a typical corporation. Setting up an LLC is fairly simple, and I would recommend having a lawyer review the articles of formation before everything is filed.

Then the final step will be to secure financing for your business and conduct initial meetings with legal and financial advisors and mentors.

Partnerships, in this example, will usually not include mentors, however if you decide on a partnership there are a few more things to consider. Ensure you and your partner(s) consult an attorney beforehand. Include in your agreement the relative percentages of the business each receives, responsibilities, liability, articles of formation, and administrative duties. When going into business with a partner, your partner needs to complement you, not duplicate you. If one is good with the bookkeeping, fulfilling purchase orders, managing the shop, payroll, etc., the other partner should have people skills with customer service, salesmanship, generating business, and managing employees. An entrepreneur needs to find someone who has the other set of marketable skills that the business needs to succeed.

Finally, find the financing and the deals.

Corporations are similar to setting up an LLC but require additional legal work and structure. Legal liabilities are established when creating a corporation. Taxation needs to be addressed. Entrepreneurs then distribute shares to the board members and any investors. You'll need articles of formation and operation for the company are required. Documented quarterly board meetings are needed to keep yourself on track.

Finally, the hardest part of the enterprise, you the entrepreneur to locate the funding and the "deals" for your business venture.

I have briefly gone over the three types of businesses that include other partners or mentors. It is up to you to do your own research; in the references section I have provided you with articles to look at, but should still do your own additional research. However, going over all of the intricacies with the pros and cons of each would require an entire book to itself. That is why you will have to do your own research regarding which structure is best, and then read your state and federal laws. Granted, you are not going to be able to start your company tomorrow, but I hope this places your mind in the right direction as opposed to going it alone.

## 5. Buy an Existing Business

Acquiring revenue is easier than generating new revenue. You may choose to buy an existing business. Whether it is real estate, technology, small businesses, farms, factories, oil rigs, natural resources, fisheries, etc., you have to go out there to find the deals. Today, the Internet has made easier than ever to go out and acquire the businesses you want or purchase the assets your businesses need to start and grow. Another deal a business founder may consider is government contracts to fulfill for your business. My view is that government contracts are great for businesses since governments overpay for everything they order. However, that means that it is bad for us taxpayers, and for our businesses due to over-regulation along with taxation.

First let's talk about acquiring businesses. Just conducting a web search for "small businesses for sale" will pull up a plethora of resources. A few websites that pop up include bizbuysell.com, businessbroker.net, and businessmart.com. My personal favorite is bizbuysell.com, but businessbroker.net is okay too. Find one that you like. Now make sure always to do your due diligence before writing checks, especially when you are borrowing the money. Most of these things you can find online either by the website they are selling on, reviews, and other online sources.

When purchasing a business make sure you are purchasing the assets of the business, and not purchasing stock or membership interests in an LLC or corporation. Purchase the real assets of the business so you have control over those assets, and then ask the owner about the sales taxes and payroll taxes.

If the seller of the assets or business has back taxes in sales taxes or payroll taxes, the state tax authorities can come after you. Most businesses use a payroll service; this allows you to check if they are current on their taxes. A prospective buyer needs to go to the state tax authorities to get a "clearance letter" stating that the seller is current on his sales tax, property tax, and payroll taxes at the closing date. A buyer needs to search to see if the business has any debts, such as a mortgage on real estate, or if he is leasing the real estate.

If so, you should find out how much time remains on the lease term and whether the landlord is willing to let you assume the seller's lease "as is," without an increase in rent. If the lease has less than two years to run, you might want to spend the money now to negotiate a new lease with a five-year or longer term. Also, find out if the landlord is holding a security deposit. Your seller will probably want you to purchase his security deposit on top of the agreed-upon purchase price for the business assets. If the seller is including the security deposit in the purchase price, make sure that's spelled out in writing somewhere.

Then it's time to consider pre-paid expenses.

Taking into consideration that a business is typically bought during the year, the business may have pre-paid expenses. Just like a security deposit, a seller's pre-paid expenses are assets for the business such as pre-paid advertising that is expensed throughout the year. Considering that the seller does not include pre-paid expenses in the purchasing price, ask him or her for a list of "closing adjustments"—amounts the seller has prepaid that will have to be pro-rated—so you can budget them accordingly to have no surprises at closing.

Once you have taken into consideration the pre-paid expenses, you need to look at the accounts receivable the business has.

Most businesses have accounts receivable, where customers owe the seller money on the closing date. Who is going to be responsible for collecting these debts? It can either be you or the seller. You may purchase the accounts receivables for a discount to reflect that some customers will default on the debt, or you have the seller collect the debts at his leisure. If the seller collects the account receivables, it will decrease the purchase price of the business since an account receivable is an asset of a business, and typically included in the asking price.

A letter of intent is a two- or three-page agreement between the buyer and seller of a business that spells out all the important terms and conditions of the sale. For example, it will include the purchase price, how and when the purchase price will be paid, the assets that will be sold to the buyer, the assets that the seller keeps, the terms of the seller's non-compete agreement, and so forth. While this is a non-binding contract, it gives both parties a written document of what to expect from the sale of the business and business assets. This also helps the lawyers form the sales documents correctly on the first or second draft; the investor saves money from having to draft the legal documents multiple times.

Two major legal issues you need to consider are bulk sales laws (if your state has them) and receiving an indemnity from the seller. With regard to bulk sale laws, you will need to notify all of the business's creditors and the government that you are taking over the business. An experienced lawyer will be able to help you with this issue and others. Even when an investor's lawyers, accountants, and other advisors have looked through everything at least twice, you should still obtain an indemnity, it is not worth a lawsuit for something the seller failed to do before an investor took over his or her business.

After the process is completed, make sure the seller remains during the transition period and until you know the employees to ensure a successful acquisition of the business, or business assets.

There are special considerations for assuming government contracts.

Research both the contract and the laws regarding government contractors.

Make sure you have the capacity to fulfill the government contract. There are sources on the Internet you can search with regard to becoming a government contractor. The best resources are found on government websites regarding contractors, and government contracts. It may be wise to start small with cities and municipalities to gain experience for state and federal contracts.

Conduct your own research, I can't do that for you! Section *5. Buying an Existing Business* is incomplete with regards to all of the necessary information to acquire an existing business. This section's intention is to explain a step in the blueprint, and introduce this concept to an individual. Consult the proper attorneys and accountants for all of the conducive and pertinent information regarding your specific situation.

I am an entrepreneur who is triple majoring in Accounting, Business Information Systems, and Supply and Value Chain Management. I am not a lawyer or a licensed accountant. Seek the necessary legal and financial counsel for your personal needs.

Now, how do you finance your deal and dream?

## 6. Financing

Acquiring the money to finance your company or your entrepreneurial dream is the step that people believe is both the most difficult and most important. I disagree with the conventional wisdom that raising capital is the hardest or most important part of the process. In fact, it is the easiest step out of the whole process, and probably least important for these two reasons. One being that the deal or company is the hardest item to accomplish and makes financing pointless if you do not have a deal or a company. When you have a dream team, it makes financing easier. The reason why is that the company has credibility, and there are individuals who have a track record for financiers to review. A dream team makes financiers feel more comfortable; therefore, more likely to finance the business.

So, how do you get the money? I know you have been patiently waiting for this topic. First, here's a list of possible sources of capital.

## Partial List of Sources of Capital

Angel networks
Businesses
Barter
Commercial banks
Corporate private equity
Credit cards (not usually a good choice)

Crowd funding
Family
Friends
Hedge funds
Governments
Insurance company fund
Investment forums
Leasing
Online resources
Peer lending
TV shows for entrepreneurial pitches
Self-Capitalization
Venture capitalists (VC) and private equity

There are many ways to finance your deals, your inventions, or your companies. There are many online resources that will aid you in your quest to find more information on how to raise capital. Here are a few ideas.

## Angel Networks, VCs, Private Equity

Angel investors are not angels! They care more about the return of *their* capital, not so much the return on capital. They will take as much of you company as you let them. Angel networks, venture capitalist, and private equity firms are a great way to raise money; however, there is a downside. A significant downside is losing control of the company, and I would never want that happen.

Investors are wonderful people, but they want the best investment possible. However, some may want to take over a startup rather than partner with the prior investors to build the company. Another pitfall is a "vulture capitalist" who seeks to buy a company below book value (purchase the company for less than the equity value) and sell the assets at a higher price to make profit. The majority of these investing networks want to invest in a successful business and make money. A personal rule of mine is to raise equity when multiple investors control similar portions, and no one investor has control over the company. For example; 10% of the shares are owned by the founding board members leaving 90% for the entrepreneur, during the first round of refinancing an entrepreneur gives up 25% ownership to an angel investor, during the second round he or she gives up 20% to a private equity firm, during the third round 15% to an investment firm, and then gives up 10% of the company for the Initial Public Offering (IPO). The founding Board of Directors should end up with 10% ownership, an angel investor with 25%, a private equity firm with 20%, an investment firm with 15%, the public owning 10%, and the entrepreneur owning 20% of the business. During each step of this process, the entrepreneur should maintain control to the point when they finally relinquish control to multiple interests. This type of strategy reduces the risks of a takeover or a "vulture capitalist".

I would not negotiate a deal with someone who cares more about his or her position than the well-being of the company. It should be understood that there is no room for this type of thinking in any organization under your control. You should walk away from any such deal. Most venture capitalists would say that I would rather have a small portion of a big thing than a large portion of a small thing. Wrong! I have the company, the idea, and the work ethic to grow the company exponentially. You have the company; they don't! Period! So they can have a nice portion of a big thing or no portion of a big thing. The choice is theirs to make. The world is flush with cash, and they have competition.

Like I've said before, it's harder to find the deal or create the proper company than finding the financing. I see too many entrepreneurs give up too much to finance their deal, so do not pass up your best offer.

## Commercial Banking

Commercial banks are a great source of funding. Typically, they do not desire equity. However, they always want collateral. If they really like your company, they may want an equity kicker. Now, I am fine with that. It's a great compliment.

Commercial banking comes down to perception, presentation, and the business. Here are a few brief points before I defer to an in depth source created by a well-respected and credible individual. Perception; act and look successful to be successful. Wear apparel that a banker would. Improve your communication ability, speak slowly in a measured manner, and if you happen to have a thick accent try to mitigate it. Walk tall and sit with good posture. Presentation; Your presentation should contain documents containing brief paragraph concerning each key mentor with contact information, another folder containing the appropriate information about your accounting and law firm. Your presentation should include what you want from your audience, why you are there, what you can do for them, and what they can do for you. My referral is Dan Pena Sr. book *Your First $100 Million*.[xxxvii] His book is free at: http://www.danlok.com/daniel-s-pena/books/building-guthrie/

It all comes down to focus, commitment, and courage. Pursue at least two presentations per week to targeted institutions asking them to finance your deal. Find the right partners, do your own due diligence regarding the institution that you are marketing to. Ensure your proposal aligns with your marketing effort.

## 7. Develop Your Business

Building the foundation is critical, but so is growing. You can't grow unless you take care of the fundamentals.

✓ Clearly state the need that is being fulfilled by your product or service.

✓ Understand the market or industry you are operating in.

✓ Know the size and your competition.

✓ Make sure you can clearly state your target customer's base and whether it is business-to-business or business-to-consumer.

✓ Define your competitive advantage over the competition, and why you will succeed.

✓ Provide any overview of how you are going to deliver the value to the customer.

✓ Describe your business processes to complete the goals, and prioritize them.

✓ Then just do it. If you have bumps in the road, which you will. Be prepared to alter the plan to meet your goals. Then *just do it*.

## 8. Have a Strong Work Ethic

Just do it! Typically, you have a strong work ethic, or you don't. If you don't, you can train yourself to become a high-performance person, but it is up to you. You can adapt and change to make yourself a successful individual. If you do not want to start a business and have the responsibilities of a business owner, then create your personal plan with a CFP and then just execute the plan. No matter your approach, it still comes down to *just do it*!

## 9. Be Resourceful

In business and life, we are not always going to have the resources to pull through—yet we all have abilities to utilize our resources more effectively. Resourcefulness is a more compelling tool for you, because the more resourceful you are, the more the resources will come to you. An entrepreneur has the responsibility of fulfilling unlimited demand with limited resources. If you care about your personal finances, then being thrifty will result in greater savings and more capital to deploy.

## 10. Create and Deliver Value Where People Need It Most

People need value such as food, energy, products, and services. Fulfill that need for value to humanity and be a blessing to others. Start a business that provides value and provides livelihoods, products, services, etc. and you'll truly be a blessing to others.

Remember it is your job to deliver value to the customer. Delivering is more important than the product itself. If you can create value, but fail at delivering value, no one enjoys that value. When the next financial crisis comes, people are going to be clamoring for real assets, real wealth, real people, and real value—not the paper promises or claim checks that will be wiped out in this next financial calamity. So, be that person to help others, and provide value for people!

## Critical Path

The critical path method is an over view of the most fundamental process, and I utilizing it to summarize and crystalize the process.
1. Research and Analysis
2. Identifying systemic risks, and undervalued markets
3. Create your plan and/or business plan
4. Assemble your Dream Team
5. Launch company or product, or purchase existing business
6. Expand and Grow your business or enterprise

Continual adapt and deliver value

# Chapter 10: A Game Plan for Personal Investing

I'll bring together all the pieces of the first nine chapters in this one chapter. We'll see how to create your game plan to protect you and your family from the future financial crisis, and position yourself to take advantage of the future economic boom. This chapter focuses on wealth management, wealth preservation, and financial positioning. The template needs to be customized to your needs, and consulted with your personal financial advisors. Please refer to the previous chapters to grasp any of the concepts discussed in the game plan.

Before I dive right into the game plan, let's quickly review the major concepts I discussed in the book concerning personal finances.

Protect your wealth by limiting counterparty risk and diversifying your counterparty risk. Utilize the wealth cycle's principle to identify overvalued and undervalued markets. An investor develops their wealth pyramid to diversify properly between paper assets and real assets while having a stable foundation for personal finances.

## The Six Parts of a Financial Game Plan

1. Be your own central bank
2. Build your wealth pyramid
3. Invest using the wealth cycle principles
4. Asset(s)-backed leveraging
5. Wealth diversification
6. A personal financial insurance policy

### 1. Be Your Own Central Bank

I believe a prudent course to any financial plan is becoming your own bank. A common fear investors and individuals have is whether their money is safe in a bank. It's easy to eliminate that fear: basically, create your own bank.

The central banks of the world own and hold gold and physical currency. An individual needs to create the foundation for capital formation, and that is his or her savings. It's also the first foundation of the wealth pyramid. Personally, I only have enough cash in my bank accounts for emergencies and to fund my business on a monthly basis. Cash is held for deflationary purposes and possibly cover no more or no less than six months of expenses. Cash is short-term savings.

The next forms of savings are gold and silver, and industrial metals.

Gold and silver perform the role of long-term savings. An ounce of gold stores an enormous amount of wealth. Every individual needs to start with silver first, then work their way toward gold. I believe that investors start with constitutional silver, also known as "junk silver," but please do not call American coinage "junk"! Constitutional silver, for practical purpose, criminals have not attempted to counterfeit constitutional silver at this point.

Coin dealers would easily detect counterfeit constitutional silver, and there is not enough market incentive to counterfeit silver dimes, quarters, and halves. A dime currently is $1, a quarter $2 to $3, and a half dollar is a little over five dollars. Remember it is about the ounces, not the dollar sign. Once a person has 100 ounces in constitutional silver, which is roughly $140 in face value of constitutional coinage, it is time to move onto one-ounce coins. American silver eagles, Canadian maple leafs, and other government-minted coins are wonderful to start with. Diversify between government minted coinage and bullion coins.

After roughly 400 ounces of one-ounce coins, then start investing in 10-ounce bars, or even 100-ounce bars. Do not buy numismatic coins! That is a no-no! Unless you are a coin collector, stay away from numismatic coins. Let me give you an example of why you do not buy a numismatic coin such as a peace dollar or a silver Morgan. A friend of mine was buying silver Morgan dollars for $60 a coin; meanwhile, the spot price for silver was $30 an ounce, and a silver Morgan contains .77 ounces of silver or $23 worth of silver per coin. When you sell a silver Morgan dollar back to a dealer, they will typically offer you melt value. So, he bought a coin from a dealer for $60, and if he turned around to sell it back, the dealer would have offered him $23 for the coin. Stay away from numismatic, unless you like to collect coins and understand the collectible coin market.

Buying gold coins utilize the same practices as you do for silver. Start small and work your way to the larger bars.

---

On to industrial metals.

You'll buy them in large bars. A pound of copper is currently $2 to $3, or a ton of copper is $4,000 to $6,000. Storage may be problematic; as precious metals store more value in less space. Focus on industrial metals such as copper, nickel, platinum, and palladium. Copper and nickel are understandable, and the physical form is for the long-term. Platinum and palladium do act as precious metals since they store an incredible amount of value in one ounce. Be aware that platinum and palladium are greatly affected by the supply and demand factors of the industrial sector and by the cyclical nature of the market; a contrarian point of view will provide the best view of when to buy industrial metals.

**This Is What I Would Not Do!**
- Do not panic.
- Do not become paralyzed by fear or depression.
- Do not procrastinate; take action to improve your financial situation.
- Don't sell all your assets and panic into cash.
- Don't sell all your assets and panic into gold and silver.
- Don't take on more unproductive debt or consumer debt.
- Don't use excessive leverage.
- Don't gather financial information from only one source. Instead, do your due diligence and research.

I hope I never hear about a person who reads my book panicked, sold their assets, and went all in gold, silver, or one specific asset. Right now I am stating that's a financially stupid decision. If that person chose to sell all their assets and panicked into one asset, that was his or her decision. I do not make recommendations. Remember, I tell people what I will do and what I am currently doing. I state my beliefs regarding what investors should or should not do.

A crisis investor does not panic in the first place; they do not sell all their assets to position themselves solely in one asset. A crisis investor diversifies risk, positions, and can pivot from one asset class to another.

## 2. Build Your Wealth Pyramid

There are a few points I want to make concerning building your wealth pyramid. First, I will make a few generally dos that I believe could benefit anybody, and then I'll break it down for beginners, prime investors, and retirees.

Please find a certified financial planner to start a financial plan with you, to go over this book for a second opinion, to keep you on track to reach your personal finances goals, to have yearly financial health check-ups, or to answer any of your questions when it comes to personal finances.

Please continually educate yourself in finances, monetary history, investing, markets, assets, and business. You can find a list of these resources in the back of the book.

Please pay attention to the news and listen to alternative media outlets to get the full picture, a list of these resources are in the back of the book as well.

### What Could Beginners Do (Millennials)

If you, my dear reader, are currently starting out, and I mean you're starting with zero dollars to your name, the question I will answer for you is: "How do I begin?"

Most importantly you need to educate yourself about the topics discussed in the book, especially the topics in the resource section of the book. Then start to save!

Millennials, you and I are in the prime *saving* years of our life, not the prime *spending* years of your life. Financial advisors may tell you to take on more risk to earn more reward. Their reasoning if you lose money now, you can make it up later in your life.

Their reasoning is wrong and unsound.

Recall Warren Buffett's two rules:

Rule number one: Do not lose any money.

Rule number two: Remember rule number one.

Losing money as an investor not only sets you back in the present but also the future. Another reason why not to follow the conventional wisdom of the financial community is that the greater the risk does not guarantee greater the reward. Recollect that the reward depends upon the evaluation of the asset, not necessarily the risk involved.

Starting out from zero dollars you first have to save. Build cash (short-term) savings of a minimum of three months to the maximum of six months' expenses. Then build your (long-term) savings starting with silver working your way to gold and the industrial metals.

Once you, the investor, have total savings of $25,000 in current dollars, it's time to make your first investment. I hope you utilize the wealth pyramid; it's just one strategy, and if you find one that fits you, great! Use that strategy. I'm going to show you how to utilize the wealth pyramid so you and others know how to implement this strategy.

Complete the foundation first, which is savings. As your investments increase, increase your savings as well.

For most individuals, investing in productive farmland, oil rigs, or residential real estate is almost out of the question. More than likely an individual will be a passive investor, investing $1,000 at a time, making the stocks and bonds level of the pyramid the only feasible level. Using the principle of wealth cycles, invest in markets and companies that are currently undervalued and trending in a bull market. Continue to increase your savings foundation while you add to and grow the stocks and bonds level. Eventually, there will come a point in time to use asset-backed leveraging to move into another level. A point in time will come when your savings can collateralize a cash-flow residential real estate transaction.

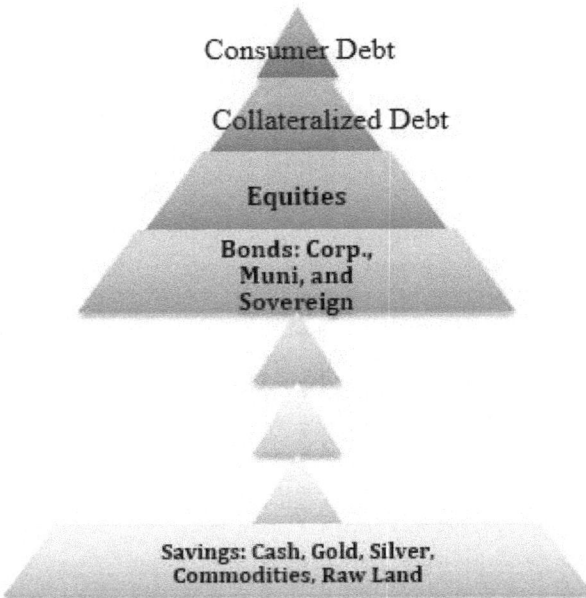

Consumer Debt

Collateralized Debt

Equities

Bonds: Corp., Muni, and Sovereign

Savings: Cash, Gold, Silver, Commodities, Raw Land

## What Could Prime Investors Do (Generation X)

I hope that during your prime saving years you saved enough to start utilizing asset-backed leveraging. When developing your cash-flow real estate portfolio, consider that you will have to be more involved with the asset and in the geographic property market. Using asset-backed leveraging can greatly enhance the return and wealth creation. The key to success is keeping constant cash-flow streams, using those streams to pay down debt as quickly as possible to move to the next deal. This process can be repeated in the other asset levels, and then at your discretion with the valuation tools that I have provided as well as your own, begin to move into other levels and other assets to build your pyramid strong. It's okay to have a little top-heavy pyramid in the begin, provided there is very little debt at the top. Then fill in the middle of the pyramid, and grow your bottom. Remember to take some of your winnings off the table.

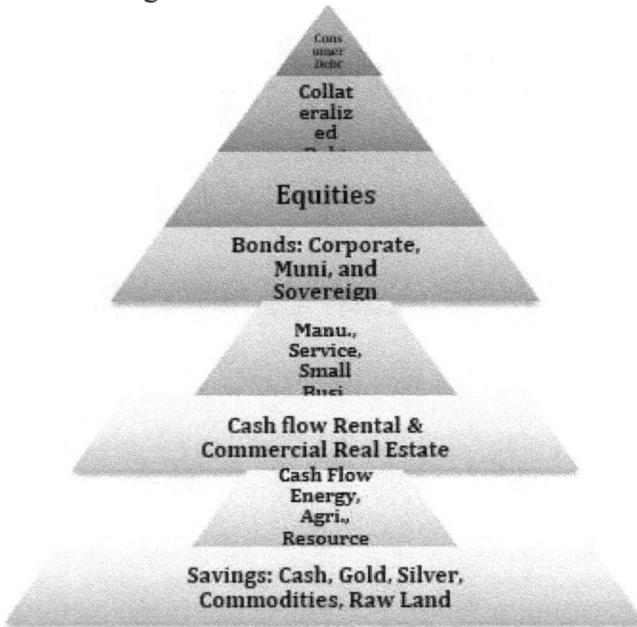

## What Could Retirees Do (Baby Boomers)

The greatest risk today facing baby boomers and part of Generation X is the counterparty risk and the systemic risk with their retirement plans. Some refer to the stool with three legs: your pension, Social Security, and 401k. All of these plans have counterparty risk, and all your assets are invested in the claim check financial system of stocks and bonds unless the pension has in its prospectus allowing it to invest in real assets. Social Security invests nearly all assets in U.S. Treasury securities, and your 401K is invested in bonds and stocks at your own choosing. For myself, I would start diversifying into real tangible assets, but do not empty out the portfolio. Consult a certified financial planner to see how much you could diversify out of your 401K. With that being said, if the CFP says "none," consider another Certified Financial Planner. CFPs do not make money on your real estate income or on any other real asset that you physically possess.

Now onto to a more in-depth conversation about what an individual could do if they are in a retiring position. When my father (a baby boomer) read this book. He loved the book and thought it was great for Millennials and Generation X. So when I heard that, I knew I had missed the mark in addressing the area of actions that retirees could take, if they conduct their own research, do their own due diligence, find good lawyers and accountants, vet businesses, build partnerships, and make their own investment decisions to take control over their assets and future.

I am going to make an example Wealth Pyramid of a Baby Boomer, who has $1 Million of investable assets with no debt. In my example, I will show you what I would do, and elaborate on how I would do it.

First is the savings base, savings is fundamental to wealth preservation because it allows the individual to utilize their wealth without liquidating a productive asset. Cash is the liquid asset to allow an individual to make it through a cash crunch. The only time an individual should liquidate some of their precious metals position is if they need to, or if precious metals blow off into a bubble. Sell the precious metals, and an individual should look to utilize that capital in an undervalued market.

Raw farmland or ranchland is also a form of savings and can produce cash flow. The average acre of land is currently selling around $3,000 an acre. A $150,000 purchase would yield roughly 50 acres of land. Farmland can be leased to a farmer or a rancher, however, expect a low ROI of 1% to 3%.

*General Wealth Pyramid Example*

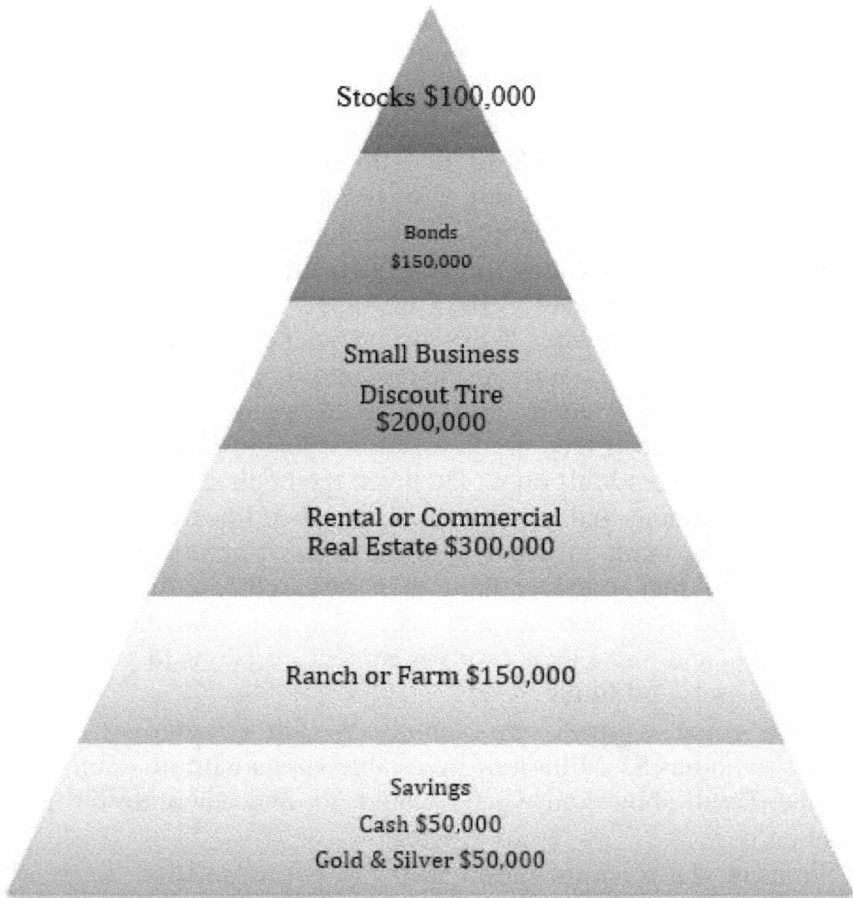

Stocks $100,000

Bonds
$150,000

Small Business
Discout Tire
$200,000

Rental or Commercial
Real Estate $300,000

Ranch or Farm $150,000

Savings
Cash $50,000
Gold & Silver $50,000

An owner may also lease their land to hunters if their land is better suited for hunters. Facilities along with water and electricity on the property will allow an owner to charge more; however, the ROI will remain roughly the same or slightly increase. An owner or investor would have to do their due diligence. Timberland is great, but the only way to earn a return of 3%-5% or more is to have a facility to store a portable saw mill, and have the clientele who want custom wood. Carpenters, craftsmen, and artisan want some type of hardwood, oak, some type of cedar, or another type of wood to use for the projects or businesses. The large timber companies will not service this clientele, and this allows for a niche opportunity. I view farmland, timberland or ranches as the safest form of bond to own. Land is a low yield bond with no chance of default that is why the yield is so low. The land itself is another form of savings. A 50-acre productive farm will require more investment than the original $150,000. Joel Salatin, a practicing Virginian Farmer, uses methodologies enabling a nice return or living from farming. I would encourage anyone interested in ranching or farming to search and research Joel Salatin and Gabe Brown. Farmland is a bond, low yield and safe, and then there are higher yield investments in real estate.

Rental and commercial real estate is a higher yielding investment. In my opinion, an investment in rental or commercial real estate should generate 8% return or higher to justify the effort and investment. As of right now (2016), commercial real estate is considered by most pundits to be in a bubble, which means it is definitely in a bubble. I would be very careful when investing in commercial real estate; however, in a couple of years once the bubble pops there will be great opportunities. Rental real estate is another avenue of investment.

Real Estate is all about location, location, and location. You and I have heard this all before by a dozen or more realtors. However, rental real estate is all about tenants, tenants, and tenants. I assure you that is the critical part, which plays into location, location, and location. Tenant selection is key to a successful and easy investment, such as: medical professionals, professionals, college students (parents), government employees, and anyone else that has guaranteed income or very solid income stream. Small business owners or struggling entrepreneurs are not ideal tenants because the last check written is to the landlord. The other expenses are paid first, and then you're paid. There are many books and videos for educating individuals of how to invest in real estate. Conduct your own research before you invest, I can't do that for you. I like to listen to Phil Pustejovsky, YouTube him to find his free content. Now onto a small business.

One great retirement investment avenue that is underappreciated, and neglected from the financial planning community are small business investments. In the pyramid above, I have a $200,000 Discount Tire business. Nevertheless, this is just an example; I would diversify the small business portfolio (you may do this with your real estate portfolio as well). What I would do is make a company and find 4 or 5 partners, which can be friends, co-workers (in a similar financial position as you are), or other investors in your investment community (web search and find organizations). Form the company, I would then find 3 to 5 investments and diversify the $200,000 into 4 businesses, or $50,000 individual investments. I will only consider investments for small businesses that yield 15% or higher ROI. The reason why is time, money, and risk-reward, I don't waste my time with low-performance investments. Low reward and high risk is a financially stupid investment. High reward and low risk investments take time, dedication, and will power to find, acquire, and run. There is a plethora of small businesses that are great to own for retirement purposes. **Here is a list of possible businesses:**

1) Discount Tire
2) Goodyear
3) Storage Units or Storage facilities
4) A/C businesses (Partnership)
5) Plumbing business (Partnership)
6) Computer repair
7) Automotive shop
8) Body shop
9) Computer training
10) Computer test center
11) Rent a room (real estate)
12) Tutoring service
13) Car washing and auto detailing services
14) Welding service
15) Granite countertop business
16) Phone accessory and support business
17) Liquor stores
18) Yoga and meditation instructor
19) Tour guide
20) Wine taste testing store
21) Franchises (location and industry)
22) Franchise (Yogurt)
23) Franchise (Ice Cream)
24) Franchise (Pizza Hut, Papa Johns, Little Caesars, etc…)
25) Franchise (Subway)

26) Franchise (Starbucks)
27) Franchise (Fast Food)
28) Gas stations
29) Land Surveying (Real Estate)
30) Restaurants (Existing Legal & Finance)
31) Barber or Beauty School
32) Electrician Business (Partnership)
33) Concrete Business (Customers governments and businesses)
34) E-Cig and Vapor Stores
35) Midas, Pep Boys, Autozone
36) Tool and Appliance Store
37) Garage Organization & Storage Business
38) Medical Spa
39) Swimming Pool Servicing (Partnership)
40) Ranch & Farm Supply Store or Feed Store (Rural areas)
41) Patent your Invention
42) Publish your book
43) Free Lance Writing or Editing (Small cash on the side if you enjoy this type of activity.

Chapter 9 Blueprint will be a great guide to point an individual in the right direction to build their small business portfolio. Also, I would read over Dan Pena's QLA methodology for business owners or entrepreneurs.[xxxviii]

A few things to note before I continue to stocks and bonds. The partnerships in parenthesis can be formed in one of two ways: starting a business with a partner, or investing in an existing business. My father is a blue-collar worker, and he has co-workers who own their own plumbing company or automotive company. You may look opportunities there, or simply ask to speak to the owner of the plumbing company to see if you can't become a passive investor.

The last $250,000 of the portfolio is diversified among stocks and bonds. This part of the portfolio may be managed by a Certified Financial Planner. Hopefully, you will find a competent manager, with an ROI for the portfolio of 8%. Analyzing the portfolio, it should be diversified much of the portfolio is in hard assets producing cash-flow, and with minimal counter-party risk. The potential ROI for the $1,000,000 portfolio is: farmland $150,000 3% ROI $4,500, rental real estate $300,000 8% ROI $24,000, small business $200,000 15% ROI $30,000, stock and bond portfolio $250,000 8% ROI $20,000.

The net income is $78, 500 or a 7.85% return on hard assets that an investor owns outright. Little counter-party risk, limited systemic risk, no chance of losing wealth in a bank default, and the whole portfolio can be diversified in each category. Conduct your own research do your own due diligence and utilize professionals. Remember, you must investigate before you invest. I cannot do that for you!

This pyramid is a further breakdown of the previous pyramid in regards to diversification of every part of the portfolio. The number in parentheses is the number of companies or positions that could be taken in that portion of the pyramid. The total dollar amount is the amount invested per company or position. When I say company, I mean the company that an individual founded with the dream team, partners, and investors. A position is what I am referring to an investment made in a public company or a debt security.

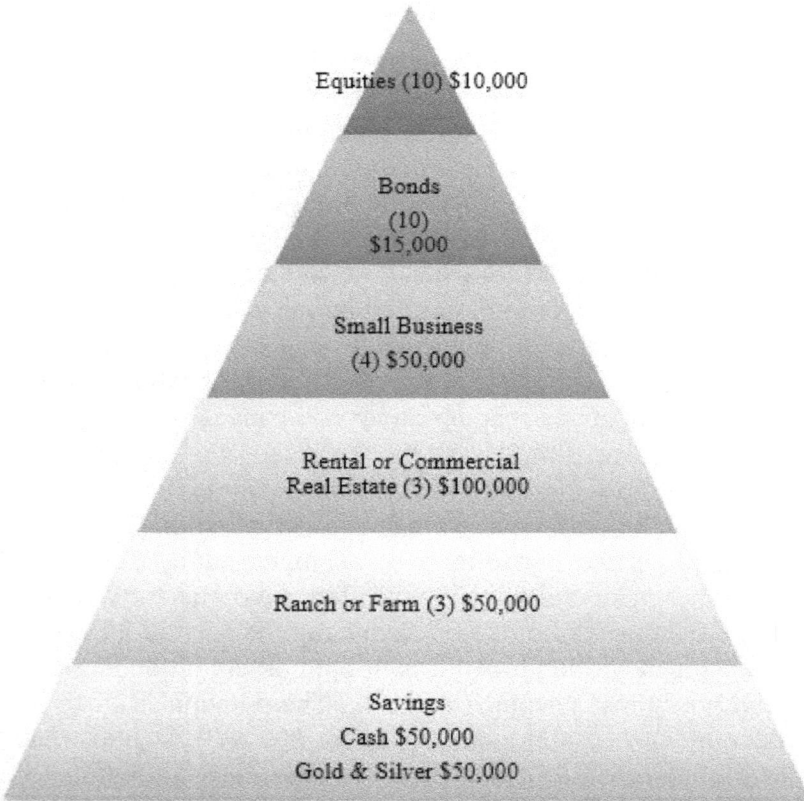

Equities (10) $10,000

Bonds
(10)
$15,000

Small Business
(4) $50,000

Rental or Commercial
Real Estate (3) $100,000

Ranch or Farm (3) $50,000

Savings
Cash $50,000
Gold & Silver $50,000

## 3. Invest Using the Wealth Cycles Principle

Mike Maloney is the creator of Wealth Cycles Principles. I am a practitioner of them. In Chapter 8, I only briefly went into what I have learned about the Wealth Cycles Principles. Mike Maloney is my Ben Graham. He is a wonderful mentor and teacher, so I suggest listening and learning from him. His website is wealthcycles.com. Mr. Maloney provides free content on his YouTube channels, as well as free articles on his website, and puts an enormous amount of effort into educating the public. He also provides an insider service, which has proprietary data and analytics that helps investors understand how to invest in his Wealth Cycles Principles.

I have learned a few things about how to invest using the Wealth Cycles Principles:

1. Measure markets against markets to determine the real value, and invest in the undervalued market. (Conduct your own market research).
2. Purchase undervalued assets in the undervalued market.
3. Utilize those assets to produce cash flow for your portfolio.
4. Organize assets and start businesses in those undervalued markets, and grow the business in the growth phase of the market.
5. Once an asset becomes *overvalued*, sell it and invest in an *undervalued* market. Better yet, use the cash flows to invest in the undervalued market, and maintain the overvalued asset's cash flow.
6. Utilize the information in Chapter 7, do your due diligence, and conduct your own market research.

## 4. Asset(s)-Backed Leveraging

A financial technique that I love to use and have personally developed is called *asset-backed leveraging*. Leveraging is borrowing money to make more money, so what does "asset-backed" mean? Asset-backed leveraging is buying an asset (preferably a cash-flow asset) and then collateralizing that asset to buy a cash-flow asset on debt, leveraging your returns. This leveraging significantly limits your risk in the leveraged asset in two ways.

First, the asset backing the leveraged asset can pay off the debt if needed, limiting your chance of defaulting. The worst-case scenario is selling one of the two assets to repay the loan.

Secondly, if the asset backing the leveraged asset produces cash flow, you have a greater ability to repay the loan quicker and easier, limiting your chance of defaulting.

Let me show you an example. (TH = Town House, SH = Small House, MH = Medium House)

| Age | Asset(s) | Loan | Save (Payment) | Cash-Flow | Months Earlier |
|---|---|---|---|---|---|
| 22 yrs. | $0 | $0 | $800 | $0 | N/A |
| 26 yrs. | $40,000 Condo | $0 | $800 | $400 | N/A |
| 26 yrs. 4 mo. | Saved $5,000 | $35,000 4yrs. 5% | ($800) | $400 | 17 mo. |
| 29 yrs. | 2 Condos | $0 | $800 | $400 | N/A |
| 30 yrs. 3 mo. | TH  Saved $25,000 | $75,000 10yrs. 5% | ($800) | $800 | 67 mo. |
| 34 yrs. 10 mo. | 2 Condos 1 TH | $0 | $800 | $800 | N/A |
| 37 yrs. 4 mo. | SH Saved $48,000 | $150,000 30yrs. 5% | ($800) | $1,600 | 287 mo. |
| 43 yrs. 5 mo. | 2 Condos 1 TH 1 SH | $0 | $800 | $1,600 | N/A |
| 46 yrs. | MH  Saved $75,000 | $225,000 30yrs. 5% | ($1,200) | $2,800 | 295 mo. |
| 52 yrs. 5 mo. | 2 Condos 1 TH 1 SH 1 MH | $0 | $1,200 | $2,800 | N/A |

I want to accomplish two objectives in this section:
1. Show you the principle of asset-backed leveraging.
2. Show you how to make it applicable to any individual.

In this scenario, this individual graduated from college, and their starting salary is $35,000 a year, a figure that is just above the median income of $29,500 in the United States. For the first four years right out of college, the individual needs to save $10,000 a year. They've moved backed with their parents or are renting cheaply with a roommate. Federal, state, and local governments will in some shape, way, or form consume taxes at approximately $11,550 a year (33%), leaving $23,450 in net income. This individual budgets $6,000 a year for rent (roommate), $2,450 a year for food, utilities $3,600, transportation $2,000, cable and Internet $1,000, health insurance $2,000, car insurance $750, and fun money $600. Regarding your car note, you should have *none*. All cars should be purchased by cash— period! This individual has $7,050 a year for savings.

We can't forget about student loan debt. The average student loan debt in the U.S. is roughly $35,000. This individual's yearly payment, for ten years, is $4,200 a year, so they're left with $2,850. Now, this individual can pick up a part-time job or freelance to make up the extra $7,150, or live with parents. Sorry, this is just the reality you and I have to live with.

When this individual turns 26, they purchase a condo and rent it out, and save for the next five months for a $5,000 down payment on another condo. A bank loans this individual $35,000 for four years, and with decent credit along with collateralizing the other property at 5% interest rate, this individual uses the cash flow from the rental property to pay off the loan 17 months early.

With his or her condo paid off, it's time to save for a townhouse and move up. As this individual repeats this process the cash flow grows, real estate equity increases, credit is built, only short-term debt is taken on that is manageable, debts are repaid early, and the individual is saving money from the smaller interest payments.

My example above shows that the individual would have $680,000 of real estate equity, and yearly cash flow of $33,600 at the age of fifty-two. Add your 401K and possibly Social Security (if it's still there), and you will have a wonderful retirement. In thirty years, this individual will have two condos, a townhouse, a small house, and a medium house with 100% ownership of all the properties. If the individual purchased the medium house at 26 years old, and he or she saved $40,000 and somehow managed to purchase the medium house with 5% interest for 30 years. This individual would have only $300,000 worth of real estate equity, no cash flow, and they would have paid $242,500 of interest payments over those thirty years.

The interest payments are a major reason why people are poor, or struggling with retirement: stay away from banks as much as possible!

Let's say this individual who has used the asset-backed leveraging principle waits for one more decade, by repeating the last step of purchasing the medium house. The individual would have $1,580,000 worth of real estate equity, and a yearly cash flow of $105,600 at the age of sixty-three. I love the miracle of compound returns!

Now, what about cars? In my high school money matters class, I watch a Dave Ramsey video about personal finance. Dave Ramsey's[xxxix] idea or principle was to purchase a car in cash, and then save what would be the monthly payment for the average car then purchase a newer car. This strategy saves the individual from paying interest payments on the car.

Starting out with $5,000, an individual saves $300 or $400 a month, and at the end of the year sells the old vehicle and purchases a newer one in cash. Saving $3,600 a year, an individual can have a $23,000 car paid for in cash in five years. A car note is a big "no-no." Do not pass go, do not collect your $200—just *no*! Another reason why someone is broke is because of that car note, and the car is losing half its value when you drive it off the lot. Asset-backed leveraging is a principle that can be practice with any asset and in any business.

## 5. Wealth Diversification

In this section, I want to crystallize a point to you. You are very intelligent and probably have a great grasp of this principle from my previous chapters. Nevertheless, this principle belongs in the template, and I can clarify the whole principle at once.

An investor, in my opinion, should diversify between *claim check assets* and *real assets*. Most Americans are heavily invested in claim checks assets, and due to the instability in the current economic system claim checks assets contain above average risk. An investor should properly diversify between both, focusing on cash-flow assets, diversify amongst the various assets class. A person needs to take into consideration the fact that markets perform by the combined movements of all the assets, not just one. Manage the risk of the assets; evaluate the risk-reward relationship, and personally invest in due diligence. Continually add to your own long-term savings base. Take into account the liquidity of all your assets, and then factor into account the liquidity your short-term and long-term savings add. The ability to pivot from one market to another or being able to sell when a crisis starts to unfold will allow an investor to protect themselves.

## 6. A Personal Financial Insurance Policy

Long-term savings is your personal financial insurance policy that you pay to yourself. In this section, I will show how an investor could structure this policy. Earlier in the book, I discussed gold, silver, platinum, palladium, copper, nickel, and other stores of value. A question might be, "What do I buy to start saving?" An investor, in my opinion, should start with Silver. Gold is the gut reaction, and Silver is the smart reaction. Silver is a Precious Industrial metal; the second most widely versatile commodity with over 15,000 uses (behind oil), and is easier and cheaper to liquidate.

Silver is currently $15 an ounce; if an individual saves $200 a month in silver, that will equate to nearly 10 ounces of silver. In this case, if an individual needs to liquidate $200, $300, or $500 they can easily do so, but compared to one ounce of gold you will lose currency spent on the premium. However, silver does have a drawback; it is a very volatile metal. Volatility is fine with me in the insurance policy, reasons I will state in the last paragraph of this section. The amount of silver you want to accumulate will depend on the investor's personal preferences; 500 ounces may be the chosen amount before moving onto another metal.

Platinum and palladium are industrial precious metals. They are similar to silver in that regard but do not have as many applications, and they are expensive for most manufacturers. These metals allow an investor to store a significant amount of savings in ounce coins. Again, how many ounces to accumulate will depend upon the investor and the amount of savings needed to support the wealth pyramid. After that, investors could consider gold in his or her insurance policy.

Gold is just a precious metal; it has a small role in the industry, primarily in jewelry. The lovely aspect of gold is that nearly all civilizations have recognized gold as a store of value. Gold is also a stable store of value, with very little fluctuation in value. A Roman citizen could purchase with an ounce of gold a fine handmade toga, a sash, and sandals. Today, an ounce of gold will purchase a fine suit, a belt, and dress shoes. Gold will maintain its value with consumable goods. Mike Maloney's Wealth Cycles Principle shows that as an asset, gold will either gain or lose value compared to other assets. I understand why gold is the gut reaction, but in today's modern world precious industrial metals will perform better than gold, their precious metal counterpart. Copper, nickel, and other industrial metals need large storage areas if you have these facilities, then great; if you don't, you could continue to invest in silver.

There are a few things to be aware of when purchasing metals from dealers.

An investor has to calculate the premiums. I have had countless people tell me they were buying silver Morgans for $60 or more when the spot price was at $30. Do not buy numismatics and do not purchase collector coins for the insurance policy. When you need to liquidate immediately, the dealers will only pay spot, not what you paid for the coin. I could spend a chapter on the dos and don'ts; please use the resources in the back of the book. Perform your own due diligence: use a search engine or watch YouTube videos that pertain to how to buy gold and silver.

This is a personal financial insurance policy, and can be cashed out at any time. However, this policy is only for emergency, or an investor could use some of the long-term savings to purchase cash flow assets (Mike Maloney's Wealth Cycle Principle). When market circumstances permit, use the overvalued metals to purchase undervalued assets.

What happens when the price of the metals falls? Great, I love it when my insurance policies fall in price because now I can buy more ounces. Volatility, in this case, provides great opportunities. I care about how many ounces, not the dollar amount because I want to accumulate real wealth, and only use the policy when I can purchase undervalued assets. I do not want to have to cash out because I am having financial difficulties. Hopefully, nobody needs to dip in, but it's always there if an investor needs to use their policy.

Many people want to know what I think could happen in the future, or what my predictions are. I believe the future will be fantastic; however, there are unstable systems in the economy. My next chapter is intended to raise awareness of these unstable systems, and what could happen in the future.

# Chapter 11: My Predictions for The Years Ahead

I'll begin by saying that the market knows all and I know little. So-called experts and analysts are often incorrect about their predictions because the market knows all. I'm discovering that the older I become, the less I know. Some would say it is just a process of becoming wise. We can only prepare to react to a situation before it happens. However, we can draw conclusions logically from the current economic, social, and political systems to try to see how the future could unfold.

*"To know is to know that you know nothing. That is the meaning of true knowledge."*
*- Socrates*

## The Coming Global Depression

Bear in mind from Chapter 2 and the booms, busts, and economic cycles that we are always somewhere in a cycle. The recovery and expansion phase of the current cycles started in 2009. Currently, we have had six years of economic growth with no recessions or slowdowns. Historically, we see a slowdown or a recession every three to five years, and at the most nine years for an expansionary period. One of the longest and largest expansionary periods in U.S. history was from 1921 to 1929. Eight years of credit expansion, speculation on Wall Street, consumer credit, overconsumption, and rapid economic growth was followed by the Great Depression that lasted for eighteen years.

I believe we are heading towards another bust in the years to come. A credit contraction will soon approach, followed by a downturn in the business cycle, and then an economic recession or possible depression to follow suit. The expansion of credit created primarily by the Federal Reserve's monetary policy, low-interest rates, and lack of credit standards by financial institutions have created a large and long expansion. But this economic expansion will develop into a recession or possible depression. I fear we will see a larger contraction in credit and liquidity in the system than we did in 2008, resulting in a worse business downturn and liquidation than we had in 2008, and aligning for a horrible economic recession or depression than we could have ever have imagined in 2008.

It is my personal belief that the overall economy will be worse than we saw in the 2008 Financial Crisis, but follow a similar pattern. Where 2016 will look like 2007, but worse, 2016 will be the calm before the storm. 2017 will look like 2008 but worse overall in the whole economy. 2018 will look similar to 2009, but much worse. The recovery will take much longer, and with very low growth. My reasoning is because the governments of the world transferred the bad debts and bad books of large "too big to fail" companies onto the public's balance sheet. Now, these "too big to fails" are larger with more debt than in 2008. Then the governments of the Western World have been running large deficits, and accumulating ever-larger debts, since the time they accumulated the large debts of these multinational banking corporations. I believe the economic system will rebalance; however, the events I believe that will transpire are just my predictions.

First, we will see a real deflation in commodities prices and in earnings (rising unemployment and stagnant wages) with sporadic inflation in particular goods and services that are influenced by taxation and regulation by the governments who want to "stimulate" inflation, next we will see governments hyper inflate the currency supply to counteract the contracting credit currency supply, governments may initiate a bail-in of the banks while simultaneous conducting "helicopter drops" (printing currency to give Americans tax refunds or cutting taxes and paying the larger deficits with the newly created currency), deflation will cease with rising inflation in commodities and necessities with real wages lagging behind. I believe this scenario will end in two ways: a catastrophic deflationary depression with governments restructuring their debts, initiating a bail-in, and backing their currencies to the SDR known as Special Drawing Rights (IMF currency) to rebalance the economic system, the second is a hyperinflationary depression where the wipe out much of the debt, issue new national currencies that are backed by the SDR, and rebalance the economic system.

## The College Bubble

$1.2 trillion of college debt!

Isn't that a way to start a section, unless you are in my position of paying for college? The class of 2015 graduated with $35,000 debt per graduate, and this does not include their savings, along with the income, or parents' contributions used to pay for the costs to earn that degree. These statistics do not state the amount of debt non-graduates take out to go to college, making the economic situation for non-graduates worse. I infer that the typical college graduate will pay well over $50,000 to earn a college degree and probably a little over $75,000.

The rising cost of education is just a symptom; the underlying problems are the lending standards and the easy access to credit. I can state for a fact, since I recently went through the whole financial process, that lenders do not check your credit, you don't need any income or a job, and you do not need assets to collateralize the loan; all you need is a pulse. I have heard this before: "No income, no job, and no assets" (NINJA loans), but you're able to acquire loans of $20,000, or in the instance of Kelly Space $200,000[xl] to finance a Sociology degree. Sounds like the NINJA loans from the housing bubble are back; remember that history does not repeat but rhymes.

Wait a minute! I thought the politicians in Washington said something like this would never happen again.

Needless to say, Americans are seeing a similar bubble inflate in tuition, in on-campus housing, and in student loan debt. The consequences of this when the bubble burst will be astounding. Tuition will fall dramatically, and enrollments will decline as the public views higher education as an unsound investment. If the government permits individuals to liquidate student loan debt through bankruptcy, a large deflationary pressure will build in the economy, and colleges and universities will find themselves in a financially difficult position. Especially if institutions took out debt to develop real estate that has a high maintenance cost. I believe this bubble will burst within a few (3 to 5) years.

## The Bond Crisis

Record low yields and record amounts of debt create a perfect storm for the bond market. Bonds have been in nearly a 35-year secular bull market that is coming to a close. In a falling interest rate environment, debt is seen as an asset due to the capital appreciation. On the contrary, in a rising interest rate environment, debt is seen as a liability due to the capital depreciation of the bond. Currently, the United States is financing the largest debt the world has ever seen with historically low-interest rates.

People who have been buying bonds and institutions that have been leveraging themselves to make money off of the bond market will find the worst margin calls in their lives. If interest rates double from 2% to 4%, the bonds will be worth half as much as they were when interest rates were at 2%. If interest rates were 6%, the bonds would be worth only a third of what they were. Since we have had historically low interest, I believe we will see historically high-interest rates, and how high-interest rates will go only the market knows.

One of the largest crashes looming in the future will be the bond market collapse. We have seen in Greece and Puerto Rico that sovereign bonds can be worth little to zero compared to their face value. If the Fed prevents interest rates from rising through their quantitative easing efforts, the Fed will have to issue massive amounts of new currency, or better yet more money printing to purchase the bonds from investors, institutions, and foreigners that dump their bonds on the market. Creating fears that capital will be wiped out if interest rates rise, currency creation through quantitative easing will cause a rapid depreciation of the dollar against gold, silver, and some other currency. However, the dollar index could still rise due to the rapid depreciation and devaluations of other nations' currencies.

## The Great Dollar Devaluation

One day we may very well have a dollar crisis on our hands. The reason for that is due to the enormous amount of currency created by the Federal Reserve and spent by the federal government. Since the crisis of 2008, the Federal Reserve has *quadrupled* the base currency supply of the United States. Certainly it does sound like the perfect recipe for hyperinflation even though we haven't seen anything resembling out of control inflation, yet!

Remember that the base currency supply has to be leveraged into fractional reserve banking. I believe in the future that we will see a real deflation in the overall currency supply, the central banks of the world will print more than you could imagine, triggering a high inflationary period, and if people lose confidence in central bankers or the fiat currency, possibly a hyperinflationary event will result. We will see a great devaluation of the dollar relative to gold and silver. Whether extreme inflation or a hyperinflationary event will happen or not only the future knows. Personally, I believe we will see an inflationary period, but not necessarily hyperinflation. First though we must go through a large deflationary event to trigger panic in the banking system to pressure the central banks to print more currency.

The purchasing power of the dollar will decline rapidly as the ordinary American citizen will see prices rise much faster than their pension funds, stock portfolios, Social Security checks, and other fixed income sources. Prices are not rising due to a shortage of goods or services. The rise in prices is an inverted correlation to the purchasing power of the dollar: prices rise as the dollar falls. There must be a great devaluation of the dollar to sustain the debts occurred over the past two decades. If central banks save the dollar, they do so at the expense of the financial and banking institutions who will see liquidity dry up as their paper assets fall in price, creating the worst deflationary period the history of the U.S. However, if the central banks preserve the financial and banking system along with its insolvent institutions, it must sacrifice the dollar to do so.

You may be wondering what will happen to real estate since it is so interconnected to the financial and banking system. Let's find out.

## Real Estate Catastrophe

Real estate is one place that many Americans store a large portion of their wealth. How will real estate respond when the bond market collapses and interest rates skyrocket? People do not buy real estate, or even cars, for that matter, on the price tag alone. Typically, a person buys real estate off of a percentage of his or her take-home pay. This means that prices of real estate are determined by two factors. The first is a person's income, and the second is the monthly payment, or in our case the credit available and the cost of credit, meaning the interest rate.

Rising interest rates will create larger monthly payments, unless the price of real estate falls to compensate for the rising interest maintaining the same monthly payment.

Let's say a $300,000 house was financed with a 30-year mortgage at a 3% interest rate, making the monthly payment $1,264, which is a price most people could afford. Now in a period of rising interest rates where the interest rate for that 30-year mortgage is now

6%, that $300,000 house needs to sell for roughly $210,000, or a decline in prices of 30 percent. Six percent is a normal interest rate to see in the U.S., but we have been at historically low-interest rates, so let's raise the interest rate even more to 9 percent. Our house would need to sell for $155,000, or 48% less than what we paid for it.

Let's double the interest rate to match what interest rates were in the late 1970s and early 1980s. That $300,000 house would need to sell for $85,000 on a 30-year mortgage with an interest rate of 18 percent.

The destruction of the bond market with the rise in interest rates necessarily implies that real estate will share the same fate. Real estate is typically bought on credit. The credit markets directly affect the price of real estate: instability, credit contraction, and tougher lending standards will negatively affect the price of real estate in the years to come. However, if the central banks of the world in coordination with the governments of the world make a concerted effort to sustain this historical bond bubble by sacrificing the nation's currency, housing prices will stay flat or sharply rise only due to the decreasing purchasing power of the dollar. Nevertheless, the real value of housing will fall against commodities, particularly the precious metals.

I believe that residential real estate will have a negative long-term outlook as the large generation of the baby boomers will start to downsize to smaller forms of housing. A seller must have a buyer, and the buyers are Generation X and the millennials who are financially burdened by student loan debt, unlike their parent's generation. If millennials and Generation X do not have the financial capacity to purchase real estate at historical highs, then baby boomers must liquidate their assets at lower prices—not only their real estate assets but also financial assets such as stocks.

## The Stock Market Crash

If the stock market has a nominal crash caused by the contraction of credit, liquidity drying up, and people selling stock to acquire cash to protect them from market volatility and deflation, the bond market may temporarily go up in prices as bonds are perceived as a form of safety. If the Fed intervenes by providing liquidity to the stock market through negative interest rates, and quantitative easing, then we will see the nominal prices of stocks stay flat or rise.

The stock market is now determined by interest rates and access to credit. Margin debt is near all-time highs; this is a flashing warning sign. Large corporations are leveraging their balance sheets through stock buybacks by issuing bonds to purchase the stock. Credit allows you to outbid your competitors, but it is a double-edged sword since you have to pay back the principal plus the interest, putting financial stress on any balance sheet. Listening to the Federal Reserve address Congress and the world about their policies, actions, or inactions, I have observed the responses by investors, financial institutions, and banks. If we had a free market without government intervention, investors, financial institutions, and banks would not care what the Fed would say if they did not yield great control over the economy and the financial markets.

Eventually, the market overpowers all, and there is only so much the Fed can do to keep interest rates artificially low. Rising interest rates will negatively impact the stock market; one reason is from the margin debt, and the second follows Ben Graham's (Warren Buffet's mentor and professor)[xli] investing principle. Value investors use the ten-year Treasury note as a tool to evaluate the risk and rewards of the stock market. The higher the yield, the more appealing U.S. bonds look over equities. Interest rates affect the price of the stock market. The supply of stocks will increase, selling stocks to then purchase bonds, and the demand shifts from stocks to bonds. Those actions would cause bonds prices to rise and yields to fall; however, if the Fed raises rates to curb speculation, yields will continue to rise as the stock market falls. Essentially the cash and the capital are moving towards paying down debt, not purchasing assets.

On a long enough timescale, the Federal Reserve will eventually make a terrific blunder to undermine the confidence of central banks and their respective currencies. Confidence is the basis of the Federal Reserve's policy for economic growth, development, market stability, and the management of investors' expectations. Regrettably, confidence is not an economically sound fundamental to grow an economy and prevent financial calamities. Savings, production, proper regulation, no government or central bank interventionism, and interest rates determined by the free market create a sound economy. Historically low-interest rates imply historical speculation, over consumption, and over-leveraging by Wall Street, investors, businesses, and speculators. A rebalancing of historic proportions will one day arrive.

## Commodities and Real Wealth on the Rise!

Commodities are some of the most undervalued assets in the world. The world has been in a blizzard of paper wealth that is tearing itself apart. Human perception has only just begun to change back from paper to real wealth, making commodities, productive farmland, mines, oil rigs, and other real assets the foundations for an industrial, service, and informational society. Without real tangible wealth, we could not have the industrial, service, or information age.

Farmers and ranchers have been in decline to the point we will see in the next decade a significant shortage of farm and ranch owners, operators, and labor to support the demand for agricultural products. Due to the instability in the system people are rushing to the precious metals first. Proof of this is seen in the demand for American Silver Eagle sales, which stands counter to the recent fall in price.[xlii]

A first move typically seen by the investing community is to move paper assets through precious metals and then into real productive assets. Investment in agriculture, resources, and energy will grow at a substantial rate compared to other markets. For the past 35 years, many investors and investing institutions have had little or no interest in commodities other than exchange traded funds (ETFs), which I see as a paper vehicle to trade on the underlying asset. ETFs are not an investment in these types of real assets, only claims on the real assets. In the next decade, we will see great interest in markets that produce real tangible wealth, while those markets and companies have very little to do with real wealth will struggle to acquire those assets for the value-added companies. The blow off phase of the future commodity bubble may happen in the 2030s or 2040s.

## Bullet Points of My Predictions for the Overall Economy and Markets

- I predict that we will see a similar but larger financial crisis than we did in 2008. First we'll see a deflationary wave of defaults and credit contraction as the economy cannot support the debt service. A business downturn will cause the economy to go into recession with large-scale unemployment (10%<X) and underemployment. The trigger point will be seen in the debt markets and derivatives markets utilized primarily by financial institutions, and the sovereign bond markets of the world. The financial system will seize up as the parties involved won't trust the counterparty risks associated with the financial transactions. Simply put it, there will be too much debt.

- European nations will become more problematic due to their unstable financial systems in congruence with bankrupt and cash-strapped sovereign nations, which will cause enormous economic problems that will be felt around the world.

- China's real estate bubble will collapse. In 2015, we have already seen the collapse of their stock market. Real estate will follow the same pattern culminating with the Chinese financial system either will come to a crisis or an outright implosion in 2016 or 2017.

- The slowdown in China, East Asia, South America, and Europe will cause a slowdown in the world economy, affecting the U.S. economy. We will see the world's central banks, the IMF, and the World Bank trying to solve these financial problems before the inevitable collapse of the financial systems. Cyber wars between nations will erupt in an effort to weaken the grid and financial markets of competitors. Cyber wars have already begun—just read the newspaper or web search "cyber wars."

- Stocks and real estate prices in nominal terms will temporarily fall, including real assets in the commodity markets. U.S. bonds may soar to historical highs as other sovereign nations default on their debt, or go through restructuring. The U.S. dollar will strengthen compared to other currencies. The reality of the situation won't hit the public domain until late 2016, possibly as late as 2017.

- We will see defaults in ETFs, derivative contracts, and gold and silver fractional reserve ETFs, and banks will fail.

- I predict the Federal Reserve in conjunction with other central banks will act to subdue the volatility in the financial markets through more quantitative easing efforts, lowering real interest rates to negative rates, and trying to recapitalize failing institutions by bail-outs and possibly bail-ins.
- The Federal Reserve will sacrifice the dollar to preserve the banking system, and try to sustain the unsustainable debt the U.S. government has occurred, as well as the debt of the private sector. Central banks around the world may follow suit.
- Nominal prices of real estate and stocks will rise if negative interest rates are induced on the market, along with the massive currency creation of central banks. Real prices will fall in the real estate market, stock markets, and bond markets. The bonds market will lose tremendous value even though we will see negative interest rates. Inflation will wipe away the value of the bonds and value of the dollar.
- A massive devaluation of the dollar will occur against other nations' currencies, regarding purchasing power, and against gold and silver. I believe the foundation will be laid in 2016, and won't see the Great Devaluation until sometime in 2017.
- Commodities, real wealth, and companies who produce real wealth will see a rapid rise in price and will gain real purchasing powering. This event could be seen in 2017. Until 2017, I expect commodities and precious metals will fall first before a rapid rise in price and purchasing power.
- After 2017, we will see a recovery being led by real assets, particularly in agricultural, resources, and energy. Value-added businesses will follow the trend of the real assets concerning growth. We will see a return in manufacturing if the political environment permits it. The services industry and the information industry will be the last sectors of the economy to recovery.

---

# Warning Signs

The bullet points already show a few warnings signs, but I want to clarify a few of them. We need to understand that the U.S. economy is the center of the world economy. Developing nations surround the U.S. economy. So, if you want to see the macro picture of a developing macro crisis, look towards the weaker countries. Emerging markets, particularly China, are flashing the largest warning signs. China's real estate bubble is imploding, their stock markets have free fallen, and their economic growth has considerably slowed. Manufacturing is the basis of their economy; their economy consumes enormous amounts commodities. Copper shows the pulse of developing nations, and copper's supply is steady, so a fall in price means demand has fallen.

Emerging markets such as Brazil, South Africa, and India are showing recessionary signs. Their economies slowed, causing a fall in demand in the commodities market. Credit is contracting: investors and individuals are paying down debt, climaxing in deflationary pressures. Commodities are typically the warning sign for inflationary periods and deflationary periods. The further commodities prices fall, the greater the threat of a deflationary recession or depression.

Sovereign debt crises are coming; however, municipalities will come first. One example is Detroit, which was bailed out in 2008 by U.S. taxpayers before declaring bankruptcy in 2013. Puerto Rico gave a nice haircut to its bondholders and defaulted on August 1st, 2015.

Chicago is insolvent—they just haven't declared bankruptcy. My sister was recently visiting colleges in California, and my father and mother traveled with her. My dad loves to read newspapers; as they traveled throughout southern and central California, he noticed the newspapers contained many articles about municipalities defaulting or declaring bankruptcy. There is a warning sign. The PIIGS of Europe (especially Greece) and Puerto Rico are colossal warning signs to any investor that claim check wealth is evaporating. Scan the financial headlines and you will be able to see the warning signs.

## A Red Flag, China!

For the past few years, China has been the economic growth engine of the world. That has great benefits and pitfalls. Economic growth, prosperity, and a rising standard of living has benefitted China and the world. Wealthier countries can trade more goods and services with each other, as opposed to a wealthy country trading with a poorer country. Trade always benefits both countries through comparative advantage with both countries producing more efficiently and trading the surpluses with one another. The result for the trading nations is a higher standard of living. However, there are pitfalls with this economic interconnectedness.

A few pitfalls are the reliance on each other's economic growth, financial sustainability, and political stability. If a nation's economy falls into a recession, for this instance China, then their trading partners' economies, namely the U.S., will have a negative drag on growth. Credit contracts causing businesses to close, which leads to a downturn in the economy of the recessionary country (China). The effect this has on the trading partner (U.S.) is negative due to the dependency of production and consumption each nation has with each other. Both nations economic activity depends on production and trade, so each nation consumes the surplus production of their trading partner. When one nation experiences an economic downturn, it inevitably leads the trading partner in to an economic downturn as well.

China is a red flag since it is the manufacturing powerhouse of the world. Recall the credit cycle, followed by the business cycle, and the economic cycle. A credit contraction means that individuals are paying down debt; this creates a business downturn which leads to an economic recession or depression. The world purchases China's production, specifically the United States purchases a significant portion of China's manufacturing output.

U.S. consumers have been decreasing their spending. The 4th quarter of 2015 saw one of the worst quarters of retail sales since the last recession. Europe's economy is in a mess with the Greek and PIIGS situation. If Americans and Europeans under consume to pay for their previous overconsumption; this affects the demand for Chinese manufacturing products. China will probably close down many plants and businesses, similar to the example in Chapter 2 about businesses closing their doors (Pg. 16).

The United States is the world's number one importer and the number two exporter. China is the world's number one exporter and the number two importer. A developing middle class in China has been purchasing more imported goods, particularly from the western civilization. Contrary to popular belief, the Chinese purchase IPhones, IPods, clothing, cars, construction equipment, and other products from Western nations. Yes, some Chinese are peasant farmers, but there is a significant portion of the population who can afford the western lifestyle. If U.S. consumers slow down their purchases of Chinese products; Chinese manufacturing will decrease, and layoffs will ensue. The loss of income the Chinese will experience will directly affect their purchases of Western products. Creating a decrease in demand for American and European goods, western countries will start to close down their manufacturing. American retailers will also decrease the labor force due to the decrease in demand.

A factor in the rapid decline in the price of oil is the slowing demand from the Chinese economy. A growing economy needs increasing amounts of energy. I believe in the near future Americans will see jobs losses in oil, manufacturing, and retailing. These job losses will be followed by job losses in the financial and business consulting industries due to the decrease in demand from their business clientele.

Stay alert on China's $11 Trillion economy. Where the U.S. goes, so does China. Where China goes, so does the United States economy. Due to globalization of the world economies; the credit cycle, business cycle, and economic cycles are now becoming synchronized. Politicians and members of the press are demonizing Chinese prosperity. They're stating that this prosperity is to the detriment of the U.S. economy. Of course, they are totally wrong. Economics 101 states that both economies are better off and are wealthier with trade due to the principle of comparative advantage. Also, the wealthier and interconnected the Chinese become, the more peaceful they will act. Examples of this are Japan after World War Two, Great Britain after the War of 1812, and Russia after the collapse of the Soviet Empire. Prosperity encourages cooperation rather than war because people and governments want to live comfortable rather than in a war-torn nation.

The greatest threat the Chinese government perceives is not the American people, but their own people. Red China is still communistic; however, they are adapting capitalism and free market principles. A capitalistic economic system has never existed underneath a communistic political regime. Capitalism has only existed under democratic republican systems (Democracies, Republics, or Constitutional Republics). As the Chinese government utilizes a more capitalistic system and increasing economic freedoms, the Chinese people have and will continue to advocate for a classical liberal political system. The Communist of China want to stay in power and retain their political power; this is at odds with their people. The Chinese government is trapped in a paradox. The more prosperous the Chinese people become; they rely less on an authoritarian government and see this government as tyrannical and a kleptocracy. China's concern is with the United States government (not the people) militaristic ambitions, and antagonistic politicians. These politicians are a minor concern compared to the political instability that is developing in China.

Fear mongering by U.S. politicians and officials about China becoming the new Soviet Union is just that, fear mongering. China wants to increase its sphere of influence to protect its sovereignty from foreign rule (read China's history, they were essentially a subservient territory of European powers until World War Two) while the United States wants to maintain its supremacy as the world's lone superpower. Is this a problem? Yes. However, I believe both nations will resolve this peacefully. The only thing I fear (really concerned with) as an American is the Chinese plunging into another Civil War. A Chinese Civil War would cause the world's worst world-wide depression. Hopefully, the Chinese government will relinquish power peacefully and transform into a Constitutional Republic similar to the United States; only the future will tell.

## Bail-Outs and Bail-Ins

From the 2008 Financial Crisis, everyone is familiar with bailouts. Central banks and governments will make or want to make larger bailouts than we saw in 2008 to support the financial system. Interest rates hikes or spikes will be the cause of the financial system collapsing. The bailouts will have to be necessarily larger to take on the bad debts, derivatives, and obligations of the "too big to fail" financial institutions. I believe that the government and the banks won't stop there, observing the Cyprus banking crisis with the banks "bailing-in" as opposed to the government bailing out these banks. A bail-in is the process of taking depositors money to make the bank solvent. In Greece, we see bank runs by depositors fearing that the banks were insolvent (which they were), and the citizenry is only being permitted to withdrawal only 50 euros a day.

I believe that Americans for the first time in a long time will see bank runs, bank holidays, limited withdrawals, and bail-ins. When you deposit your money in the bank, you are an unsecured creditor. Why keep your money in a bank? There is no return, yet extreme risks are associated with the banking sector, fractional reserve system, and rampant leveraging and speculation from too many banks. An unsecured creditor is the riskiest creditor to be, and the lowest form of a creditor. So again, why keep your money in a bank? There is no incentive for people to keep cash in their bank accounts, and since there is no incentive in conjunction with the high risk of losing your deposit. There will be bank runs, period!

## New World Monetary System

I want to revisit history before we continue onto the main subject of the possibility and probability of a new world monetary system. America's last great bank runs and bank failures occurred back in the Great Depression. In the 1930s, the money was physical gold and silver while the claim checks were the paper currency that was backed by the real wealth (gold and silver). Today the money is the paper currency while the claim checks are the digital dollars. When they nationalized gold (they did not nationalize silver) people had to trade in their money (physical gold) for paper currency (claim checks). Then the government devalued the dollar against gold.

Today we have a system with digital claim checks on the paper currency. We have a similar situation today where the claim checks or the digits in our bank accounts greatly outnumber the paper currency. This increases the possibility of banks runs taking place. When people lose faith in the solvency of the banking system, the fear of not getting their "money" paper currency out of the bank will cause bank runs.

I believe that governments around the world will try to force their respective populations to use a cashless system. We are already moving to a cashless system with debit cards and credit cards. Nevertheless, if there is a banking crisis that causes bank runs, one action that the governments will take is suspending the redemption rights of withdrawing paper currency from banks. The next step is to devalue the currency, but against what? You can't devalue an identical digital currency from its respective paper counterpart. However, you can devalue a nation's currency against the currency of other nations, devalue a currency through rampant inflation (great loss of purchasing power), or devalue your currency against gold and silver.

Moving on to the world's monetary system, we have seen nearly 45 years of a dollar standard system, and that system is beginning to break. Emerging markets and emerging countries, particularly Brazil, Russia, India, and China (BRICs), are setting up their own world banking system and monetary fund. The creation of the Asian Infrastructure Investment Bank (AIIB) is a direct competitor to the World Bank, International Monetary Fund (IMF), and the Asian Development Bank (ADB). From what I have read, China has 26% of the voting rights followed by India 7.5% and then Russia 6 percent. These three countries hold 40% of the voting rights, and the U.S. has not considered even applying for membership to the AIIB. In the IMF, voting rights for the first five countries total roughly 37%; U.S., Japan, Germany, France, and U.K hold these rights.

AIIB is a threat to the primarily Anglo-American-European-controlled IMF. China is leading the charge with the BRIC nations following to set up their own monetary and international banking systems to undermine the power and control of the IMF and U.S. and European countries over Asian countries. China along with the other BRICs and Asian nations do not feel that they are accurately represented at the IMF, and feel that their interests are undermined.

China is setting the yuan or renminbi to act as a trade currency, but not yet pursuing a world reserve currency. Their deals with Russia, Iran, other Middle Eastern nations and other Asian nations show the trend of establishing the yuan as a trade currency. Establishing a trade currency, setting up their own trade systems with nations, buying up thousands of tons of gold, and establishing the AIIB are allowing China to one day be able to dump the dollar and dump what they consider worthless U.S. Treasury notes.

Many pundits say that China needs us to sustain their economic growth. However, once they build the necessary financial infrastructure and establish export trade around the world to sell their goods, and encourage the rising Chinese middle class to be consumers as well, dumping the dollar will be a painful transition that will allow China to invest its excess reserves in the AIIB, their country's

---

infrastructure, and their future Treasury markets. Rendering the U.S. dollar and Treasury market as an utterly pointless, worthless investment, since the U.S. Government is just as much insolvent as the PIIGs of Europe or Greece.

What is the trigger point? As long as the Chinese are producing and then reinvesting in our Treasuries market, and just as long as the U.S. keeps on consuming, the monetary system will hold. However, if the Chinese economy spirals downward, look for the collapse of their stock market (this may come sooner than expected) or their real estate and other financial bubbles to burst. The producing side of the equation will weaken, and weaken United States consumption. (On the flip side, if the U.S. falls into another serious recession, the consumption component may trigger the sudden monetary debacle of world currencies.) Nevertheless, if the Chinese can increase their efforts in building the AIIB, their yuan, and trading partnerships, we can see a new monetary system when the Chinese quit reinvesting and investing in the U.S. debt markets.

The United States has exported dollars around the world to import real tangible products. More than half of all dollars are outside of the United States. What will happen when many of those dollars start following back to the United States? We will see a devaluation of the dollar as well as inflation—hopefully not hyperinflation, but very high rates of inflation when foreigners repatriate the dollar for tangible goods.

As the dollar dies, there will be a great movement of nations along with international organizations wanting a new reserve currency to conduct trade. We have already heard and seen countries publicly stating that they want to replace the dollar with a new currency. I believe that the new world reserve currency will come out of the IMF or the AIIB. This reserve currency will only be used in trade, and will not replace national currencies. I believe that the reserve currency will be a digital fiat currency as oppose to a fiat paper currency. Nations will also move toward a cashless system within their borders. The possibilities of how this will unfold are endless. The instability in the system is there for the old monetary system to collapse and a new world reserve currency to rise.

Do not be afraid; most people who read this have already gone through a transition like this in the 1970s when the U.S. defaulted on the Bretton Woods agreement, and the dollar standard rose out of the ashes of the old Bretton Woods system. This is just a transition period; the world will continue.

The rest of this book is dedicated to the wonderful prosperity we will have in the future, and how the world will change for the better!

## The Recovery

In scouting, we have a saying: "Hope for the best and plan for the worst." My previous predictions are worst-case scenarios with the possibilities that these situations may occur. However, even in the worst-case scenario, we will see humanity evolve, and the world becomes a better place to live.

Two things generate the important foundations for progress in society.

The first is the average person knows and will try to produce more than he or she consumes, and save the difference. This action creates capital.

Secondly, scientists, engineers, and technology engineers will create the technological advancements for society to progress. Currently, there are more scientists and engineers alive today than all of the deceased scientists and engineers in human history combined. Scientists and engineers will continue to produce new technologies provided there is sufficient capital saved so these advancements can be financed. I am partly pessimistic if there is enough capital in the world because all of these foolish governments around the world are wasting capital (in the form of national debt) it took generations to save.

Currently, the world economy is stagnating, and the economic system is unbalanced. We are now seeing and will continue to see the economic system rebalance itself. After this rebalance, I believe the economic development of the world will advance at a rapid rate due to the technological advancement.

Governments have full control over their fiscal and monetary policies, and they can choose to kick the can down the road in the years ahead by raising their debt ceilings, increasing deficit spending, and issuing more bonds. The worldwide investment community can choose to place their capital in the hands of governments. Nevertheless, the investment community could revolt by not buying their bonds, selling the bonds they hold, and then directing their investment elsewhere in the private market, sending interest rates soaring.

However, I believe governments will use monetary policy to drive interest rates down further to negative territory. This action may result in massive inflation, causing claim check wealth to lose real purchasing and real wealth gain in real purchasing. In Chapter 7, the base of the unstable inverted pyramid will expand rapidly while the top of the inverted pyramid remains the same in dollar terms or slightly grow. Eventually, the inverted pyramid will transform into a pyramid, so the system is rebalanced.

This event may take a year in a hyperinflationary scenario, or in a few years with very high inflation. Once the system rebalances, growth in real wealth will continue with commodities, agriculture, manufacturing, and energy leading the way. Technology, biotechnology, and services will follow the real wealth with finance, and financial services are the last to recover. If my timeline plays out, we will see the recovery begin early 2018 with growth slow at first, but by 2020 worldwide economic growth and development will boom. Yet, the governments can postpone the rebalance to 2020, 2021, and 2022, which is the next likely time of the credit cycle contracting. They possibly could postpone it further, though the economic stagnation will worsen. As an individual crisis investor, I will prepare for both inflation and deflation, or other situations.

Finally, my dear reader, you are on the last leg of the book. I know Chapter 11 wasn't a wonderful flower garden, and there are very serious topics discussed in the book. I have been saying I am very optimistic about the future, and my next chapters relate to positive change in the future.

# Chapter 12: Energy Drives the Economy

Energy is the most important component that allows trade to occur. If I could give you all the wealth in the world but no energy, you could not enjoy your wealth. Imagine a car without gas, or a home with no electricity; they are completely useless unless there is available energy to utilize wealth. For economies to grow, they need ever-increasing amounts of energy to fund economic growth. Primarily in this chapter, we will be discussing oil, due to its utility as a portable liquid energy. Oil's unique characteristics make it is the most widely used commodity with over 30,000 uses. The development of oil production allows insight to oil production future.

Whale oil had been used to power and lubricate machines and other industrial materials. The oil that came primarily from sperm whales had been depleted due to overharvesting and overfishing of the whale population. Eventually, the prices of whale oil soared, and the market looked for other alternatives.

In August of 1859, Edwin Drake made the first successful oil-drilling rig in a drilled well on Oil Creek near Titusville, Pennsylvania. The first principal product of oil was kerosene, which replaced whale oil.

Soon rigs began to spring all across Pennsylvania, New York, the Virginias, and eventually the largest discoveries came in Texas. What I call the 2 x 4 rigs: that literally look like oil producers slapped together 2 x 4s and sunk a pipe into the ground and oil came spewing out in a gusher. They did not need to pump the oil. The oil just gushed out of the ground and flowed everywhere. Exploration was much simpler since oil seeps were where the drilling primarily took place while the oil industry grew new utilizations for oil developed.

Oil pumped from the ground began to gain prominence in the U.S. by the 1870s. More products that required oil in congruence with the developments in processing oil increased demand for oil. Oil production continued to explode due to the need for energy to fuel the industrial revolution. Eventually, oil became harder to find since the oil producers had drilled the easiest to find, the easiest to extract, and the closest oil deposits for distribution.

Oil companies had to increase their costs for exploration to find oil deposits, to extract the deeper oil deposits, and to travel farther to distribute oil from the field to the growing industrialized cities. The need to find more oil deposits lead to the development of new technology for exploration purposes. Oil companies began to develop and construct larger rigs to drill deep and then had to begin to pump the oil to extract it from the earth. The energy required extracting more energy began to increase.

Fast-forward to today, and the oil industry worldwide has been increasing production and increasing the need to evolve technology to find and extract oil. The oil industry is extracting oil offshore on huge ocean oil platforms, drilling all the way down to the ocean floor. That requires much more energy, and the oil finds on the ocean floor are not as large or plentiful as the oil finds on the continents.

## The Law of Diminishing Returns

In economics, the law of diminishing returns refers to the decrease in the marginal (incremental) output of a production process as the amount of a single factor of production is incrementally increased, while the amounts of all other factors of production stay constant.

In other words, the same effort produces a smaller result than it used to.

This is what we call an energy cliff. If you are familiar with exponential functions, this is similar to one, except this is an exponential function that will eventually hit zero as opposed to going straight towards infinity.

Now this is a rough estimate of oil, but oil production can be broken down by region. "Return on energy" is the oil output (energy extracted) divided by the oil input (energy needed to achieve extraction). For example, three barrels of oil might be produced for every barrel of oil input. In the oil industry, it is stated as "energy returned on energy invested" (EROEI). In the United States, the EROEI is anywhere between 3:1 to 10:1. Tar sands and oil shale is nearly 2:1, while oil returns in the Middle East are higher than 25:1.

In the future we will have less available "cheap" oil to extract; that has been the historical trend for centuries. Not only for oil, but for coal, uranium, and other non-renewable energy sources.

Cheap oil will be in the rear view mirror, and society will have to adapt to operate on expensive oil. While oil becomes more expensive, alternatives will hopefully be developed or discovered. Unfortunately, I see little urgency on the part of the humanity solve these problems with cheap oil as opposed to solving these problems on more expensive oil.

Nearly 33% of our domestic oil production supports agriculture. This is a great Achilles heel to any farmer, rancher, or investor due to the increases in their costs related to oil. These costs will also be transferred to everyone on the globe. Very poor countries whose income mainly goes to food will see tremendous upheavals in social, political, and military. The oil industry will need to figure out an exit plan if they want their companies and their stockholders to survive.

## Energy is the Primary Driver of a Sustainable Recovery

*"If we want to reduce poverty and misery if we want to give to every deserving individual what is needed for a safe existence of an intelligent being, we want to provide more machinery, more power. Power is our mainstay, the primary source of our many-sided energies."*
*- Nikola Tesla*

For an economy to recover, it needs a growth of energy to form the foundation for economic development. We need energy inputs to extract the natural resources of the earth, energy inputs to convert the raw materials into goods, energy inputs to transport those goods to market, energy inputs to service those goods, and energy inputs for the human labor that was a part of the whole process.

Energy is the key ingredient to extract, produce, transport, and maintain the economy that we enjoy. Every economy from the beginning of time has used energy to generate economic growth. The availability of energy and the utilization of energy are both important to develop a person, a business, and an economy. When an economy shrinks, it can be caused by a lack of supply of energy or a lack of demand due to the economic cycles. Please do more research regarding the supply and demand factors of the energy markets and the new developments in the energy market. Then you can one day invest successfully in these companies, or be the one who launched the company that revolutionized the world!

# Peak Oil, Peak Everything. No! Transformation

Before you pass judgment on this section in skepticism or pessimism, I have a brain exercise. If we live on a finite plane, can we expect to have an infinite amount of resources? Well, no. A few thoughts come to my mind: one, recycle; two, we won't run out of energy due to the sun, so I do not worry about the energy component; and three, humanity needs to manage better the world's resources.

Oil first has to be found before it can be pumped. World oil discoveries peaked in the late 1960s. U.S. oil discoveries peaked in the 1930s while our production peaked in the 1970s (remember the oil crisis). Discovery peak to production peak is anywhere from 40 to 50 years. It may take a little bit longer due to the fracking miracle, which has almost caused the U.S. to pass the peak set in the 1970s.

One day we will run out of that finite resource, but oil is not the only resource.

Other resources are showing the same pattern such as gold, silver, other industrial metals, other non-renewable energy, coal, natural gas, etc. The world will not come to an end, but in our lifetimes, we will see a large transition from the old energy systems to a future energy system. Since there is a great change, there are great opportunities. Typically, a crisis erupts, and that is the time to seize the opportunities to gather land, labor, and capital to create something that will solve the world's energy problem and benefit humanity.

## Renewable Resources

Renewable energy sources such as solar, wind, and geothermal can replace coal and uranium. What is going to replace the liquid energy such as natural gas and oil? At this point, I have absolutely no idea. I still maintain my faith and optimism that we will find a solution. Two solutions may be the electric car and the hydrogen power car. Both types of cars will require energy from renewable sources, but this is still far out into the future.

I have more faith in hydrogen cars than purely electric cars. One reason is the amount of lithium required to create the batteries for the cars, and lithium is a non-renewable depleting resource. Hydrogen, on the other hand, does not have this problem. The hydrogen acts as the battery, not the energy source. The reason why we do not have and will never have hydrogen as an energy source is due to the Second

Law of Thermal Dynamics. Hydrogen is also problematic, for the major reason that it is highly explosive. Combustion engines will need to be reconfigured to compensate for hydrogen's explosiveness as oppose to gasoline's combustion. Hydrogen is not a lubricant, unlike gasoline engines, of which the primary lubricant is oil. Tires are also made out of seven gallons of oil apiece, and I for one do not want wood to replace the rubber tire.

With these problems I believe we will see radical improvements in these areas once it becomes economical to do so.

A mixture of hydrogen with biofuels may provide a solid solution to replace oil. Nevertheless, we will need engineers to figure out how to practically use this fuel in our cars, jets, buses, and other forms of transportations. This includes the development of the distribution system to deliver these forms of energy. There are companies and individuals who are trying to solve these problems, such as Elon Musk with Tesla; become one of them, and become a problem solver.

## Producing Energy and Creating a Profitable Business

Starting companies to produce energy, discover new alternative forms of energy, innovate technology to improve the utilization of energy, and create inventions that will help energy efficiency have been gold mines for creating generational wealth. Look at where the large fortunes that were made in human history. Finance, industrialization, transportation, technology and energy are the major areas that have generated generational wealth.

Recall the Rockefellers, Jerry Jones, Glenn McCarthy, Waite Phillips, T. Boone Pickens, and other families who made fortunes in oil, natural gas, and coal power plants. Energy is one sector that can create enormous fortunes because the demand for energy is nearly infinite. Energy is found not only in oil, natural gas, and wind turbines but also in agricultural products that are a source of energy to power human bodies.

If you follow my blueprint, which is the same blueprint that is guiding my journey, I believe you will have a good chance of succeeding in this industry. It's all about finding the right mentors, building your plan, and then executing with focus and determination. I believe you will go far in life. Investing in wind energy or solar energy is extremely smart not only for personal use to power your home but to diversify your exposure to the non-renewable energy market. Some of you readers love the TV show *Shark Tank*. I do too! I remember watching an episode with a man pitching his invention to the sharks. Essentially the invention was a large shake weight with an electromagnetic inducing current from the magnet that moved up and down due to the motion of the ocean waves. Essentially he was transforming the energy from the wave into electrical power.

Investors need to grasp a better understanding of our energy industries. As investors, this is the single most important industry to study, and following it will increase your odds of winning in the stock market. Most traders have no clue how the energy industry affects other stocks and the overall economy. Cheap oil will eventually decline in production replaced by more and more expensive oil due to the law of diminishing returns. The human race will then begin to search for new energy sources and develop technology to utilize these resources. The future will look brighter—it will just have a few bumps in the road ahead.

# Chapter 13: The Coming Agricultural Revolution

Agriculture created the foundation for civilization to flourish by eliminating the hunter-gatherer economy, elevating humanity out of huts and into cities. Agriculture periodically goes through revolutions due to newly discovered techniques, and the influences of technological advances. The last agricultural revolution occurred at the beginning of the 20th century with new machines that were powered by oil.

The modern agriculture revolution, referred to as the "Green Revolution," succeeded the British and Scottish agriculture revolution, which coincidently created the Industrial Revolution. That in turned created the groundwork for the modern agricultural revolution to take hold. Cycles are seen throughout human history, and agriculture has played a large role in facilitating those economic cycles.

This next agricultural revolution will have a drastic impact on how we grow and manage our food supply. Agricultural historically produced more energy than the input required. Now our modern agricultural practices for our agricultural products are net *consumers* of energy instead of net *producers* of energy. This consumption of energy will have to change to benefit the agriculture industry and society as a whole. Energy is the main part of the equation of why change will occur.

Nearly one-third of our domestically produced oil supports our agricultural industry. Recently, shale oil production has caused our domestic production of oil to increase, alleviating the stress on our oil production to support agriculture. Increasing the oil supply will ease the tension, but what if the trend from the 1970s continues and our oil production continues to decline? What consequences will result in this? One, the United States will become more dependent on the oil import market, and two we will have more problems maintaining the infrastructure associated with agriculture. Due to the mechanical innovations of humanity over the past 300 years, agriculture is an energy-intensive industry.

Technology is decreasing the amount of labor-intensive work, and will transition farming and ranching to a very management intensive work. The utilization of machines, combines, and other equipment requires and will require increasing amounts of energy to sustain the agriculture industry. Certain management techniques will utilize energy more efficiently. The rise of farmers marketing directly to consumers will decrease the oil used in the transportation systems used to deliver agricultural products from field to home. Alleviating the need for drastic increases in oil production means that other alternatives must arise to replace energy derived from oil. Wind farming will help replace oil by utilizing electrical power generated by the wind turbines.

## Toxicity of Modern Agricultural Practices

Oil has played a major part in agricultural production, and some evidence shows a direct correlation between oil inputs and food related disease and allergies.

Statistics show the negative health effects of modern agriculture in conjunction with genetically modified organisms (GMOs), genetically enhanced foods (GEs), and chemical fertilizers. Even though there is significant evidence towards the negative health consequences of the practices of modern agriculture, this may only play one part in our society's health decline. Prescription drug abuse, cultural attitudes, lack of exercising, modern advances in technology, and many other factors also play parts in the decline in health and an increase in healthcare costs.

Sadly, farmers and ranchers are seeing the horrible effects on people's health, the environment, and their income (*Food Inc.* is a great documentary to watch) of these products that they have bought to build better farms and ranches. Herbicides, pesticides, insecticides, GMOs, chemical fertilizers, etc. have been destroying the soil fertility of farms and ranches (research conducted by farmer Gabe Brown)[xliii]. The future yields without these harmful products will fall, but once the soil is cleansed of the toxins yields will return. Farmers, ranchers, consumers, and investors will be dramatically hurt, and the great collapse will not happen to any of these people. It will happen to the big agricultural corporations who cannot sell their toxic products anymore. We have already seen this in Europe with bans on GMOs and GEs. I believe there will be more bans in the future.

*"Land degradation did not start with chemical agriculture. But chemical agriculture offered new tools for annihilation."*
*- Joel Salatin*

Consumers have long had an innate understanding that modern agricultural practices that utilize chemical-based herbicides, pesticides, and fertilizers can cause health issues. Supplies of goods are produced in response to the demands of consumers, and consumers have been turning towards organic agricultural products. This drive in demand could cause a revolution in how farmers and ranchers produce their agricultural products.

## A Looming Agricultural Crisis

Before you start pondering in fear of what I could mean, let me define this coming agricultural crisis. We will still have food, we will still have agriculture, we will still have farms and ranchers, and the agricultural industry, along with civilization, will carry on. However, a "crisis" or an inflection point is in the future, probably a decade or two away.

Why is there going to be a crisis in agriculture? Simple—we lack in the four economic resources: land, labor, capital, and entrepreneurship!

First I will define lacking, and that is we are eating our seed corn by running shortages in these four resources. Land by acreage is somewhat a problem; in the past two decades we have lost a total of 8% of our farmland to urban development. In 1995, we were producing on more acres than we do today.

What has compensated for this? It is the increase in yield, which has been substantial.

However, farmers and ranchers have been making less in real terms over the past decades. How can that be when capital costs are going down in real terms (less land to purchase and maintain), and productivity is increasing per acre? I will make a hypothetical guess that the expenses column has been increasing: taxation, regulation, purchasing GMOs, chemical fertilizers, the equipment to utilize these chemicals, etc., have all decreased the real income of farmers and ranchers. I don't have proof, but I am making an inference from the data and my reasoning.

Seventy-five percent of farmers and ranchers make less than $50,000 a year[xliv] and are working 12-hour days, six days a week, taking on legal liabilities, running their businesses, and barely scraping by. What incentives are there for the younger generation to produce agricultural products? Especially since societal attitudes towards farmers and ranchers are very negative: uneducated, poor, destitute, etc. Well, there are no incentives! Incomes are representative of the price of labor. When prices are too low, supply decreases while demand increases, creating a shortage. The supply of farmers and ranchers is decreasing with the baby boomers dying, Generation X leaving the profession, and millennials not entering into the agricultural industry.

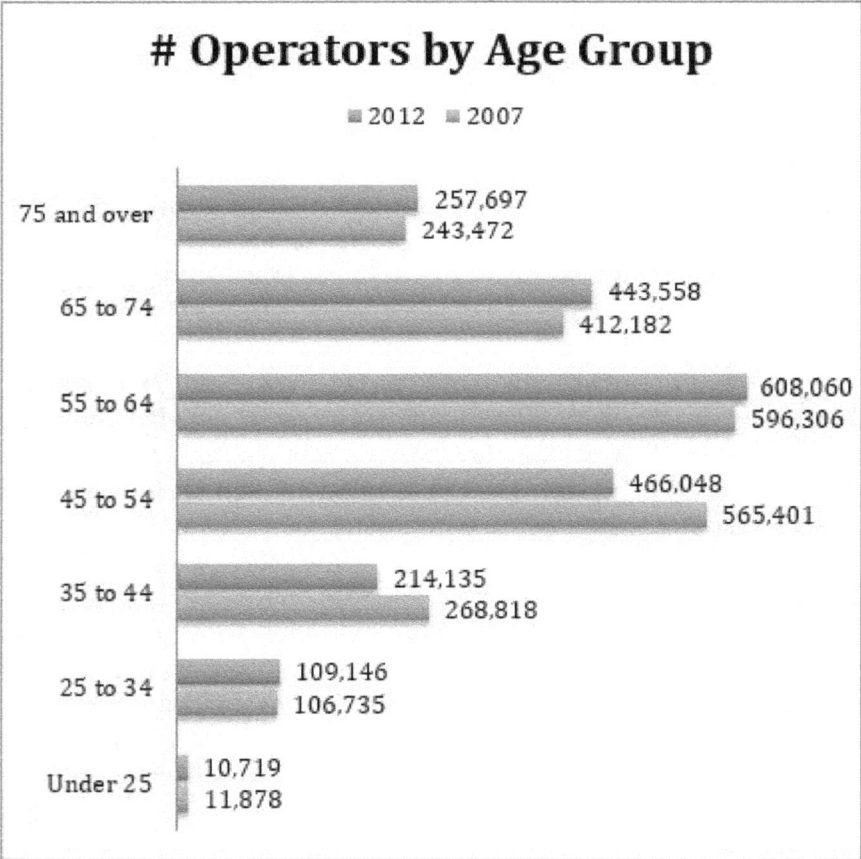

# # Operators by Age Group

■ 2012  ■ 2007

| Age Group | 2012 | 2007 |
|---|---|---|
| 75 and over | 257,697 | 243,472 |
| 65 to 74 | 443,558 | 412,182 |
| 55 to 64 | 608,060 | 596,306 |
| 45 to 54 | 466,048 | 565,401 |
| 35 to 44 | 214,135 | 268,818 |
| 25 to 34 | 109,146 | 106,735 |
| Under 25 | 10,719 | 11,878 |

(Data Sources:
http://www.agcensus.usda.gov/Publications/2012/Preliminary_Report/Highlights.pdf)

Looking at the chart above, we see that baby boomers are becoming older. Generation Xers (35 to 54 years old) are leaving the agricultural industry, and there are barely any millennials entering. We desperately need the labor and entrepreneurs to participate in agriculture. If not, who is going to grow our food?

Of course, I know that many politicians and special interest groups who would love to ship these jobs over to China. Unfortunately for them, they can't do that.

The future crisis I see is the American people realizing that there are not enough farmers. Food prices will rise gradually, and the rate of increase will gradually rise as well. Americans will find food more expensive, possibly causing social instability since the poor are least likely to adapt. Agricultural products, profits, and incomes will out of necessity have to increase to incentivize Generation X, and millennials will become professionals in the agricultural industry.

A question I can't wait to be answered is at what price (incomes) will it take to incentive Generation X and millennials to become farmers: working 12 hours a day six days a week, working outside in the elements, taking on the legal liabilities of operating a farm, managing the business, etc. What will it take? Generation X and millennials have been flocking to Wall Street careers and financial jobs working 40-, 60-, or 80-hour workweeks in air-conditioned offices, with benefits, not carrying any legal liabilities, not having to manage the business; and typically these jobs start at $50,000 as opposed to the 75% of farmers and ranchers who make less than $50,000 a year. Remember during the dotcom bubble, the real estate bubble, and now this bond bubble, when people went to the stock market as brokers, analysts, started technology mutual funds, and set up hedge funds. Then the real estate bubble people were flipping real estate, opening mortgage companies, and creating these paper contracts to sell to Wall Street. Then Wall Street flipped them and sold these contracts around the world. Kids fresh out of college were making seven-figure incomes! What dollar mark will it take to incentivize these two generations to go out into the fields and produce agricultural products?

First we have to have the land, which we do. However, due to the environmental degradation caused by these GMOs, GEs, and chemicals used in modern agriculture, soil fertility is at a historical low. Soil health and fertility will have to be generated in conjunction with the weaning off process of taking these chemicals out of the agriculture industry.

Second is the labor and the entrepreneurship part of the equation. This will coincide with the increase in operating incomes and profits.

Lastly is the needed capital required to build the needed infrastructure, businesses, equipment, and technology to transition into this new age of agriculture. Currently in real terms, we have the same capital expenditure for agriculture as we did in the 1920s even though we have four times the population. Two contributing factors for this lackluster capital expenditure are the growth in technology and machinery, and that we needed to utilize the capital built up from the mid-1940s to the early 1980s. This factor only partly explains for the problematic capital expenditure, and we should at least be 50% above current levels at a minimum.

## Technological Advancement

A blessing of our modern age has been the rapid development of technology. This technological development is a major element that will transform agriculture in the decades to come. We'll see more aquaponics (hydroponics), internet buying clubs, computer programming and automated combines, robotics, artificial aquifers and springs, and more! The future is very bright in agriculture, and is one of the last frontiers that mainstream technology companies haven't yet focused on.

One day farmers and ranchers will be sitting on their patios with a laptop wireless connected to a GPS and an electronic guidance system that will sow and reap the fields for them. Farmers will complete this intensive part of farming on a computer, instead of having multiple people who have to be trained and then operate the combine. Robotics will also be heavily incorporated into farms. Lely is one company that has entered this space by creating the Lely Vector, which can feed and milk cows, freeing up the time that would have been spent by the farmer or laborer.

Development of technology is not only limited to robotics and computer programming. Aquaponics will make its mark as another solution to our agricultural crisis. Aquaponics mimics a cycle in nature where fish waste (fecal matter) is filtered through plants (crops), cleaning the water of fish waste, to then be cycled back into the fish tank. This idea has made, and will continue to make, its mark in urban areas. Gotham Greens is an agricultural company that specializes in producing agricultural products on top of a rooftop in New York. They grow organic and wholesome food on top of grocery store rooftops. One acre of their aquaponics system is the equivalent of producing 20 acres of the same crop. A major challenge to the project is that it's very capital intensive to build the greenhouses, construct solar energy units to power the greenhouses, and the aquaponics systems themselves.

However, a major benefit is that it reduces the carbon footprint and consumption of oil to transport food from field to store. Literally, a person just harvests the crops and sends it downstairs to be stocked on the shelves. Transportation is a key factor in the energy input out of the equation. The creation of internet buying clubs will further reduce these costs and energy consumptions.

Web sites to organize buying clubs are already in development with the goal of directly sending a farmer's product to the doorstep of the consumer. People will be able to go online in the comfort of their own home to shop for groceries. They'll have a list of the products they want, click on the particular item, and then have a choice of farmers to choose from based on price, quality, and delivery. Transporting food from field to grocery store, and then the consumer driving to the store and then back, all just to purchase groceries, will be simplified. I believe we will see the efficiency of essentially being able to FedEx the product from field to door with just one car delivering the food. Of course, that car and the driver can be replaced when the evolution of Amazon.com drones to deliver food packages to the consumer.

One of the innovations I am currently working on for my business is the development of artificial aquifers and springs.

Our water resources are the most important resources we have. Here in North America, we have abundant fresh water resources at our disposal. Regrettably, we as a country in conjunction with the rest of the world have poorly managed our water resources. We are polluting our rivers and aquifers with these toxic chemicals from factors and farms, overconsuming our water to have perfectly manicured lawns. A good example is the water crisis in California that they are going through right now.

Water is a precious resource, and it should not be politicized, but, unfortunately, we live in a society that loves to politicize everything, including our water. California's water is subsidized not for poor people but to help the big agricultural companies. Tax dollars are being used to help suppress the price of water since the price is artificially lower than what the free market would set. This policy leads to the overconsumption of water with a shrinking supply. Agriculture companies comprise 80% of the water usage in California: to water their crops that they grow out in the desert (growing crops in the desert is unwise because it multiples the water usage compared to what crops would use in temperate climates). The price of water was artificially low; farmers, ranchers, and big agriculture did not concern themselves with using water more efficiently and practicing conservation.

I am a Texan; in our state we go through periods of droughts, followed by floods, and then a year or two of normal rainfall before we enter another drought cycle. In California, they have these same cycles. The two cycles are differentiated by time span, rainfall, water collection, and water conservation. Currently, California is going through the drought phase of the rainfall cycle, and then you will see them slide down the mountain when it eventually floods.

California typically has a two or three years of drought, followed by a year or two of floods, and then three to five years of adequate rainfall. They have gone through four years of drought, meaning they are likely to see floods very soon. The rub is they only have about eight months of water left. If their next rainy season (October to March) fails, Californians will have to wait nearly another year for the rain season again, which will be too late.

Here in Texas, we typically have four to six years of drought (sometimes longer), then followed by two to four years of floods, and then one year or two of adequate rainfall before cycling through the cycle again. In Texas, we take our water supply seriously, because most of our state is in some form of a drought for a very long time. California weather is incredibly lovely, so Californians do not worry so much about their water supply. This lesson will be a painful lesson to learn! Conserving water and setting the price of water by the free market needs to be the norm, instead of water policy being set by bribed—oops, I mean lobbied—politicians and bureaucrats who only want to please the big agricultural industry in California. If you have time, there is a great VICE News YouTube video that describes California's fresh water crisis.

## Future Organic Practices of Agriculture

The agriculture industry will change dramatically due to consumers increasing demands for organic foods produced without chemicals, herbicides, pesticides, GMOs, etc. This shift in demand will be dramatic when people find out that the foods that they have been eating are likely to increase the risk of cancer, heart disease, liver disease, and other diseases, leading to expensive medical bills. Practices, techniques, and technology will change within the agricultural industry.

Biodiversity is one of the key components of this transition. In the African plains there are the water buffalo, birds, and a plethora of other species that are integrated together. In modern agriculture, everything is segregated into cages, pens, or fields. North American plains did not used to be like this. Recall the bison in the millions that would roam the plains eating and defecating. The birds would follow the bison to eat the bugs off them, and to peck through the feces to eat other bugs. Essentially the bison were the fertilizers for the plains, and the birds would spread the fertilizer around while sanitizing the pastures.

A farmer by the name of Joel Salatin is operating a farm on this principle of mob grazing and biodiversity.

Soil regeneration, health, and fertility are important to the bottom line of agriculture, and biodiversity is one part of the solution. One harmful practice in the agriculture industry has produced barren soil. The sun's UV rays and heat destroy the microorganisms that live in the soil. A few ways to combat this are no-till systems and cover crops. Cover crops cover the soil and add nutrients back in the ground. During the rest cycle of the field, a farmer can use cover crops to help feed cattle and use biodiversity to add the needed nutrients into the soil.

When it comes to the large monocultures we see over the plains, they may look impressive, but one superbug could destroy an entire crop. Take a look at nature; are there any monocultures in nature? No, and not even in prairie grass. Four square feet of prairie grass has over 150 species of grasses, legumes, and weeds. Polycultures can be utilized in agriculture to protect the soil from the strain of one crop, protect the soil from UV rays and heat, and benefit the soil health.

Gabe Brown is a farmer who has performed extensive research on his farm and has an incredible video detailing his findings on YouTube.

This next agricultural revolution will move away from oil-based production and towards renewable energy and naturalistic cycles to increase product yields. Biodiversity on farms will increase yields and polycultures will be introduced to lower the need for oil-based chemical inputs. America's farmers and ranchers are dying off. It will be up to entrepreneurs and millennials like me to step up and improve the agriculture industry. Right now there is a startling demographic decline in farmers resembling an inverted pyramid. We may for the first time in U.S. history see a labor shortage in the agriculture industry.

With both opportunities and catastrophes, this new reality will create many fortunes for some and spell disaster for others.

# Chapter 14: Another Great Enlightenment and a Future That Looks Brighter

I hope my book has kept a realistic tone throughout its entirety, but that, of course, must be a subjective opinion formed by you, the reader. If you feel a little depressed, this part of the book that will cheer you up! If you are already optimistic and ready to pursue your dreams in the world, great! This chapter will super-boost your attitude! Throughout history, we have been in similar situations before, and we know the results from these situations. History does not repeat, but history certainly does rhyme.

In the past, the access to information and the spread of ideas has drastically changed human society. Once again, access to information and knowledge has transformed the world. Today's modern communication, particularly the use of the Internet, has caused the spread of ideas, knowledge, and information to every corner of the globe.

Change will occur, and it's a guarantee that it will occur: history is just an example of this. Do not fear change, because change is just part of history, and humankind has changed for the better. Human beings have progressed from the swamp to the stars, from caves to houses, from hunters and gathers to farmers and ranchers, from clans to civilizations, from warriors who looted wealth to self-made men who produced wealth, from despotism to democracy, from monarchies to republics, from biological impulses to philosophical thought. History is bountiful in the number of humans who have left a positive mark in the world.

We try to learn from the mistakes and hardships of history, but the reason why financial history and calamities either repeats or rhymes is because of the human element. The human element where we believe that we can get something out of nothing by writing more claim checks than real wealth or production that is in existence. Human beings will progress further in philosophy, in science, in innovation, in industrial production, distributing knowledge, in agriculture, in government, and everything we interact with today. Today we have the Internet, which allows people all over the world to connect and spread information. The Internet is causing the greatest disturbances in technology, science, education, knowledge, philosophy, politics, etc. in history! Right now you can feel that the world is not in equilibrium, and seems like everything is tearing apart and flying out of control.

We have been here before in history. Yes, terrible events did occur then as they are occurring now. Humanity continued on and created change for the better for our posterity. One such period was the Great Enlightenment; which historians say lasted from the 1620s to the 1780s. However, I disagree, I believe the Great Enlightenment lasted for centuries, from 1436 with Gutenberg's invention of the printing press to the late 1800s when the world denounced slavery.

## The Great Enlightenment

The Gutenberg printing press was the Internet of its day, allowing people to print and distribute books, sonnets, poetry, scientific papers, pamphlets, and other intellectual and artistic content on a scale never before imagined. It was amazing technology for the 1400s. Unlike today, where the Internet is creating a Great Disturbance and another Great Enlightenment in a matter of decades, it took centuries to fully utilize the technology of the Gutenberg printing press.

People in Europe were very religious, and the first thing that was mass-produced by the printing press was the Bible.

Martin Luther wrote his Ninety-Five Theses in protest of the Catholic Church's practices of accepting money to forgive sin, as well as many of the Holy Roman Catholic Church's other teachings and practices. When the Church ordered him to stop, he refused, and the Catholic Church excommunicated him and then influenced the emperor of the Holy Roman Empire to condemn him as an outlaw. Despite official opposition, Luther's writings, works, and speeches spread through Europe, inciting the Protestant Reformation.

The Protestant Reformation caused a mass social upheaval in Europe, sparking the European Wars of Religion. These were wars you may have heard about in history class, such as The German Peasant War (1524-1525), Schmalkaldic War (1546-1547), Eighty Years' War (1568-1648), French Wars of Religion (1562-1598), Thirty Years' War (1618-1648), and there are more.

Once people had distributed those new thoughts and ideas of religion using the technology of the Gutenberg press, people began to utilize the Gutenberg press for scientific and philosophical thought.

Science and scientific development exploded at this time. Scientists learned from the books produced by the Gutenberg press and wrote papers to be printed and distributed throughout the universities and libraries of Western Europe, allowing people to self-educate themselves. People could now educate themselves on the topics of physics, astrology, biology, geology, and the other major sciences of the day. A new birth of scientist arose; for example, Nicolaus Copernicus posited that the Sun was the center of the universe instead of Earth. This is known as heliocentrism. Here is a small list of many other scientists and natural philosophers who left their mark during this period: Leonardo Da Vinci, Galileo Galilei, Athanasius Kircher, Sir Issac Newton, Giovanni Battista Riccioli, Cornelius Drebbel, and many more. The rate of new scientists, chemists, mathematicians, and other hard science professions increased exponentially as a direct result of the advancement in printing technology.

A new understanding of the physical word and how the physical world around us works created the foundation for inventors and innovators to use this knowledge to produce goods and services that increased the standard of living for everyone. Technological developments were made: the microscope, invented by Zacharias Janssen; Galileo, the first thermometer, Hans Lippershey, the first refracting telescope; Dom Perignon, the world's first Champagne; Giovanni Branca, the steam turbine—the creations of human beings are endless. Nevertheless, we did not simply rest on our achievements in just the physical sciences, but we explored philosophical thought as well.

The more information people had, the more they began to question their own existence and the existing structure of society. The main focal point of the structure of society was the government. In the 1500s to the early 1800s, monarchies were the primary forms of government. These were governments based on Aristocratic rule by birth and which controlled the populous by dictate rather than the populace rightfully having the sovereignty to self-rule.

Great Enlightenment thinkers and philosophers who greatly affected the social, political, and even economic structures of societies included: Francis Bacon (1561-1626), Cesare Beccaria (1738-1794), Rene Descartes (1596-1650), Benjamin Franklin (1706-1790), Hugo Grotius (1583-1645), Thomas Hobbes (1588-1679), David Hume

(1711-1776), Thomas Jefferson (1743-1826), John Locke (1632-1704), Thomas Paine (1737-1809), Jean-Jacques Rousseau (1712-1778), Adam Smith (1723-1790), and Voltaire (1694-1778). These gentlemen left an incredible mark that still influences culture and our principle interactions with one another.

All of this new information with new ideas and the accessibility to this information transformed the world for the better, even as we saw some of the greatest atrocities in human history. All of this information with all of these thinkers, idealists, scientists, and inventors caused many revolutions to overthrow aristocracies and tyrannies, replacing them with self-government and liberty. Millenniums-old monarchies were overthrown and superseded by democracies and republics.

Granted, all of this success did come at a cost.

The Great Enlightenment caused many revolutions; most notable is the American Revolution from 1776 to 1783. America's revolution was based on three philosophical principles: the individual's right to life, liberty, and the pursuit of happiness. No king, tyrant, or even elected leader has the authority to infringe upon these rights that people hold dear. The sovereignty of the nation and the government of the nation were now held by, of, and for the people.

Our great journey and discovery did not end with the American Revolution or the Declaration of Independence; it is a continual process that was launched by the founders of America. The responsibilities were up to us, "We the People of the United States, in Order to form a more perfect Union," to pursue the expansion of liberty for ourselves and for posterity. We were not created in a perfect nation; we were part free, and part slave, part suffrage, not universally suffrage, and the founders and Enlightenment thinkers did know and did regret the wrongs that operated in society since the beginning of civilization. They could not fix it in their time, so it was our responsibility to make a more perfect union—We the People.

We defeated the greatest sin that had plagued humanity since the beginning of time, which was slavery, that had been implanted purposively and destructively by the aristocrats and the royal family of England to divide We The People against each other. We expanded civil liberties to all minorities. We believed that the individual rights and liberties were the foremost important principle in our society and our law. No other nation has ever accomplished so much in such little time. Our story of America does not end here.

After the Great Enlightenment caused by the Gutenberg press, new inventions were created for communication: the telegraph, the telephone, the radio, the television, and the film industry. All these inventions caused great disturbances in society in the early 20th century. We had two World Wars that changed the political, social, and economic landscape of the world forever. Terrible things did happen, but look at all of the beautiful things, creations, events, and success humanity has had over these centuries.

Before we had religious freedoms we had religious wars, before we had the scientific revolution we had rudimentary tools and technology, before we had freedom and liberty humanity lived in slavery and tyranny, before we had democracies and republics we had despotism and monarchies, before humanity operated economically by voluntary trade called capitalism, we had forceful slavery. Why have we had all of these travesties? Human ignorance, human greed, human fear, and psychopathic human beings who manipulated good human beings to commit atrocities were the factors in all of these wrongs that have plagued humanity.

*"Those who can make you believe absurdities can make you commit atrocities."*
*-Voltaire*

The future will be better because at this moment we are experiencing the greatest disturbance in human history! The Internet has allowed for the greatest access to information, knowledge, and a podium for people to share and express their ideas, thoughts, inventions, research, data, and more. I can access the world's knowledge just from my smartphone, which can fit in my hand. A person can set up their own website and create whatever platform they can imagine. The power of the Internet is up to you, the users and creators!

Would you have ever thought we could have internet radio, called Pandora? What about a social network site for business contacts that have replaced the Rolodex, called LinkedIn? Take into consideration what phones have replaced. Phones have replaced the contact book, calculators, handheld Gameboys, notebooks, the calendar, and alarm clocks. You can place stock trades with your phone. Need to look up the weather? There is an app for that—and it goes on and on. Yes, there is an app for whatever you need. You can surf the web with your phone. You don't even have to purchase a desktop PC to surf the Internet anymore.

There is no reason to be bored or ignorant, because the Internet has Netflix, Hulu, YouTube, and more sites I can't even think of. Ignorance is not an excuse, because anyone can teach himself or herself using the Internet to do so—just look at Khan Academy. Sorry, but you do not need an Ivy League degree to succeed. Look at Mark Zuckerberg—he left Harvard! Elon Musk dropped out of Stanford. Bill Gates dropped out of Harvard; he's a high school graduate worth nearly $80 billion. The richest man in the world does not have a college degree.

## America's Story

*"We the People of the United States of America, in Order to form a more perfect Union...."*
*- U.S. Constitution*

The Founding Fathers were just people, after all; they knew that America was not perfectly formed, we still had the British Imperial system of slavery we had to overthrow, women could not vote, and other ailments that remained from the looters' continents of the old world. Humble the founders were to write the first sentence of the Constitution "We the People... in Order to form a more perfect Union", a more perfect Union, it is up to us, their descendants, to make America a better place.

In 1776, America declared independence and fought a seven-year revolution to free itself from tyranny. In 1861, America was torn apart by a bloody Civil War; 600,000 Americans died to free people who did not share their own race. This war was fought on America's principle of our virtue, "We hold these truths to be self-evident, that all men are created equal, that they are endowed by their Creator with certain unalienable Rights, that among these are Life, Liberty, and the Pursuit of Happiness."[xlv] In the 1930s and 1940s, America found herself in the midst of a Great Depression and then a World War. A war fought against tyranny in the same form but disguised with

---
176

different names called Fascism, The National Socialist Workers' Party (Nazi), and the Emperor of Japan.

Roughly every 80 years America experiences a rebirth: The American Revolution 1776 – 1783, The Civil War 1861 – 1865, and The Great Depression and World War II 1929 – 1945. Tensions build due to injustices, financial profligacy, or foreign enemies, the tensions erupt, and We the People overcome, making America a better place for all. For 6,000 years, the world only knew tyranny and slavery. Tyranny in the forms of despots, monarchs, and aristocrats of the state ruling against the will of the people and other nation's people with the oppressive economic imperialistic system called slavery. For 6,000 years tyranny and slavery ruled the world, and then there was America. I pay my greatest respect and tribute to the men and women who served and sacrificed for this noble idea we call America.

An idea that holds self-evident truths and the virtues of establishing "justice insure domestic Tranquility, provide for the common defense, promote the general Welfare, and secure the Blessings of Liberty to ourselves and our Posterity." Now seventy years after our last great struggle we again see the tensions build up socially, economically, politically, and militarily. What will the 2020s hold? We are in the midst of another rebirth in the American experience. We may see some very difficult hardship, but we will become stronger, freer, and more prosperous on the other side.

## "To Make Money"

America was the creation of the idea that "We the People" could live freely and harmoniously with each other on the understanding that each individual controlled their own destiny. That we would not allow the government to use force or coercion to control or enslave the populous. There would be no tyranny of a monarch, from an aristocracy, from the majority, from the minority, or from a kleptocracy. We would not operate under an economic system of imperialism and oppression, but one under voluntary trade, utilizing free markets and free people. Through the centuries we formed "a more perfect union" expounded upon the principles that every individual has a right to "Life, Liberty, and the Pursuit of Happiness", and with these principles, we prospered. We built the Erie Canal, transcontinental railroads, a mass communication system of telegraphs then telecommunication, created the process for mass production, constructed the first airplane, flew for the first time, invented interchangeable parts, the television, microwave ovens, modern air conditioning, hearing aids, global positioning systems (GPS), the internet, and successfully landed a man on the moon then had him return safely home. With all of our successes and economic production, "We the People" coined a phrase "To make money."

Have you ever thought about this phrase? A phrase containing those three words. Some people have contempt for this phrase, and regard it as a disgraceful thought pertaining only to greed, corruption, and comprises only of ill-intent. They regard money as evil, and those who love to make money as corrupt. Who are these "they" I am speaking of? They are the rotted cultures of the looters' continents. The monarchs, the rulers, the despots, the emperors, the dictators, the military juntas, the aristocrats, the kleptocrats, the communists, the fascists, the socialists. So, what is this money that with great vitriol they damn?

Money is merely a tool to exchange economic value for economic value. Money rests on the idea that individuals may trade with each other on the principle that they, to the best of their abilities, produce goods and services for others, and accept a promise that others will choose to produce goods and services to fulfill their needs or wants. Money is only made possible by the production of those individuals; who voluntarily choose to meet the needs and satisfy the wants of others.

What if there was a world without this "evil" money?

How would individuals obtain the necessities to clothe and feed themselves?

The only solutions are to coerce their fellow human beings through a muzzle of a gun, barter, or physically create the goods and services to satisfy their needs and wants. I ask these people to try to fill their car with gas by drilling their own well and refining their gas to power their car; try to create a solar panel to produce the electricity to light their homes or power their A/C units to keep them warm in the winter or cool in the summer, try to obtain things by physical exertions, and they may find that people's sacrifices and works are the creation of all the wealth in the world. Money simply represents their endeavors.

Is this what they consider to be evil?

Or was it those capitalist who love to make money are corrupt and evil?

American's love for money is not for what it can buy, but what money symbolizes. Money is the symbol of the virtues of individuals who wish to coexist with one another with collaborative trade, not dictatorial force. It represents our efforts and time to create value for one another, and to generate utility to increase our fellow individuals' standard of living. "We the People" understand that money demands that we trade our talent to the customers' intelligence, not to their gullibility. Money demands that it buys the best products and most efficient services, not the lousiest of goods.

Money was made in the mass production of the car, but the looters' cultures claim that this money was made at the expense of those who purchased the Model T. Henry Ford created his product for the benefit of his fellow man, so they could travel miles more comfortably and faster than on horseback. Money was merely a tribute, a symbol of his customers' appreciation for his effort and sacrifice.

Money cannot purchase intelligence for the willfully ignorant, praise for the lethargic, respect for the deceitful, looks for the vain, good decisions for the reckless, nor good conscious for the immoral. Money is such a noble tool it will not support a person's depravity. The person who condemns money has acquired it shamefully. The person who loves and cherishes their money has worked for it. Money will not serve an individual who does not or cannot respect it.

Money demands the greatest respect and the highest attention. If a person does not respect money, money will surely discipline those individuals in the appropriate manner. Such as Conrad Hilton, who found himself $500,000 in debt because he was not attentive enough to what money was telling him. He, like others, learned the lesson the hard way, but through resilience and perseverance, he achieved his success. Money was merely an arbiter to ensure that he delivered value for value, a measurement of weights and balances in the supreme court of capitalism.

"We the People" live by trade, with our imagination, intellect, and efforts deciding the marketplace, not legislated by aristocrats and bureaucrats. For that reason, we choose the best products, the best services, the noblest ideas, the most creative performances, and reward them respectfully. We reward individuals with the best reasoning, highest ability, and greatest efforts, not by a person's political connectedness. We reward based upon their performance and their productivity. This is the standard of America's economy, whose tool and symbol is money.

Is this why, they call money and our capitalistic system evil?

America's economy is represented by the word capitalism. The collective Socialists of the Old World shame those who identify as capitalists or industrialists. Socialists' state that capitalism and democracy are incompatible with one another and will only lead to ruin and chaos. Yet, I ask, what is capitalism? Capitalism is the highest form of democracy. Capitalism operates on the ballot box of the free market with free individuals casting their votes on every product, on every service, on every business venture, on every idea, and on the character of the entrepreneurs. Individuals vote on the most useful tools, the most creative content, the most enjoyable performances, the ecologically minded businesses, the most efficient and effective business processes, and every economic action an individual or an entrepreneur makes. Capitalism rest on the axiom that every correct decision is rewarded accordingly and every incorrect decision is disciplined accordingly. Profits are privatized; losses are privatized, not socialized. Bankruptcies for the financially incompetent, not bail-outs.

Is this what they consider to be evil?

I see the Fascists, the Communists, and the Socialists privatizing the profits to them, the politicians, the bureaucrats, their special interest groups, big corporate donors, and the politically well-connected while socializing the losses onto the backs of the middle class and the poor. Bail-outs for the rich at the expense of poor. Bail-outs for the politically well-connected at the expense of the taxpayers. Bail-outs for the Socialist and statist at the expense of the capitalists and the people.

Communists, Fascists, and Socialists have erected walls, not to keep foreign enemies out, but to keep their people in. These totalitarians have massacred and assassinated political dissent while capitalists and constitutional republics espouse the virtues of the freedom of speech, the freedom of the press, the freedom of assembly, and the freedom to petition and protest. When the political and power elites seize a country, they disarm the people and then silence their voice. They mislead the people into believing that they are here for their benefit that they are only do-gooders, and denounce those who voice their grievances of the atrocities the elites are committing.

In their speeches, they advocate that they are the most responsible with power, and the people should transfer their responsibilities, rights, and with it their power to a centralized political system and bureaucracy. Always remember, that power to the people is liberty while power to the government is tyranny. More power to the government eventually corrupts a government. It's simply not that power corrupts, but it is the corrupt who seek power.

They divide people based on social class, political party, sex, gender, creed, ethnicity, and race. Some politicians state that "We the People" are racist and need to be regulated and controlled by the government for our own benefit. I have *not* known Americans as a whole to be racist. 600,000 Americans died to free a race from slavery installed by the British Empire and upheld by an ignorant government, against the will of the people. "We the People" marched on Washington to demand the government to treat the races equally. It was the government who enforced slavery; it was the government which legislated Jim Crow Laws to force people to discriminate and treat each other differently. How is it that a black single mother working for $1 a day as a washerwoman, goes on to start her company in the deep south selling hair care products to become the first female millionaire in 1919? If the American people were racist would she have ever become a millionaire? No, "We the People" reward our fellow Americans based on merit, effort, ability, and character.

Capitalism is the arbiter to reward productivity, and discipline wastefulness. Capitalism requires rugged individualism over collectivism. Capitalism requires collaboration over coercion, competition over political graft, integrity over corruption, reason over authoritative dictate, perspective over speculation, adaptation over stagnation, free people over political subjects, liberty over tyranny.

Capitalism only approves transactions to occur from the un-coerced decision of individuals. Free markets only allow individuals to create goods and services worthy for purchase by other individuals. This principle means individuals in a free market must generate value and utility, not at the expense of others, but for their benefit. Capitalism demands the best that you and I can offer. Capitalism demands of us our best intellect, our best inventiveness, our best integrity, our best ethics, our best abilities, and our best work. Capitalism is the product of our innovation and work. Capitalism means that individuals must create value, not violence to acquire wealth.

Kleptocrats (Socialists, Fascists, and Communists) use a government as a tool to cement their control and power over the people. Before they can enforce their authority, they must first subvert the government. You will see the coming to power the men and women of double speak, doublethink, and of the double standard; those who use dictatorial force to tax, nationalize, and confiscate from those who produce wealth, the capitalist. In a moral, capitalistic, and constitutional society, the laws are written to protect you from the thieves and looters. Laws will either be neglected by the elites or rewritten by the elites to serve their interest, not ours. Power elites believe that they can dictate what can be produced and when; how much of the profit is reinvested, how much of the profit is taken by the government, the bureaucrats, the party elites, the financial elites, the special interest groups, and how the meager crumbs are "redistributed" to members of society; you will see society starve and struggle. Society then divides and destroys itself between the haves and the have-nots, the power elites and their victims, and between the government and the people. If you want to know when the kleptocrats have control, watch money.

Money is the weight that free people in a free market society measure their value of trade with one another. Kleptocrats will first destroy this measure to destroy the tool on which a free society operates with, money. When you see the kleptocrats destroy money, debasing money and replacing our money with a counterfeited paper currency stamped with their seal, and enforced by their edict. When you see their currency being transferred from those who produce to those who create political deals. When you or I are forced to acquire permission to establish our businesses, our business philosophy, our business processes, to produce our goods and services from the kleptocracy who produces nothing, then you will know when the kleptocrats, not We the People, are in control. When you see America dying, do not ask who is killing her, We the People are.

We The People have the responsibility since we have the power. We The People are responsible to ensure that government serves us, and only our interest. We The People have the responsibility to protect America from threats both foreign and domestic, not the government. We The People are responsible since we have the rights, and we as people enforce our authority over government. We The People is an idea that is the newest and most innovative idea; that government is beholden to the people, not the people to a government.

The Founding Fathers and the First Generation of Americans new that if government had immense power, then a few would try to subvert to control that power. So, they wrote a Constitution to clarify what the government could *only* do; if that power was not granted by the Constitution it was held to the States "We The People", and government could *not* have that power or authority. However, the United States Constitution is just a piece of parchment, We The People enforce the Constitution on our government, not the other way around.

Unfortunately, We The People have allowed politicians, power elites, financial elites, special interest groups, big donors, the new monarchs, to divide ourselves and try to make us apathetic through small welfare payments, so they can acquire more power and profit.

We have allowed them to replace our money, Gold & Silver, with a paper currency that they call a Federal Reserve Note. The same edicts the monarchs of Great Britain wrote to confiscate America's money, and replaced it with paper script.

We now stand with the greatest idea of the greatest productive nation in world history, and forgotten our money and our virtue. People look at money the same as the degenerates of the old world, and are taken back by America's stagnation. The phrase "that money is evil" comes during a time when money was created from the backs of the slaves of Egypt, of Rome, of the British Empire, of the Soviet Union, of the monarchies, of the aristocracies, and now the kleptocracies. The phrase "to make money," shows part of our virtue and principles. The Founding Fathers and We The People realized that money must first be produce before it is stolen by the aristocracy. American capitalists, We The People, decided to make money. A nation of production, not conquest. A nation of justice, not violence. A nation of opportunity, not of economic immobility. A nation of entrepreneurs, not conquers. I have the greatest reverence to America, a nation of morals, justice, tranquility, reason, innovation, production, and money. However, we have forgotten our three virtues guiding our journey; the rights to Life, Liberty, and the Pursuit of Happiness.

These three virtues stand on the axiom where everyone has these rights to Life, Liberty, and the Pursuit Happiness, and no one has a right to inflict their version of Life, Liberty, and Pursuit of Happiness upon another individual. If you believe that you have a right to inflict your version of your world upon others, do not be surprised when others try to do the same to you. You and I find it totally inappropriate and immoral to tell each other in our own homes of what is correct or incorrect for what to buy, who to buy for, who to love, who to talk too, what to talk about, and so on. Then why is that we allow people to go to government to tell other people how they should live their lives; shouldn't that be inappropriate and immoral in a civilized society?

If you believe that you have the right to tell others who they can love, then others will tell you who you can marry. If you believe you have the right to force others to purchase healthcare, then they may try to force you to purchase firearms or to supply the military industrial complex. If you believe you have the right for government to tax others to subsidized energy companies, do not be surprised when they tax you to fund their environmental movements, studies, and activities. If you believe you have the right to infringe upon Americans' second amendments rights, do not be surprised when they infringe upon your fourth amendment rights and your right to privacy from a surveillance state. If you believe you have the right to tax others to pay to criminalize selling or smoking pot that are merely pieces of plants, do not be surprised when they use government force to criminalize selling and holding gold and silver that are merely pieces of metals. If you believe you have the right to have the government tell people what they can and cannot do with their property, do not be surprised when they use government to tell you what you can or cannot do with your body. The Founding Fathers wanted us to determine our own fates, our own moral codes, and our own lives, not having the populous voting to tell government what others in society can or cannot do. We The People cannot allow ourselves to divide each other. The Founding Fathers knew that if we did; then those corrupt individuals who love to seize power by dividing the people to conquer the government and control the people. They will surely take over and create a kleptocracy.

United we stand, divided by the politicians and the kleptocrats amongst race, ethnicity, sex, gender, sexual orientation, creed, political ideology, or political party, we will surely fall. America rests on our shoulders, our greatest power comes within ourselves, We The People.

I hope that as Americans, we continue towards the future hand in hand. That we look to ourselves to solve poverty, we the people solve homelessness, we the people care for each other, we the people protect the environment, we the people create businesses and jobs, we the people create innovation, we the people deliver equal opportunity, we the people prosper together, we the people are united by this one idea. This American idea of Life, Liberty, and the Pursuit of Happiness, and we all, as a people, respect those rights. Misguided individuals who support Socialism, Fascism, or Communism do not understand that when a government uses force it obliterates those rights, and the promise of prosperity will turn into an ash heap of misery and totalitarianism, because force is antithetical to prosperity. Liberty means you and I have the freedoms to make social and economic decisions for ourselves, not made for us by an autocratic edict. With these freedoms mean we have the responsibility to provide for ourselves socially and economically; look after one another during financially distressful times, and watch for the political danger that may threaten those liberties.

Our next greatest enemy will not be some far distance oppressive aristocracy, not some decrepit, vulgar economic system of slavery, nor the totalitarians who ruled the European and Asian continents. No, America's next greatest fight is happening between We The People, our greatest obstacle is our divisiveness and our apathy, our greatest threat is allowing the kleptocrats to seize power, our greatest struggle is ensuring that politicians serve the people, not themselves.

Until and unless we see money, capitalism, and ourselves as a source of good, equal opportunity, and prosperity, then we cannot solve our problems of an out of control government, and out of control political system. I believe that the American people are intrinsically good, and we are the greatest innovators in human relations. We must have the courage to choose to act. We are coming towards another inflection point in American history with a decision to make in how we conduct our relations with ourselves. Whether we choose to reestablish the virtues of our founding principles of America, or profess that a small group of power "elite" in a far distant capital can dictate our fate better than we can decide for ourselves.

This decision is for you, I, and "We The People" to make, so we may form "a more perfect Union."

## The Trivium

Our Founding Fathers gave us three virtues I and others call the *trivium*: life, liberty, and the pursuit of happiness. The three virtues are derived from and understood by the use and understanding of grammar, logic, and rhetoric. These virtues are not solely enough standing by themselves; it takes We the People to implement these virtues in our lives, our communities, and our country. Grammar is very important since it forms the basic structure of language. Logic is the reasoning conducted to construct our arguments for life, liberty, and the pursuit of happiness to others, and reveal the tyranny that is still in our world. Rhetoric is the identification of symbols, words, and actions to help us reveal to others the terministic screens politicians, bureaucrats, and the military industrialists use to obfuscate what sins they are committing against us or other nations. Educating yourself in grammar, logic, and rhetoric is essential and is the foundation of a classical education. Please improve yourself in these disciplines.

*"Genius without education is like silver in a mine."*
*- Ben Franklin*

## A Future That Looks Brighter

I believe in the deepest part of my heart that we will see positive change in the world in all aspects. There will be so many wonderful things that will happen in this world. We are going to develop new technologies to utilize energy. Discover new sources of energy. A large energy revolution will occur because we will have a crisis, and that crisis will spark change for the better. Cars are going to be powered by electricity, hydrogen, or something that perhaps I can think of! Homes will become self-powered either through solar panels, wind turbines, or something that hasn't yet been invented.

Our agriculture industry will change for the better. Production will shift to favor healthier food, healthier agricultural practices, and more nutritious food. We'll see financially independent farmers and ranchers working on large estates, with robots feeding the animals, milking the animals, moving the portable fences around for the animals to move them to new pastures. They will operate large combines from the front porch, sitting there with a beer and T-bone steak; they'll control their combines with their computers. Farmers, ranchers, and people who invest in agriculture will see enormous gains in income and purchasing power.

But that's not all.

Our healthcare system will see a leap in bounds in biotechnology, stem-cell research, cancer treatment, male birth control pills, and more. The amount of growth and development in biotechnology that will extend our life expectancy will increase dramatically. New life-saving technology will be introduced. All of this will be possible with the advancement in access to information, research, and data, and from all of these institutions putting this information online for other researchers to use. Artificial limbs, artificial joints, maybe artificial eyes to solve blindness, artificial ears to cure the deaf—the sky's the limit.

What about space exploration?

Space exploration will be the new and ultimate frontier. Elon Musk says he can put someone on Mars in 2025.[xlvi] If you don't believe it is possible; I and Elon would say to you, that we can achieve the impossible when we believe that it is possible. I believe that I will see a man and a woman land on Mars in my lifetime. If my parent's generation had a man on the Moon, why can't my generation put a man and a woman on Mars? I bet we will see asteroid mining to extract the plentiful resources from the asteroid belt to build the new cities, the new technologies, the new companies, and the new inventions here on Earth.

We will improve in technology, the sciences, our economy, our agriculture, and our healthcare system. We will see improvement in human society: when it comes to government, hopefully, we move away from politics and towards philosophy, and we'll see progress in civil liberties, male and female interactions, world issues, domestic issues, and other social elements. Granted this is my hope and faith that we will see great improvements in the human element. I believe we will because of the Internet, which will unlock the next level of human conscious.

We The People, not just in America, but the people around the world will stand up to the kleptocrats in governments, and take on the responsibilities to provide for ourselves thereby acquiring power, and with that power we expand our social and economic liberties.

Political and economic freedoms will be acquired by the people of the world over their respective governments. People should never fear their governments, because it is governments who fear their people. Unfortunately, the media does not cover this great awakening. People in China, North Korea, Iran, the Far East, and the Middle East are questioning their totalitarian regimes. When they acquire the information about the principles of Life, Liberty, and the Pursuit of Happiness. I believe they will make the correct choice, as we will, and as the trend has been throughout human history. That people will choice freedom, liberty, and prosperity over the dictatorial chains of a centralized, governmental regime of power elites. This by its very nature means that the future will be better, due to the positive changes that have and will continue to occur.

# Chapter 15: Live Your Dream

What are your dreams? Are you even pursuing your dreams? People who succeed have the motivation to pursue their dreams. Every single day they are pursuing their dreams. No excuses—just do it! All successful people have that mentality. Find people who are successful and personally resonate with you. "Show me your friends, and I'll show you your future," says Dan Pena, and he is right. Take pride in yourself, have some self-confidence, and possess the courage to take action to complete your dream.

## Spirit

Certainly, there will be times when the economy will be horrible, and there'll be personal financial difficulties, family issues, health issues, and what have you. However, do not make an excuse, because I have pointed out people who have overcome more than you, and accomplish more than you have. My point was made with Madam C.J. Walker. She was a black single mother who became the first female self-made millionaire in the 1910s, long before the Civil Rights movement of the 1950s and 1960s.

If the world goes to hell in a hand basket, your life doesn't have to!

Many of your friends, relatives, and society will either passively or actively try to undermine your self-esteem and dreams. Do not become angry or upset with these people; they are just victims of the same dynamic. Have only pity for them, and try to ignite their spirit that's within them. Go and find people whether it is friends or certain family members who you resonate with. Do not let someone's opinion of you become your reality. Write your reality! Pursue your dream, make your game plan, build your dream team, and take action.

*"Our deepest fear is not that we are inadequate. Our deepest fear is that we are powerful beyond measure. It is our light, not our darkness that most frightens us. We ask ourselves, 'Who am I to be brilliant, gorgeous, talented, fabulous?' Actually, who are you not to be? You are a child of God. Your playing small does not serve the world. There is nothing enlightened about shrinking so that other people*

*won't feel insecure around you. We are all meant to shine, as children do. We were born to make manifest the glory of God that is within us. It's not just in some of us; it's in everyone. And as we let our own light shine, we unconsciously give other people permission to do the same. As we are liberated from our own fear, our presence automatically liberates others."*
*-Marianne Williamson[xlvii]*

Live your life! Let's say the dollar collapses, the stock market crashes, people are rejecting the food at the supermarket because of these toxins they use in the agricultural industry, gasoline goes to $10 a gallon or more, and any despotic or dysphoric event you can think of happens! The world will continue to improve, because I believe humanity is intrinsically good. All of these crises are just events that most people fail in; you don't have to fail! You can always succeed in any situation. Most financial calamities have the best opportunities to succeed. Examples I have provided were in Chapters 5 and 6. After the crisis the boom come, so start your business, patent your invention, or whatever it may be during the crisis to take advantage of the future boom.

*"The world is my canvas, imagination is my paint, and I shall be the one who determines my fate."*
*-James J. Hobart*

The world will over time become a healthier, happier, and wealthier place to live. Be a part of this future world, and live that dream of yours. Because the future will be better than we imagine; yes, I believe the future will be better than we can imagine it.

Do something that you love and pursue your dream. How many people fail at something they hate because they were told not to pursue their dreams, to play it safe with a job, to not become the next Bill Gates, Elon Musk, or Oprah Winfrey; so they work at a job to make money to buy crap they don't need. I see and hear this story all the time. Maybe you are currently in this position. Why? It doesn't have to be this way. You have the power to change your life!

## What I Hope You Take from This Book

My overarching point to this book is that you can, in nearly any circumstance, live your dream! Granted, the economy will perform poorly and make it harder, but you need to persevere to succeed. And if you now understand or have gained a better understanding of how to operate in these financial crises and calamities, you can create a better life for yourself. Lifelong learning is essential in this day in age just as it has held true for every age. The Founding Fathers were lifelong learners and loved the power of knowledge.

Have dreams and pursue those dreams. It's all right to fail at your dreams. It's not all right to fail at something you hate. Dreams can be as ambitious as building the next futuristic automobile company, becoming a billionaire hotelier, or creating the next great beauty care product. Dreams can be opening your own small computer store, a restaurant, writing a novel, writing the next great computer software program, earning certifications in medicine, law, accounting, or any occupation, opening up a repair shop, and anything else. Make a plan; this book contains many tools you can utilize, as well as the tools in the resource section of this book. Do not be afraid, and be an inspiration for others to follow.

## What You Can Do

You may be wondering what you can do, not only for yourself but also for those whom you care for. Right now, you may find yourself in the same position I found myself, trying to warn and help friends and family about protecting themselves from financial crises. I tried many methods of verbally explaining it and presenting some information. However, it will take me over 70,000 words to give the full picture, with some exploration in the resource section of this book. Before you can do anything for others, you must be able to support yourself. This is very important, because you need to lead by example. Then start helping your friends and family.

First they need to understand the principles found in this book. Presenting these principles, information, and facts are extremely important; however, do not just approach them and lecture. When you are conversing with them, direct the conversation towards the economy. If you're anything like me, then you might try to explain the whole picture; but do not do that. Articulate a few strong points based solely on information (not an argument), recommend the books you have read, recommend the YouTube videos you have watched, or financial podcast you have listened to. Hopefully, they will watch, read, or listen to some of the information and hopefully this will lead towards positive action in their life. This eliminates conflict and allows your friend or family member to engage; and it will not create the perception to your friends or family members that you have lost your nut.

There will be good times and there will be bad times. Help people prepare for the bad times and succeed during the good times that will roll around. If you have very close friends and family members whom you care about and they refuse to prepare, then prepare for them, if you can.

I have personally done the best I can to prepare. I have educated myself and saved as much as possible. I have been following and accomplishing my plan and my dreams. I wrote this book to help others, because back in the Financial Crisis of 2008 and in 2009 when my friend's parents were committing suicide since they were losing their jobs, I wanted to know what was going wrong in the world. It would have been lovely if someone could have handed me a book to explain to me what was going on, what I could do, and where to start. Now I have this book to hand to people I care about whenever a financial crisis erupts. I care for my friends, my family, and everyone; and this includes you, my dear reader. My hope is that you not only help and protect yourself but help others as well.

I just have one action to ask from you. Please, go to your loved ones and tell them how special they are in your life, and tell them how much you love them.

## Your Legacy

We have discussed in this book a few things: first was economics, next financial and monetary history, and then how to protect yourself from a financial crisis, how to spot a financial crisis developing, how to profit from the coming boom, constructing your blueprint, and creating your own financial game plan. All of that is fantastic, and I hope you have received at least a few insights that will help you financially. However, there are more important aspects to life than just making money. Recall that money is just an inanimate object; it can't be evil or good, but it's just a tool to store your economic energy. What's important is how you utilize money for not only the betterment of your life but the lives of others.

*"If a man is proud of his wealth, he should not be praised until it is known how he employs it."*
*- Socrates*

I hope in your endeavors that you become fabulously wealthy. Nevertheless, it's the real friends, families, business relationships, and relationships in this world that will give you true purpose and meaning. Too many people become wealthy and yet they are completely miserable. Others become wealthy and are revealed to be crude bullies with inflated egos.

Accomplishing your dreams may bring you happiness; however, are those dreams making a positive impact in the world? Is your business creating livelihoods, valuable products and services to your customers, and raising the standard of living for those in your community? Are you making relationships and sharing experiences with your family, friends, and loved ones? Do not become a person who only focuses on money, because money is merely a representation of one thing, economic value. The value you generate for others—whether for money or civil service—is important. My question for you is this: What will be your legacy? What type of positive impact will you have on the world?

*"Do not change the world to make yourself happy and free. Change yourself to make the world happy and free."*
*- James J. Hobart*

# Informative Resources

Books

## *Essentials*

***Intelligent Investor***, Ben Graham
ISBN-13: 978-0060555665
ISBN-10: 0060555661

***Security Analysis***, Ben Graham
ISBN-13: 860-1404298264
ISBN-10: 0070140650

***Guide to Investing in Gold and Silver***, Mike Maloney
ISBN-10: 1937832740
ISBN-13: 978-1937832742

## *Fantastic Reads*

***Currency Wars***, James G. Rickards
ISBN-10: 9781591845560
☐SBN-13: 978-1591845560

***Death of Money***, James G. Rickards
ISBN-10: 1591846706
ISBN-13: 978-1591846703

***The Ascent of Money: A Financial History of the World***, Niall
Ferguson
ISBN-10: 0143116177
ISBN-13: 978-0143116172

*Civilization: The West and the Rest*, Niall Ferguson
ISBN-10: 0143122061
ISBN-13: 978-0143122067

*All The President Banker's*, Nomi Prins
ISBN-10: 1568584792
ISBN-13: 978-1568584799

*The Smartest Guys in the Room*, Bethany McLean & Peter Elkind
ISBN-10: 1591846609
ISBN-13: 978-1591846604

*The Creature from Jekyll Island*, G. Edward Griffin
ISBN-10: 091298645X
□SBN-13: 978-0912986456

*The Millionaire Next Door*, Thomas J. Stanley & William D. Danko
ISBN-10: 1589795474
ISBN-13: 978-1589795471

*The Millionaire Mind*, Thomas J. Stanley
ISBN-10: 0740718584
ISBN-13: 978-0740718588

*Liar's Poker*, Michael Lewis
ISBN-10: 039333869X
ISBN-13: 978-0393338690

*Flash Boys*, Michael Lewis
ISBN-10: 0393351599
ISBN-13: 978-0393351590

# *Personal Finances*

***Buy, Hold, and Sell***, Ken Moraif
ISBN-10: 1118951492
ISBN-13: 978-1118951491
***The Financial Peace Planner***, Dave Ramsey
ISBN-10: 014026468X
ISBN-13: 978-0140264685

***The Total Money Makeover***, Dave Ramsey
ISBN-10: 1595555277
ISBN-13: 978-1595555274

***Dave Ramsey's Complete Guide to Money***, Dave Ramsey
ISBN-10: 1937077209
ISBN-13: 978-1937077204

***Think and Grow Rich***, Napoleon Hill, (Contributor) Arthur R. Pell
ISBN-10: 1585424331
ISBN-13: 978-1585424337

# *Business & Investing*

***Crisis Investing***, Doug Casey
ISBN-10: 0936906006
ISBN-13: 978-0936906003

***Street Smarts***, Jim Rogers
ISBN-10: 0307986071
ISBN-13: 978-0307986078

***Investment Biker***, Jim Rogers
ISBN-10: 0812968719
ISBN-13: 978-0812968712

***Hot Commodities***, Jim Rogers
ISBN-10: 0812973712
ISBN-13: 978-0812973716

***Adventure Capitalist***, Jim Rogers
ISBN-10: 0812967267
ISBN-13: 978-0812967265

***Crash Proof***, Peter D. Schiff
ISBN-10: 0470043601
□SBN-13: 978-0470043608

***The Real Crash***, Peter D. Schiff
ISBN-10: 1250046564
ISBN-13: 978-1250046567

***The Little Book of Bull Moves***, Peter D. Schiff
ISBN-10: 0470643994
ISBN-13: 978-0470643990

***The Art of the Deal***, Donald Trump
ISBN-10: 0345479173
ISBN-13: 978-0345479174

***Your First 100 Million***, Dan S. Pena
ISBN-10: 187137930X
ISBN-13: 978-1871379303

# *Economics*

***The Wealth of Nations***, Adam Smith
ISBN-10: 1505577128
ISBN-13: 978-1505577129

*A Financial History of the United States* (**Volumes 1-3**), Jerry Markham
ISBN-10: 0765607301
ISBN-13: 978-0765607300

*A Monetary History of the United States*, Milton Friedman and Anna Jacobson Schwartz
ISBN-10: 0691003548
ISBN-13: 978-0691003542

*The Causes of the Economic Crisis: And Other Essays Before and After the Great Depression*, Ludwig Von Mises, (Editor) Percy L. Greaves Jr.
ISBN-10: 1933550031
ISBN-13: 978-1933550039

*Individualism and Economic Order*, Fredrich A. Hayek
ISBN-10: 0226320936
□SBN-13: 978-0226320939

*Long Wave Cycles*, Nikolai Kondratieff, (Translator) Guy Daniels
ISBN-10: 0943940079
ISBN-13: 978-0943940076

*The Economic Consequences of the Peace*, John M. Kenyes
ISBN-10: 1479368709
ISBN-13: 978-1479368709

*How an Economy Grows and Why it Crashes*, Peter D. Schiff and Andrew J. Schiff
ISBN-10: 047052670X
ISBN-13: 978-0470526705

# *Agriculture*

***You Can Farm,*** Joel Salatin
ISBN-10: 0963810928
ISBN-13: 978-0963810922

***Salad Bar Beef,*** Joel Salatin
ISBN-10: 096381091X
ISBN-13: 978-0963810915

***Folks This Ain't Normal***, Joel Salatin
ISBN-10: 0892968206
ISBN-13: 978-0892968206

***Pastured Poultry Profit$,*** Joel Salatin
ISBN-10: 0963810901
ISBN-13: 979-0963810907

Gabe Brown's Website
http://brownsranch.us/

Joel Salatin Website
http://www.polyfacefarms.com/

Gabe Brown Speaking Engagement
*Gabe Brown: Keys To Building a Healthy Soil*
https://www.youtube.com/watch?v=9yPjoh9YJMk

# YouTube Videos

*The Case for $20,000 oz Gold – Debt Collapse – Mike Maloney – Silver & Gold*
Channel Mike Maloney
https://www.youtube.com/watch?v=tj2s6vzErqY

*Mike Maloney's Hidden Secrets of Money Season 1 (Ep. 1 – Ep. 5)*
Channel Mike Maloney
https://www.youtube.com/watch?v=DyV0OfU3-FU&list=PLE88E9ICdipidHkTehs1VbFzgwrq1jkUJ

*Why Gold & Silver? – Mike Maloney – Silver & Gold Investing*
Channel Mike Maloney
https://www.youtube.com/watch?v=E5VNAEmmBQM

*How The Economic Machine Works by Ray Dalio*
Channel Bridgewater
https://www.youtube.com/watch?v=PHe0bXAIuk0

*Accelerated Crash Course (ACC) 2014*
Channel ChrisMartensondotcom
https://www.youtube.com/watch?v=pYyugz5wcrI

*The Ascent of Money: A Financial History of The World by Niall Ferguson Epsd 1- 5 Full Documentary*
Channel Rebel Mystic
https://www.youtube.com/watch?v=fsrtB5lp60s

*William Ackman: Everything You Need to Know About Finance and Investing in Under an Hour*
Channel Big Think
https://www.youtube.com/watch?v=WEDIj9JBTC8

---

*Course 1: Beginners Lessons on BuffettsBooks.com*
Channel Preston Pysh
https://www.youtube.com/watch?v=KfDB9e_cO4k&list=PLECECA6
6C0CE68B1E

*Course 2: Intermediate Lesson on BuffettsBooks.com*
Channel Preston Pysh
https://www.youtube.com/watch?v=-
4mXnFK0ecM&list=PLD3EB06EC4A19BFB8

*Course 3: Advanced Lessons on BuffettsBooks.com*
Channel Preston Pysh
https://www.youtube.com/watch?v=1jHqCKj0PUM&list=PL4F98F8
2F436543F7

*Real Conversations: Rickards, McCullough Unplugged on Fed,*
*USD, Economy & More*
Channel Hedgeye
https://www.youtube.com/watch?v=hN7-u7Sd7Gk&list=PLuhl1D-
19WCkgKMcG5DMRaCJ4ZZWxMCMV&index=18

*Intellectual Minds 2013 Day 1*
Channel Orchid Pictures
(Jim Rickards at 9:45)
https://www.youtube.com/watch?v=mB24T6eirMY

*Jim Rickards – Death of Money – 4-30-15*
Channel NCPAIdeas
https://www.youtube.com/watch?v=2xDSgOMifo8

*TDV Internet Exclusive: Doug Casey on the Phil Donahue Show*
*1980/1981*
Channel: TheDollarVigilante
https://www.youtube.com/watch?v=easuUdhW4X0

*Doug Casey talks to James Turk*
Channel GoldMoneyNews
https://www.youtube.com/watch?v=hSyJjC_jBWQ

*Raw Footage of Doug Casey Interview from The Bubble*
Channel Jimmy Morrison
https://www.youtube.com/watch?v=YqHwTc5Jy7g

*The Big Picture with Marc Faber: Full Video*
Channel Marcopolis Net
https://www.youtube.com/watch?v=WQW6pcWp5Ac

*Marc Faber: The Global Economy Is Entering An Epic Slump*
Channel ChrisMartensondotcom
https://www.youtube.com/watch?v=bY-eFr7ug9A

*Mirror, Mirror on the Wall, When is the Next AIG to Fall? Marc Faber*
Channel misesmedia
https://www.youtube.com/watch?v=H0sS6a9RW2E

*Rick Rule's Investing Lessons*
Channel Liberty.me
https://www.youtube.com/watch?v=l4bpgGhWDVI

*Rick Rule: I Remember My First Period of Catastrophic Losses*
Channel Sprott US Media
https://www.youtube.com/watch?v=oLNdtvzwv_c&list=PLcVjw7FD
XXrYR-3thduKCTVIpCtRbbfe2&index=6

*Rick Rule: "Speculative Profits Are Made On The Delta Between Stupidity & Fact"*
Channel Sprott US Media
https://www.youtube.com/watch?v=sO2Y-Mhep4w&list=PLcVjw7FDXXrYR-3thduKCTVIpCtRbbfe2&index=19

*David Morgan-Unbelievable Lack of Trust in the System*
Channel Greg Hunter
https://www.youtube.com/watch?v=uOVFiOvktWo

*David Morgan: Silver Update Plus Debt at the Center of the Black Hole of Our Problems*
Channel Greg Hunter
https://www.youtube.com/watch?v=DspQvNVvHhE

*Peter Schiff Mortgage Bankers Speech Nov/13/2006*
Channel Peter Schiff
https://www.youtube.com/watch?v=jj8rMwdQf6k

*Market Crash 2015 – Peter Schiff & Mike Maloney (Part 1)*
Channel Mike Maloney
https://www.youtube.com/watch?v=RapC2-oxSRM

*Peter Schiff debates David Epstein of Columbia University – Nov 11 2009*
Channel Peter Schiff
https://www.youtube.com/watch?v=zM23TZxzOw8

*Peter Sage – Extreme Entrepreneur London Real*
Channel London Real
https://www.youtube.com/watch?v=hhjEavg27jc

***Rory Sutherland – Mad Men – Part ½ London Real***
Channel London Real
https://www.youtube.com/watch?v=Cq_dHUkRwP0&list=PLA0983
D7EA3E2CDD1&index=15

***Joe De Sena – Spartan Race Part ½ London Real***
Channel London Real
https://www.youtube.com/watch?v=unSO67nQrH4&list=PLA0983D
7EA3E2CDD1&index=16

***Jim Rogers – Follow the Money $$$ London Real***
Channel London Real
https://www.youtube.com/watch?v=KqhU4zggLMA&index=65&list
=PLA0983D7EA3E2CDD1

***Jacque Fresco – The Venus Project REDUX London Real***
Channel London Real
https://www.youtube.com/watch?v=aUzlhMWYSTg&index=69&list
=PLA0983D7EA3E2CDD1

***Dan Pena – Your First 100 Million London Real***
Channel London Real
https://www.youtube.com/watch?v=O0hV2cwnoLA&index=71&list=
PLA0983D7EA3E2CDD1

Extras

***Market Insights from Rick Rule***
www.sprottglobal.com/market-insights/rick-rule/

***Greg Hunter (Alternative Press)***
www.usawatchdog.com

***Chris Martenson***
www.peakprosperity.com

*Dan Pena*
www.danpena.com
www.danlok.com/daniel-s-pena/

# Sources

## Charts

DOW Chart:
http://measuringworth.com/DJA/result.php

S&P 500 Ratio Chart:
http://www.multpl.com/table

Prices of Dow & Gold:
http://onlygold.com/Info/Historical-Gold-Prices.asp
http://measuringworth.com/DJA/result.php

DOW/ Gold Ratio:
http://onlygold.com/Info/Historical-Gold-Prices.asp
http://measuringworth.com/DJA/result.php

Monetary Base:
https://research.stlouisfed.org/fred2/series/BASE/

Mississippi Bubble:
http://www.cato.org/publications/commentary/2009-charts

Current Financial Pyramid:
Derivatives
http://www.globalresearch.ca/financial-implosion-global-derivatives-market-at-1-200-trillion-dollars-20-times-the-world-economy/30944

Bond Market
https://en.wikipedia.org/wiki/Bond_market

Stock Market

http://www.marketwatch.com/story/global-stock-market-cap-has-doubled-since-qes-start-2015-02-12

Global Deposits
https://silverbullionknowledgecenter.wordpress.com/about/the-global-liquidity-pyramid-part-ii/

Household debt
http://www.mckinsey.com/insights/economic_studies/debt_and_not_much_deleveraging

Paper Currency
https://silverbullionknowledgecenter.wordpress.com/about/the-global-liquidity-pyramid-part-ii/

World GDP
https://en.wikipedia.org/wiki/Gross_world_product

Real Assets:
http://www.investmentnews.com/article/20130526/REG/305269987/frogs-football-and-financial-assets

Japan Population Chart:
https://en.wikipedia.org/wiki/Aging_of_Japan
http://www.pewresearch.org/fact-tank/2014/02/03/10-projections-for-the-global-population-in-2050/
http://www.stat.go.jp/english/data/jinsui/tsuki/index.htm

Price of Farmland:
http://agebb.missouri.edu/mgt/breimyer/2012/12PlainFinal.pdf
http://www.ers.usda.gov/media/377487/eib92_2_.pdf
http://extension.missouri.edu/p/G404

Price of Gold:
http://www.nma.org/pdf/gold/his_gold_prices.pdf

Price of Silver:
http://seekingalpha.com/article/422081-324-years-of-the-gold-to-silver-ratio-and-195-silver

Dow Jones:
http://www.ritholtz.com/blog/2012/07/dow-jones-industrial-average-since-1900/
http://www.macrotrends.net/1319/dow-jones-100-year-historical-chart

U.S. Housing:
https://www.census.gov/const/uspricemon.pdf

# Operator:
http://www.agcensus.usda.gov/Publications/2012/Preliminary_Report/Highlights.pdf

# References

"About · History." *Conrad N. Hilton Foundation*. N.p., n.d. Web. 29 Dec. 2015. https://www.hiltonfoundation.org/about/history

"Age of Enlightenment." *Wikipedia*. Wikimedia Foundation, n.d. Web. 30 Dec. 2015. https://en.wikipedia.org/wiki/Age_of_Enlightenment

"AGRICULTURAL CHEMICALS AND THE SOIL." *Agricultural Chemicals and the Soil*. N.p., n.d. Web. 30 Dec. 2015. http://eap.mcgill.ca/publications/eap1.htm

Aktar, Md. Wasim, Dwaipayan Sengupta, and Ashim Chowdhury. "Impact of Pesticides Use in Agriculture: Their Benefits and Hazards." *Interdisciplinary Toxicology*. Slovak Toxicology Society SETOX, n.d. Web. 30 Dec. 2015. http://www.ncbi.nlm.nih.gov/pmc/articles/PMC2984095/

Bitter, Alex. "What 'PIIGS' Can Tell You About What Happens After Greece." *TheStreet*. N.p., 07 July 2015. Web. 29 Dec. 2015. http://www.thestreet.com/story/13211050/1/what-piigs-can-tell-you-about-what-happens-after-greece.html

Board, Post Editorial. "The College Bubble." *New York Post*. N.p., n.d. Web. 29 Dec. 2015. http://nypost.com/2015/01/24/the-college-bubble/

Bristow, William. "Enlightenment." *Stanford University*. Stanford University, 20 Aug. 2010. Web. 30 Dec. 2015. http://plato.stanford.edu/entries/enlightenment/

"Business Plans: A Step-by-Step Guide." *Entrepreneur*. N.p., 05 Nov. 2012. Web. 30 Dec. 2015. http://www.entrepreneur.com/article/247574

"Buying an Existing Business | The U.S. Small Business
    Administration | SBA.gov." *Buying an Existing Business | The
    U.S. Small Business Administration | SBA.gov.* N.p., n.d. Web.
    30 Dec. 2015.
    https://www.sba.gov/content/buying-existing-business

"China's Real Estate Bubble." *CBSNews.* CBS Interactive, n.d. Web.
    29 Dec. 2015.
    http://www.cbsnews.com/news/china-real-estate-bubble-
    lesley-stahl-60-minutes/

"Coinage Act of 1792." *Wikipedia.* Wikimedia Foundation, n.d. Web.
    29 Dec. 2015.
    https://en.wikipedia.org/wiki/Coinage_Act_of_1792

"Coinage 1792." N.p., n.d. Web. 29 Dec. 2015.
    http://constitution.org/uslaw/coinage1792.txt

Colombo, Jesse. "The College Bubble (incl. Education & Student
    Loan Bubble)." *RSS.* N.p., n.d. Web. 29 Dec. 2015.
    http://www.thebubblebubble.com/college-bubble/

"Colonial Script." *Colonial Script.* N.p., n.d. Web. 29 Dec. 2015.
    http://www.kamron.com/liberty/colonial_script.htm

Condon, Bernard. "Bond Market May Be More Fragile than You
    Think." *USA Today.* Gannett, 05 Oct. 2014. Web. 29 Dec.
    2015.
    http://www.usatoday.com/story/money/markets/2014/10/05/bo
    nd-market-bubble/16613571/

"Conrad Hilton." *Wikipedia.* Wikimedia Foundation, n.d. Web. 29
    Dec. 2015.
    https://en.wikipedia.org/wiki/Conrad_Hilton

"Conrad Hilton." *Bio.com.* A&E Networks Television, n.d. Web. 29
    Dec. 2015.
    http://www.biography.com/people/conrad-hilton-9339383

"Conrad Hilton." *Bio.com*. A&E Networks Television, n.d. Web. 29
   Dec. 2015.
   http://www.biography.com/people/conrad-hilton-
   9339383/videos/conrad-hilton-full-episode-2071930617

"Crime of 1873." Dictionary of American History. 2003. "Crime of
   1873." *Encyclopedia.com*. HighBeam Research, 01 Jan. 2003.
   Web. 29 Dec. 2015.
   http://www.encyclopedia.com/doc/1G2-3401801091.html

"Demography of Japan." *Wikipedia*. Wikimedia Foundation, n.d.
   Web. 29 Dec. 2015.
   https://en.wikipedia.org/wiki/Demography_of_Japan

"Diminishing Returns." *Wikipedia*. Wikimedia Foundation, n.d. Web.
   30 Dec. 2015.
   https://en.wikipedia.org/wiki/Diminishing_returns

"Dot-com." *Wikipedia*. Wikimedia Foundation, n.d. Web. 29 Dec.
   2015.
   https://en.wikipedia.org/wiki/Dot-com_bubble

"Dotcom Bubble Definition | Investopedia." *Investopedia*. N.p., 27
   Oct. 2010. Web. 29 Dec. 2015.
   http://www.investopedia.com/terms/d/dotcom-bubble.asp

"The Dot-com Bubble." *RSS*. N.p., n.d. Web. 29 Dec. 2015.
   http://www.thebubblebubble.com/dotcom-bubble/

"Early American Currency." *Wikipedia*. Wikimedia Foundation, n.d.
   Web. 29 Dec. 2015.
   https://en.wikipedia.org/wiki/Early_American_currency

"Enlightenment." *History.com*. A&E Television Networks, n.d. Web.
   30 Dec. 2015.
   http://www.history.com/topics/enlightenment

"Environmental Impact of Pesticides." *Wikipedia*. Wikimedia
    Foundation, n.d. Web. 30 Dec. 2015.
    https://en.wikipedia.org/wiki/Environmental_impact_of_pestic
    ides

"Greenback." *Wikipedia*. Wikimedia Foundation, n.d. Web. 29 Dec.
    2015.
    https://en.wikipedia.org/wiki/Greenback_%281860s_money%
    29

"Fractional Reserve Banking." *Wikipedia*. Wikimedia Foundation,
    n.d. Web. 29 Dec. 2015.
    https://en.wikipedia.org/wiki/Fractional-reserve_banking

"Fractional Reserve Banking Definition | Investopedia." *Investopedia*.
    N.p., 14 Aug. 2006. Web. 29 Dec. 2015.
    http://www.investopedia.com/terms/f/fractionalreservebanking
    .asp

"Federal Reserve Act : Public Law 63-43, 63d Congress, H.R. 7837:
    An Act to Provide for the Establishment of Federal Reserve
    Banks, to Furnish an Elastic Currency, to Afford Means of
    Rediscounting Commercial Paper, to Establish a More
    Effective Supervision of Banking in the United States, and for
    Other Purposes." *Federal Reserve Act : Public Law 63-43,
    63d Congress, H.R. 7837: An Act to Provide for the
    Establishment of Federal Reserve Banks, to Furnish an Elastic
    Currency, to Afford Means of Rediscounting Commercial
    Paper, to Establish a More Effective Supervision of Banking
    in the United States, and for Other Purposes. N.p., n.d. Web.
    09 Feb. 2016.
    https://fraser.stlouisfed.org/scribd/?title_id=966&filepath=/do
    cs/historical/fr_act/nara-dc_rg011_e005b_pl63-43.pdf#scribd-
    open

FED Kansas PDF
    https://www.kansascityfed.org/publicat/econrev/econrevarchiv
    e/1983/2q83mill.pdf

Great Britain. "Statutes at Large ...: (43 V.) ... From Magna Charta to
1800." *Google Books*. N.p., n.d. Web. 09 Feb. 2016.
https://books.google.com/books?id=I643AAAAMAAJ&pg=P
A306&vq=%22legal+tenders%22&source=gbs_search_r&cad
=1_1#v=onepage&q&f=false

"Greece's Debt Crisis Explained." *The New York Times*. The New
York Times, 08 Dec. 2015. Web. 29 Dec. 2015.
http://www.nytimes.com/interactive/2015/business/internation
al/greece-debt-crisis-euro.html?_r=0

"Greece Debt Crisis." *Greece Debt Crisis: In Depth News, Comment
and Analysis from the Financial Times*. N.p., n.d. Web. 29
Dec. 2015.
http://www.ft.com/indepth/greece-debt-crisis

Hamilton, Pixie, and Timonthy Miller. "Water Encyclopedia."
*Chemicals from Agriculture*. N.p., n.d. Web. 30 Dec. 2015.
http://www.waterencyclopedia.com/Ce-Cr/Chemicals-from-
Agriculture.html

"Henry Ford." *Wikipedia*. Wikimedia Foundation, n.d. Web. 29 Dec.
2015.
https://en.wikipedia.org/wiki/Henry_Ford

"The Life of Henry Ford." *The Life of Henry Ford*. N.p., n.d. Web. 29
Dec. 2015.
https://www.thehenryford.org/exhibits/hf/

"Henry Ford." *Bio.com*. A&E Networks Television, n.d. Web. 29
Dec. 2015.
http://www.biography.com/people/henry-ford-9298747

"Higher Education Bubble." *Wikipedia*. Wikimedia Foundation, n.d.
Web. 29 Dec. 2015.
https://en.wikipedia.org/wiki/Higher_education_bubble

"How to Buy a Business." *Entrepreneur*. N.p., 05 Sept. 2005. Web.
   30 Dec. 2015.
   http://www.entrepreneur.com/article/79638

"How to Finance Your Business Yourself." *Entrepreneur*. N.p., 02
   June 2015. Web. 30 Dec. 2015.
   http://www.entrepreneur.com/article/244869

"How to Write a Business Plan | The U.S. Small Business
   Administration | SBA.gov." *How to Write a Business Plan |
   The U.S. Small Business Administration | SBA.gov*. N.p., n.d.
   Web. 29 Dec. 2015.
   https://www.sba.gov/writing-business-plan

Inquiry, The Journal Of Business. *A Summary of the Primary Causes
   of the Housing Bubble and the Resulting Credit Crisis: A Non-
   Technical Paper* (n.d.): n. pag. Web. 29 Dec. 2015.
   https://www.uvu.edu/woodbury/docs/summaryoftheprimaryca
   useofthehousingbubble.pdf

"J.P. Morgan." *Wikipedia*. Wikimedia Foundation, n.d. Web. 29 Dec.
   2015.
   https://en.wikipedia.org/wiki/J._P._Morgan
"JP Morgan." *Bio.com*. A&E Networks Television, n.d. Web. 29 Dec.
   2015.
   http://www.biography.com/people/jp-morgan-9414735

"Kondratieff Wave." *Wikipedia*. Wikimedia Foundation, n.d. Web. 29
   Dec. 2015.
   https://en.wikipedia.org/wiki/Kondratieff_wave

"Law of Easy Money." *The Economist*. The Economist Newspaper,
   15 Aug. 2009. Web. 29 Dec. 2015.
   http://www.economist.com/node/14215012

Lopez, Linette. "'China Is in the Midst of a Triple Bubble'" *Business Insider*. Business Insider, Inc, 09 July 2015. Web. 29 Dec. 2015.
http://www.businessinsider.com/china-is-in-the-midst-of-a-triple-bubble-2015-7

"Madam C.J. Walker." *Wikipedia*. Wikimedia Foundation, n.d. Web. 29 Dec. 2015.
https://en.wikipedia.org/wiki/Madam_C._J._Walker

"Madam CJ Walker | The Official Web Site of All Things Related to Madam C. J. Walker." *Madam CJ Walker*. N.p., n.d. Web. 29 Dec. 2015.
http://www.madamcjwalker.com/#&panel1-1

"Madam C.J. Walker." *Bio.com*. A&E Networks Television, n.d. Web. 29 Dec. 2015.
http://www.biography.com/people/madam-cj-walker-9522174

"Madam C.J. Walker." *Amazing Women In History*. N.p., n.d. Web. 29 Dec. 2015.
http://www.amazingwomeninhistory.com/madam-c-j-walker-self-made-millionaire/

"Market Crashes: The Tulip and Bulb Craze | Investopedia." *Investopedia*. N.p., 07 Jan. 2004. Web. 29 Dec. 2015.
http://www.investopedia.com/features/crashes/crashes2.asp

"Mississippi Bubble | French History." *Encyclopedia Britannica Online*. Encyclopedia Britannica, n.d. Web. 29 Dec. 2015.
http://www.britannica.com/event/Mississippi-Bubble

"Mississippi Bubble 1718-1720." *John Law and the Mississippi Bubble: 1718-1720*. N.p., n.d. Web. 29 Dec. 2015.
http://mshistory.k12.ms.us/articles/70/john-law-and-the-mississippi-bubble-1718-1720

"The Mississippi Bubble of 1718-1720." *RSS*. N.p., n.d. Web. 29 Dec. 2015.
http://www.thebubblebubble.com/mississippi-bubble/

"Mississippi Company." *Wikipedia*. Wikimedia Foundation, n.d.
     Web. 29 Dec. 2015.
     https://en.wikipedia.org/wiki/Mississippi_Company

"Money, Bank Credit, and Economic Cycles." *Mises Institute*. N.p.,
     n.d. Web. 29 Dec. 2015.
     https://mises.org/library/money-bank-credit-and-economic-
     cycles

"Municipal Bonds: A Train Wreck Waiting to Happen." *Fortune*.
     N.p., 05 Dec. 2012. Web. 29 Dec. 2015.
     http://fortune.com/2012/12/05/municipal-bonds-a-train-wreck-
     waiting-to-happen/

NBER PDF
     http://www.nber.org/chapters/c9101.pdf

"Nikolai Kondratieff." *Wikipedia*. Wikimedia Foundation, n.d. Web.
     29 Dec. 2015.
     https://en.wikipedia.org/wiki/Nikolai_Kondratieff

"Nikolai Kondratieff." - *New World Encyclopedia*. N.p., n.d. Web. 29
     Dec. 2015.
     http://www.newworldencyclopedia.org/entry/Nikolai_Kondrat
     ieff

"Nixon Ends Convertibility of US Dollars to Gold and Announces
     Wage/Price Controls - A Detailed Essay on an Important
     Event in the History of the Federal Reserve." *Nixon Ends
     Convertibility of US Dollars to Gold and Announces
     Wage/Price Controls - A Detailed Essay on an Important
     Event in the History of the Federal Reserve*. N.p., n.d. Web.
     29 Dec. 2015.
     http://www.federalreservehistory.org/Events/DetailView/33

"Nixon Shock." *Wikipedia*. Wikimedia Foundation, n.d. Web. 29 Dec.
     2015.
     https://en.wikipedia.org/wiki/Nixon_Shock

"Overview of Fractional Reserve Banking." *Khan Academy*. N.p., n.d.
     Web. 29 Dec. 2015.
     https://www.khanacademy.org/economics-finance-
     domain/macroeconomics/monetary-system-topic/fractional-
     reserve-banking-tut/v/overview-of-fractional-reserve-banking

Parker, Richard. "Why Buy an Existing Business?" *Why Buy an
     Existing Business?* N.p., n.d. Web. 30 Dec. 2015.
     http://www.bizbuysell.com/buyer_resources/why-buy-an-
     existing-business/01/

Patton, Mike. "The China Syndrome: Is China Headed For A
     Financial Meltdown?" *Forbes*. Forbes Magazine, 23 Apr.
     2015. Web. 29 Dec. 2015.
     http://www.forbes.com/sites/mikepatton/2015/04/23/the-
     china-syndrome-is-china-headed-for-a-financial-meltdown/

"Peak Oil." *Wikipedia*. Wikimedia Foundation, n.d. Web. 30 Dec.
     2015.
     https://en.wikipedia.org/wiki/Peak_oil

"Recession 1973." *Wikipedia*. Wikimedia Foundation, n.d. Web. 29
     Dec. 2015.
     https://en.wikipedia.org/wiki/1973%E2%80%9375_recession

"Session 4: Financing the Business." *How to Finance a Business.
     Business Loan, FICO Score, Government Small Business
     Loan.* N.p., n.d. Web. 30 Dec. 2015.
     http://www.myownbusiness.org/s8/

"The Civil War and Greenbacks." *The Gold Standard Now*. N.p., n.d.
     Web. 29 Dec. 2015.
     http://www.thegoldstandardnow.org/the-civil-war-and-
     greenbacks

"The Credit Bubble Bursts, the Financial Crisis Begins." *Anatomy of
     a Financial Crisis* (n.d.): n. pag. Web. 29 Dec. 2015.
     http://paecon.net/PAEReview/issue46/Baker46.pdf

"The Crime of '73, '93." *The Crime of '73, '93.* N.p., n.d. Web. 29 Dec. 2015. http://www.gold-eagle.com/article/crime-73-93

"The Great Inflation Of The 1970s | Investopedia." *Investopedia.* N.p., 26 Nov. 2007. Web. 29 Dec. 2015. http://www.investopedia.com/articles/economics/09/1970s-great-inflation.asp

"The Statutes at Large." *Google Books.* N.p., n.d. Web. 09 Feb. 2016.

"The United States Mint About Us." *The United States Mint About Us.* N.p., n.d. Web. 09 Feb. 2016.

"Tulip Mania." *Wikipedia.* Wikimedia Foundation, n.d. Web. 29 Dec. 2015. https://en.wikipedia.org/wiki/Tulip_mania

"The PIIGS That Won't Fly." *The Economist.* N.p., 18 May 2010. Web. 29 Dec. 2015. http://www.economist.com/node/15838029

"U.S. Housing Bubble." *Wikipedia.* Wikimedia Foundation, n.d. Web. 29 Dec. 2015. https://en.wikipedia.org/wiki/United_States_housing_bubble

Vedder, Richard, and Christopher Denhart. "Richard Vedder and Christopher Denhart: How the College Bubble Will Pop." *WSJ.* N.p., n.d. Web. 29 Dec. 2015. http://www.wsj.com/articles/SB10001424052702303933104579302951214561682

Wasik, John. "Three Reasons Why College Bubble Will Burst." *Forbes.* Forbes Magazine, n.d. Web. 29 Dec. 2015. http://www.forbes.com/sites/johnwasik/2013/09/04/three-reasons-why-college-bubble-will-burst/

Wasik, John. "Five Red Flags for Municipal Bond Investors: Wasik."
  *Reuters*. Thomson Reuters, 18 Jan. 2013. Web. 29 Dec. 2015.
  http://www.reuters.com/article/us-column-wasik-munis-
  idUSBRE90H0YN20130118

Weller, Chris. "Japan's Population Is so Old That Elderly Workers
  Are Getting Robot Exoskeletons so They Never Have to
  Retire." *Business Insider*. Business Insider, Inc, 06 July 2015.
  Web. 29 Dec. 2015.
  http://www.businessinsider.com/japanese-airport-gets-robot-
  exoskeletons-to-offset-declining-birthrate-2015-7

Wojdacz, Mariah. "How to Purchase an Existing Business."
  *Legalzoom.com*. N.p., 01 Dec. 2009. Web. 30 Dec. 2015.
  https://www.legalzoom.com/articles/how-to-purchase-an-
  existing-business

Woodman, Craig. "How to Obtain Financing to Purchase an Existing
  Small Business." *Small Business*. N.p., n.d. Web. 30 Dec.
  2015.
  http://smallbusiness.chron.com/obtain-financing-purchase-
  existing-small-business-21919.html

"What Can the Crisis of U.S. Capitalism in the 1970s Teach Us about
  the Current Crisis and Its Possible Outcomes?" *That '70s
  Crisis*. N.p., n.d. Web. 29 Dec. 2015.
  http://www.dollarsandsense.org/archives/2009/1109reuss.html

"10 Ways to Finance Your Business." *Inc.com*. N.p., 30 July 2010.
  Web. 30 Dec. 2015.
  http://www.inc.com/guides/2010/07/how-to-finance-your-
  business.html

# About the Author

Hello,

I am an Eagle Scout and Founder and President of Serenity Ranch & Farm Estates LLC. I have been in business for over a year and have gained valuable experience. I am leading my company, and I have also lead a troop of 108 scouts. Currently, I am earning my Bachelors in Business Administration triple majoring in Accounting, Business Information Systems, and Supply Chain Management. After my undergraduate degree, I will earn my Master of Science in Accounting, and my CPA.

I have spent the past 7 years conducting research and self-learning the skills necessary for building a business and investing. The past year I finally pulled the trigger to write my book *Crisis Investor*. Trying to describe and explain what I've learned and the information that I have read to my family members and friends was difficult; I learned that I had the wrong approach. One reason was all of the information in this book cannot be stated in a conversation, and the second it takes time and charts to explain, for the most part, what is going on in the world. I took my valuable time to write this book and structure the book as a stepping-stone and a starting pointing to show a person what is going on, and what they could do about it. My goal is to raise awareness of the economic problem, and hopefully initiate some drive within a person to take positive action in their life.

I know that I will be very successful in life, and I can't wait for the day I can point to my book as the methodology of how I did it. Until that time when I am on the Forbes 400, you, my dear reader, will have to go by all of the people I have learned from, many are stated in this book. You will also have to see and use the Informative Resources, Sources, and the Reference sections of this book to determine for yourself the credibility of the information, since credibility is a subjective term. I know everyone will learn something useful in life, and see how wonderful the future will be; however, there will be crises ahead, so I recommend getting prepared!

Sincerely,
James J. Hobart

# Endnotes

[i] Stock News Now. "Rick Rule - Resources: Bear Markets Are the Authors of Bull Markets." *YouTube*. YouTube, 27 Oct. 2014. Web. 02 Feb. 2016.

[ii] "The Argentine Crisis 2001/2002." *Rabobank*. N.p., n.d. Web. 09 Feb. 2016.

[iii] Bridgewater. "How The Economic Machine Works by Ray Dalio." *YouTube*. YouTube, n.d. Web. 02 Feb. 2016.

[iv] "A Quote by Warren Buffett." *Goodreads*. N.p., n.d. Web. 02 Feb. 2016.

[v] "Nikolai Kondratieff." *Wikipedia*. Wikimedia Foundation, n.d. Web. 02 Feb. 2016. (Book Citation)

[vi] "Nikolai Kondratieff." *Wikipedia*. Wikimedia Foundation, n.d. Web. 02 Feb. 2016. (Book Citation)

[vii] "Banking." - *Wikiquote*. N.p., n.d. Web. 02 Feb. 2016.
"I Bet You Thought ..." *(Book, 1977) [WorldCat.org]*. N.p., n.d. Web. 02 Feb. 2016.

[viii] Maloney, Mike. "The Biggest Scam In The History Of Mankind - Who Owns The Federal Reserve? Hidden Secrets of Money 4." *YouTube*. YouTube, n.d. Web. 09 Feb. 2016.

[ix] Cahn, Jonathan. "The Mystery of the Shemitah: The 3,000-Year-Old Mystery That Holds the Secret of America's Future, the World's Future, and Your Future! Paperback – September 2, 2014." *Amazon.com: The Mystery of the Shemitah: The 3,000-Year-Old Mystery That Holds the Secret of America's Future, the World's Future, and Your Future! (8601401251521): Jonathan Cahn: Books*. N.p., n.d. Web. 02 Feb. 2016.

[x] Maloney, MIke. "Money vs Currency - Hidden Secrets Of Money Ep 1 - Mike Maloney." *YouTube*. YouTube, n.d. Web. 02 Feb. 2016.

[xi] Maloney, Mike. "The Biggest Scam In The History Of Mankind - Who Owns The Federal Reserve? Hidden Secrets of Money 4." *YouTube*. YouTube, n.d. Web. 02 Feb. 2016.

[xii] "Current FAQsInforming the Public about the Federal Reserve." *FRB: Who Owns the Federal Reserve?* N.p., n.d. Web. 09 Feb. 2016.

[xiii] "Federal Reserve Act : Public Law 63-43, 63d Congress, H.R. 7837:
An Act to Provide for the Establishment of Federal Reserve Banks, to Furnish an Elastic Currency, to Afford Means of Rediscounting Commercial Paper, to Establish a More Effective Supervision of Banking in the United States, and for Other Purposes." *Federal Reserve Act : Public Law 63-43, 63d Congress, H.R. 7837: An Act to Provide for the Establishment of Federal Reserve Banks, to Furnish an Elastic Currency, to Afford Means of Rediscounting Commercial Paper, to Establish a More Effective Supervision of Banking in the United States, and for Other Purposes*. N.p., n.d. Web. 09 Feb. 2016.

[xiv] Great Britain. "Statutes at Large ...: (43 V.) ... From Magna Charta to 1800." *Google Books*. N.p., n.d. Web. 09 Feb. 2016.
"The Statutes at Large." *Google Books*. N.p., n.d. Web. 09 Feb. 2016.

[xv] "The Constitution of the United States: A Transcription." *National Archives and Records Administration*. National Archives and Records Administration, n.d. Web. 02 Feb. 2016.

[xvi] "The United States Mint About Us." *The United States Mint About Us*. N.p., n.d. Web. 09 Feb. 2016.

[xvii] "Transcription: Louisiana Purchase." *National Archives and Records Administration*. National Archives and Records Administration, n.d. Web. 03 Feb. 2016.

[xviii] Friedman, Milton. "Journal of Political Economy." *The Crime of 1873: : Vol 98, No 6*. N.p., n.d. Web. 09 Feb. 2016.

[xix] Roosevelt, Franklin D. "Executive Order 6102." *Franklin* (1933): 95-97. *FDRlibrary*. FDRlibrary. Web. 09 Feb. 2016. <http://www.fdrlibrary.marist.edu/archives/collections/franklin/?p=collections/findingaid&id =507>

[xx] "Panic of 1796-1797." *Wikipedia*. Wikimedia Foundation, n.d. Web. 09 Feb. 2016.

[xxi] Irwin, Neil. "What Is Glass-Steagall? The 82-Year-Old Banking Law That Stirred the Debate." *The New York Times*. The New York Times, 14 Oct. 2015. Web. 09 Feb. 2016. http://www.nytimes.com/2015/10/15/upshot/what-is-glass-steagall-the-82-year-old-banking-law-that-stirred-the-debate.html?_r=0

"Glass Steagall." *Wikipedia*. Wikimedia Foundation, n.d. Web. 09 Feb. 2016. <https://en.wikipedia.org/wiki/Glass%E2%80%93Steagall_Legislation>

[xxii] "Rep Paul Kanjorski: 11 Sep 2008 Electronic Run On the Banks." *YouTube*. N.p., n.d. Web. 02 Feb. 2016.

[xxiii] Meroney, John. "Hollywood Discovers a Real Businessman." *WSJ*. N.p., n.d. Web. 09                                        Feb.                                        2016. http://www.wsj.com/articles/SB10001424052748703574604574500264136219696

"Hilton Hotels Corporation History." *History of Hilton Hotels Corporation – FundingUniverse*. N.p., n.d. Web. 09 Feb. 2016. <http://www.fundinguniverse.com/company-histories/hilton-hotels-corporation-history/>

[xxiv] "Ponzi Scheme Definition | Investopedia." *Investopedia*. N.p., 25 Nov. 2003. Web. 09 Feb. 2016. <http://www.investopedia.com/terms/p/ponzischeme.asp>.

[xxv] Parloff, Roger. "How MF Global's 'missing' $1.5 Billion Was Lost - and Found." *Fortune*. Fortune, 15 Nov. 2013. Web. 09 Feb. 2016.

Stempel, Jonathan. "Corzine, Others Settle MF Global Lawsuit for $64.5 Million." *Reuters*. Thomson Reuters, 07 July 2015. Web. 09 Feb. 2016.

[xxvi] "James G. Rickards." *Wikipedia*. Wikimedia Foundation, n.d. Web. 02 Feb. 2016.

[xxvii] Maloney, Mike. "Rollercoaster Crash: Top 4 Reasons For Deflation - Hidden Secrets Of Money 6 (Mike Maloney)." *YouTube*. YouTube, n.d. Web. 02 Feb. 2016.

[xxviii] *Mineral Commodity Summaries, 2015*. S.l.: Geological Survey (USGS), 2015. *U.S. Geological Survey*. Web. <http://minerals.usgs.gov/minerals/pubs/commodity/gold/mcs-2015-gold.pdf>.

[xxix] "McAlvany Financial Group." McAlvany Financial Group. N.p., n.d. Web. 23 Feb. 2016. <https://mcalvany.com/>

[xxx] "Barack Obama Said Social Security and Other Federal Checks May Not Go out on Aug. 3 If the Debt Ceiling Is Not Increased." *@politifact*. N.p., n.d. Web. 02 Feb. 2016.

"Social Security." *Trust Fund Data*. Social Security Administration, n.d. Web. 02 Feb. 2016.

[xxxi] Pethokoukis, James. "Study: The US Government Has $70 Trillion in Off-balance-sheet Liabilities - AEI." *AEI*. N.p., n.d. Web. 24 Feb. 2016. <https://www.aei.org/publication/study-the-us-government-has-70-trillion-in-off-balance-sheet-liabilities/>.

[xxxii] "Harry Browne: Libertarian Politics, Articles, Books, Speeches, and Investments." *Harry Browne: Libertarian Politics, Articles, Books, Speeches, and Investments*. N.p., n.d. Web. 02 Feb. 2016.

"Harry Browne." *Wikipedia*. Wikimedia Foundation, n.d. Web. 02 Feb. 2016.

[xxxiii] Sommer, Jeff. "Robert Shiller: A Skeptic and a Nobel Winner." *The New York Times*. The New York Times, 19 Oct. 2013. Web. 02 Feb. 2016.

[xxxiv] "WealthCycles Is Expanding into A brand New Financial Publication. ." *WealthCycles-PersonalGain*. N.p., n.d. Web. 02 Feb. 2016.

[xxxv] "MarketWatch - Stock Market Quotes, Business News, Financial News." *MarketWatch - Stock Market Quotes, Business News, Financial News*. N.p., n.d. Web. 11

Feb. 2016. <http://www.marketwatch.com/>

[xxxvi] "Business Insider." *Business Insider*. Business Insider, Inc, n.d. Web. 11 Feb. 2016. <http://www.businessinsider.com/>

[xxxvii] "Building Your Own Guthrie - Dan Lok - Serial Entrepreneur - Millionaire Mentor." *DAN LOK*. N.p., n.d. Web. 11 Feb. 2016. <http://www.danlok.com/daniel-s-pena/books/building-guthrie/>

[xxxviii] "DANIEL S. PEÑA - Dan Lok - Serial Entrepreneur - Millionaire Mentor." *DAN LOK*. N.p., n.d. Web. 02 Feb. 2016.

[xxxix] "Dave Ramsey Homepage - Daveramsey.com." *Dave Ramsey Homepage - Daveramsey.com*. N.p., n.d. Web. 09 Feb. 2016. <http://www.daveramsey.com/home/?snid=home>.

[xl] Corrigan, Catherine. "Students Take Creative Approach to Paying off Debt." *CNBC*. CNBC, 01 Mar. 2011. Web. 02 Feb. 2016.

[xli] *Wikipedia*. Wikimedia Foundation, n.d. Web. 24 Feb. 2016. <https://en.wikipedia.org/wiki/Benjamin_Graham>

[xlii] "2015 SILVER EAGLE INVESTMENT DEMAND: Continues To Be The Big Winner." *SRSrocco Report*. N.p., 11 Feb. 2015. Web. 02 Feb. 2016.

[xliii] "Gabe Brown: Keys To Building a Healthy Soil." *YouTube*. YouTube, n.d. Web. 26 Feb. 2016. <https://www.youtube.com/watch?v=9yPjoh9YJMk>.

[xliv] "Farms Trees and Farmers." *AgCensus 2012* (1997): n. pag. USDA. Web. 26 Feb. 2016. <http://www.agcensus.usda.gov/Publications/2012/Preliminary_Report/Highlights.pdf>.

[xlv] "The Declaration of Independence." *Ushistory.org*. Independence Hall Association, n.d. Web. 03 Feb. 2016.

[xlvi] Wagstaff, Keith. "Elon Musk Says SpaceX Will Send People to Mars by 2025." *NBC News*. N.p., 29 Jan. 2016. Web. 07 Mar. 2016. <http://www.nbcnews.com/tech/tech-news/elon-musk-says-spacex-will-send-people-mars-2025-n506891>.

[xlvii] Williamson, Marianne. *A Return to Love: Reflections on the Principles of a Course in Miracles*. New York: HarperCollins, 1996. Print.